LIFTING THE BOUNDARIES

Also by Gregory Blann:

THE GARDEN OF MYSTIC LOVE
Sufism and the Turkish Tradition (2005)

LIFTING THE BOUNDARIES

Muzaffer Efendi and the Transmission of Sufism to the West

SHEIKH MUHAMMAD JAMAL AL-JERRAHI
GREGORY BLANN

PIR PRESS INC.
NEW YORK

Pir Press, Inc.
245 West Broadway
New York, NY 10013
www.pirpress.com

Lifting the Boundaries: Muzaffer Efendi and the Transmission of Sufism to the West
Revised and updated 2nd edition

This edition printed and distributed by Pir Press Inc., New York

Blann, Gregory
Lifting the Boundaries: Muzaffer Efendi and the Transmission of Sufism to the West

ISBN: 1-59744-038-8

Dedicated to my family
and my teachers

CONTENTS

SECTION ONE

SECTION TWO

LIST OF ILLUSTRATIONS

* photo contibution courtesy of Muzaffer Ergur.
** photo contibution courtesy of James Wentzy.

FORWARD TO THE SECOND EDITION

This new edition of *Lifting the Boundaries* revises and expands the 2005 first edition, offering a substantial amount of new material and photographs. The new edition incorporates nearly a decade of further research, more interviews and input from Muzaffer Efendi's intimate companions and family members, as well as additional Sufi teachings from archival recordings of Efendi's sohbets in America. In the second edition, we also have been able to correct minor errors in the original work, and, with help from the Ozak family, further clarify issues concerning Efendi's birth, final days and other matters.

Since the publication of the book's first edition, further interest in Muzaffer Efendi has led to a major Turkish television documentary as well as a proliferation of English and Turkish internet information concerning him which was not available previously. Naturally, information gleaned from such sources must be carefully weighed in the interest of accuracy. When gathering stories or facts from various individuals, even from eye-witnesses to events, it becomes readily apparent that, upon retelling, not only may the details tend to vary or conflict, but the stories themselves are sometimes colored by markedly different interpretations of what transpired. Such variations are natural and to be expected as stories are passed down for decades, and memories begin to fade. In each case, I have tried to offer the most likely recollection of events, sought confirmation from multiple sources, and omitted any hearsay stories that contained doubtful elements which could not be corroborated by any eyewitness account or contemporary documentation. Actual quotations from Muzaffer Efendi's own writings and recorded talks have been sought out and utilized wherever possible, as they represent the most reliable record of Efendi's own unfiltered thoughts, memories and perspectives. We also recognize that, even in the act of translating from Turkish into English, subtle, unintentional changes can occur in the meaning and context of the spoken word.

In closing, we would like to extend special thanks to Sheikha Fariha for her contributions to this new edition by Pir Press. This involved making available additional archival recordings and photos of Muzaffer Efendi, facilitating interviews with his family and other contributors, as well as sharing some of her own recollections of Efendi. Fahrettin Dal has also added a further dimension to the new edition by generously allowing the use of Muzaffer Ergür's collection of photos from the early years in Turkey.

The author has experienced many blessings from researching and humbly participating in transmitting the legacy of this Sufi emir of love to the modern Western world. It is our sincere wish that each of you who read this book will also similarly benefit from the profound spiritual nourishment and blessing radiating from this vast tradition of love, of which Muzaffer Efendi was one link in a chain of spiritual illuminaries.

DEDICATION

O Muzaffer Efendi!
You drew them with human cords, with bands of love;
(Hosea 11:4)

You love righteousness, and abhor wickedness; therefore God, your God, has anointed you with the oil of gladness above your companions. (Ps 45:8)

Blessed be the compassionate God who loves His creation and reveals His love by sending us holy messengers. Among the messengers that came to us in the late part of the last century was Muzaffer Efendi, a soul glowing with love for God and compassion for God's children. Embracing all seekers of the light, he made them feel at home in the mystical center of their own tradition.

Then those who feared the Lord spoke to one another;
and the Lord listened, and heard it, and a book of remembrance
was written before Him for those who feared the Lord,
and ruminated on His name. (Malachi 3:16)

On first meeting Muzaffer Efendi *Alav Hashalom*—peace upon him—when he came to Philadelphia to offer the *Sema* and *Zikr* with his dervishes, the moment he came to the Shaikh's post I felt him to be connected with the *qutub*, the *axis mundi*. Dervish by dervish they came in, embraced him and the other dervishes, forming a circle that became a matrix of light and love so that when the *Zikr* began the ceiling opened for me to join them in the remembrance of the living God.

After the *Zikr* was over, I was drawn to meet with him in the dressing room of the auditorium and the bond was forged connecting us.

There was the terrible time when the Three Mile Island reactor was feared to be melting down. At that time, I had come to visit the Shaikh in New Jersey and sharing my concern for my family, wanting to rush back to Pa. and evacuate them, he calmed me and predicted that the damage would be contained and it was.

Again coming to do *Zikr* with him and his dervishes at St. John the Divine in New York and later at the *Tekke* downtown, it was always a delight from which I returned home elated, inspired and more devout in my own prayer life.

The memory of the just is blessed; (Proverbs 10:7)

May his soul ascend ever higher in the bond of life and may he be a good intercessor for us to help heal the rift between some followers of the Prophet Mohammed and the rest of the world, between the children of Israel and the children of Ishmael in the Holy land.

Then Abraham expired, and died in a good old age,
an old man, and full of years; and was gathered to his people.
And his sons Isaac and Ishmael buried him
in the cave of Machpelah, in Hebron (Gen 25:8-9)

Rabbi Zalman Schachter-Shalomi

INTRODUCTION

Sufism is the mystical inner tradition of Islam, centered in the heart and in the realization that all life is one, an expression of the Only Being—the Source of Love and consciousness itself. Sufism (related to the Greek word *Sophia*) is a stream of wisdom flowing from the ocean of mystical revelation which has come down through thousands of prophets and sages, both those who preceded historical Islam, and by the Seal of Prophecy, Muhammad, peace and blessings be upon him.

The rich legacy of Sufism first became known to the West through Victorian Era English translations of its mystic poets, such as Jelaluddin Rumi and Omar Khayyam, as well as the scholarly works of Brown, Nicholson and Arberry. Though rooted in the Vedantic rather than Sufic tradition, Vivekananda's 1883 visit to the World Parliament of Religions also generated much Western interest in the mystical traditions of the East. Theosophical groups and Masonic fraternities as well brought fragments of Eastern mysticism into Western culture; but beyond a vague awareness of the exotic ceremonies of the whirling dervishes, Sufism remained relatively unknown in the West until the early years of the twentieth century. Among the many spiritual teachers who contributed to the spread of Sufi ideas in the West during the early to mid-1900's were: the Armenian philosopher, George Gurdjieff, Meher Baba, Murshida Rabia Martin, Frithjof Schuon, and Idries Shah. The first authentic Sufi master to teach in the West was Hazrat Inayat Khan, a gifted musician from India, who first visited America in 1910. He taught a universal form of Sufism, respecting all religions, and opened the mystic path of union with the Divine in a way that transcended any particular religious affiliations. While Inayat found some Western interest in Christian esotericism and mysterious hidden masters in the East, he noted in his writings that, as a result of centuries of anti-Islamic sentiment in the West, it was necessary to veil some of the more overtly Islamic teachings and practices of Sufism in order to gain their acceptance. He died in 1927, leaving behind a number of gifted Western students, including two sons (Vilayat and Hidayat), to carry on the work and to further familiarize the West with Islamic mysticism—or in the words of Inayat's own murshid who sent him abroad, "to harmonize the East with the West..."

Muzaffer Ozak was born in Turkey shortly after Murshid Inayat Khan came to the West. A bookseller and imam by profession, Muzaffer studied Sufism with several gifted Sufi masters and, in time, gained renown as an Islamic scholar, spiritual teacher and sheikh. By the early 1970's, spiritual seekers from all over the world, including non-Muslims, were coming to Istanbul to visit him; many of these were Americans who beseeched the sheikh to visit their country and share the wealth of his knowledge of Sufism and Islam.

In 1978, an opportunity opened for Muzaffer Efendi and a small group of his followers to travel to France and Germany in order to give a demonstration of Turkish sacred music and publicly perform the noble and ancient Sufi ceremony of dhikr. When the trip was extended to include a short visit to America, Efendi fell in love with the souls he met there and with America's ideals of democracy and religious freedom, which he felt more closely reflected the authentic spirit of Islam than the regimes of many traditionally Islamic societies. Due to the Western protections of religious liberty, he was able to teach openly as a sheikh in America and lead dhikr ceremonies in a way that wasn't possible in his native Turkey, a country which had adopted a secularist code of law banning Sufi activities in 1925. Visiting America toward the end of the twentieth century, Muzaffer Efendi found a society with more mosques and more openness to Islamic studies and practice than existed during the time of Hazrat Inayat Khan. Yet for many Westerners, it was the Sufi emphasis on divine love that attracted them more than the shariat of Islam. As a lifelong Muslim and lover of Truth, Efendi embraced this attraction in America, acclimating new students with a gradualist, non-compulsory approach to the fullness of Islam and its noble shariat.

This book chronicles the life of Muzaffer Efendi and provides an account of the rich legacy of Sufi teachings which he offered as a gift to the West. Like Bodhidharma's transmission of Zen Buddhism to China in the fourth century, Muzaffer Efendi is honored as an important modern pioneer in the transmission of authentic Islamic mysticism to the United States. The teachings of Sufism are love-centered and pacifist, rather than penal-centered and retributive, a much needed balance to the restrictive and often violent interpretation of Islam so often featured in the world media today.

Though this book stands alone as a spiritual biography and contemporary presentation of Sufi teachings, readers may also wish to read its companion volume, *The Garden of Mystic Love*, which covers the history of Sufism, and particularly the Turkish Halveti-Jerrahi line (Muzaffer Efendi's spiritual lineage), from the time of the Prophet Muhammad to the beginning of the twentieth century.

SECTION ONE

Muzaffer Efendi closed his eyes for a long moment, lost in exultation. Gradually, his venerable gaze focused on the vaulted walls of the New York cathedral's great nave, then on the musicians near him and the circle of dervishes turning wheel-like around his stationary form. From every corner, the charged sounds of singing and chanting reverberated: *"Hayy, Hayy, Hayy! O Living One!"*

Then the sheikh became animated. With his large arms beckoning toward the circle, he turned in all directions, inviting the audience to come forward and join the concentric circles of dhikr. His repeated gesture of invitation—opening the circle of lovers to everyone—powerfully communicated the ancient impassioned call of the Sufi saint and mystic, Jelaluddin Rumi:

> Come, come, whoever you are! An unbeliever, a fire-worshiper, come! Ours is a caravan of hope. Even if you have broken your vows a hundred times, come, come again![1]

Photo by James Wentzy

And they came, swelling the circle from a few dozen into hundreds—circles around circles, arms joined—young and old Muslims, Christians, Jews in colorful yarmulkas, Buddhists, Hindus, people in Eastern robes and Western dress—united in one great pulsating, turning mass of humanity, together chanting the Divine Names, unveiling the light of the Divine Countenance...

At the conclusion of the ceremony of remembrance, the sheikh took a seat and received questions from the audience, which were translated for him into Turkish. Asked about his policy of inviting everyone present to join in these public dhikrs, Efendi responded:

> I am a sheikh; I work in the divine service, calling people to Allah. I don't look at people's creed, nationality, race, age, or background. We are created by One Divine Source, so I serve the Divine by calling people to unity—to Allah. Humanity is the most valuable of all Allah's creations, because of the human ability to know, to seek and to find its own Essential Source. We chant and call upon the name of Allah; we go beyond the name, and seek the Reality behind it. Each mystic guide is a door to Truth, and each breath a path to the Creator. Those with

open eyes will be able to see the Divine Sustenance and gifts, as well as experience the very Person or Essence of their Creator. I invite people to Allah to get them to taste this—so we can all join in calling upon Allah. When the wind blows, you don't see just one tree swaying in the breeze; they all move together.[2]

Asked about the walls between various religions, Efendi replied:

We have lifted the boundaries between people and issued the divine call to every soul. Actually, the boundaries and distinctions between people were lifted a long time ago; it is others who keep trying to reinstate them. Islam unilaterally accepts all the holy prophets and holy books and makes no distinction between people.[3]

Muzaffer Efendi's Early Years

Haji Muhammad Muzaffer Ozak was born on December 7, 1916 in the Karagümrük section of Istanbul, the youngest child of Haji Mehmet Efendi of Konya and Ayesha Hanim, the grand-daughter of a Halveti sheikh. Mehmet was born into a long line of military men—one of his brothers was a general—but he broke with family tradition and became a merchant and an Islamic scholar. He lived in the Balkans, together with his extended family, until the area was lost during the Russian-Turkish war of 1878.

Those in the family who survived, migrated to Istanbul. There, Mehmet Efendi undertook religious studies at the Kurunlu Madrasa in the Süleymaniye area of Istanbul. Later, he was posted to the school in Plevna, Bulgaria, where he married the head sheikh's granddaughter, Ayesha Hanim. Ayesha gave birth to a son, Murad Reis, who was later killed by occupation forces in Istanbul, shortly after the end of World War I. Her next child was a daughter, named Hikmat. Then in 1916, she bore her last child, a son named Muhammad Muzaffer Ozak. According to the family of Muzaffer Efendi, Ayesha actually bore thirteen children, but most of them did not survive World War I.

After completing his religious studies, Mehmet Efendi received an appointment as a teacher of Islamic studies for the children of the sultan at the Imperial Palace of Sultan Abdülhamid in Istanbul. When the Ottoman Empire began to collapse and the sultan was deposed by the secularist Turks of the Committee of Union and Progress, seven hundred sheikhs and theologians were exiled by the revolutionaries to Sinop, on the Black Sea. One of them was Mehmet Efendi—considered guilty by association with the sultan and forced to share in the sultan's exile.

Mehmet Efendi died in exile during World War I when Muzaffer was only six months old. Muzaffer's son, Junayd, relates that before Mehmet Efendi took leave of his pregnant wife, he confided, in reference to the yet unborn Muzaffer: "Don't worry about this child. This boy will go to the new continent and bring Islam and Sufism." Mehmet Efendi's last wish was that his youngest son, Muzaffer, would give himself over to a sheikh for his education. To this end, he asked his friend and schoolmate, Sheikh Sami Efendi to see to Muzaffer's upbringing, which the latter did, becoming a virtual second father to the boy from the time he was five until Sami Efendi's passing when Muzaffer was twelve years old. In his autobiographical reflections (*The Unveiling of Love* and *Irshad*), Muzaffer Efendi speaks very highly and warmly of his childhood benefactor, calling him the person in his life from whom he profited the very most. He stepped in to morally and financially support the Ozak family after Muzaffer's older brother was killed, leaving Muzaffer, his mother, sister and two orphaned girl cousins all destitute. His older brother, Murad, following a family tradition, had become a chief firefighter in Galata and fought in the resistance against the Allied occupation of Turkey. This brother, unlike many of Muzaffer's other relatives, survived the war (1914-1918), only to be shot one Friday by British soldiers.

Muzaffer Efendi related that, as a young child, his mother used to carry him around in a clothes basket. He also recalled, with ironic amusement, an episode that occurred during his infancy, prior to the death of his older brother. There was a great fire in the Fatih section of Istanbul where he lived, and because most of the houses were made of wood, the flames spread very rapidly. In the confusion of escaping from the approaching blaze, his family forgot that he was asleep in his crib. At the last minute, as the family scurried away from their house, carrying what belongings they could, Muzaffer's brother and sister suddenly stopped the group and pointed out that their baby brother wasn't with them! Then they all hurried back to rescue him from the rapidly spreading flames.

This episode brings up an interesting question of dating, one which has been raised within Muzaffer Efendi's own family. The great Istanbul fire of the second decade of the twentieth century—one which history records as raging through the Fatih section—took place several years before 1917, the implied year in the fire story. Unless Efendi's story refers to some smaller local fire during his infancy, this evidence would suggest that he may have been born earlier than 1916, the date Efendi cited as his birth year in his autobiographical account. His family acknowledges that Efendi might have been born several years prior to 1916. One tradition has it that he was born on the same day that his future sheikh, Fahreddin Efendi, became the grand-sheikh of the Halveti-Jerrahi Order (ca. 1913). Unfortunately, all the birth certificates and family papers were destroyed by the blaze, precluding any later confirmation of his exact birth date. Although birthdays are not traditionally celebrated or emphasized in Turkey as they are in the West, when asked in America, Efendi cited December 7 as his probable birthday, and affirmed that as the date on which it should be commemorated. Another birth detail of interest is that the house in which Muzaffer was born was located next door to the Jerrahi tekke, a room which later became incorporated as part of the tekke complex in Karagümrük.

Soon after the fire, Sami Efendi came to the aid of the family. Sami's full name was Sayyid Sheikh 'Abdul-Rahman Samiyyi Saruhani Usshaki-Halveti, and he was a sheikh in three orders, the Usshakiyya (a Halveti branch), Qadiriyya and Naqshbandiyya. A noted Islamic scholar and author of many books on Sufism and alchemy, as well as Islamic law, Sami Efendi also wrote a number of ilahis which are still sung by Jerrahi dervishes today. He was a frequent visitor at the Jerrahi Dergah in Karagümrük before its closing. Under his tutelage, Muzaffer learned to read and write the Qur'an in Arabic and memorized most of the suras by the age of seven. The youngster completed his Qur'anic studies under the chief imam of the Fatih Mosque, Mehmet Rasim Efendi. Thus, by about the age of ten, Muzaffer became a hafiz, having committed all 6,666 verses of the Qur'an to memory.

Sami Efendi

According to Ibrahim Akkökler, who would later serve for years as Muzaffer Efendi's secretary, Muzaffer's first teacher, Samiyyul Usshaki Efendi, was blessed with a beautiful vision of the Virgin Mary while he was serving time in a Greek prison. He managed to procure flowers from the prison garden and create natural pigments, and in this way fashioned an exquisite artistic representation of Hazrati Mariam as she had appeared to him in his vision. The painting has survived to this day and is now considered quite valuable.

Muzaffer Efendi also elaborated on how Sami Efendi, while exiled to Greece during the revolution at the end of Sultan Abdülhamid's reign, was inspired to become a visionary portrait artist, although as a Muslim he had no previous training or experience in creating figurative art. During his exile, the Prophet Daniel came to Sami in a dream and taught him how to paint. After this, Sami began painting icons and became famous in Greece for his almost photographic likenesses. Most extraordinary of all was a series of portraits he was inspired to paint of the American presidents, supposedly without ever having seen what they looked like, yet extremely realistic. Efendi said he had seen some of Sami Efendi's beautiful paintings, and had heard that an American collector had offered half a million dollars to purchase the collection—quite a sum in those days.[4]

Muzaffer Efendi relates that after he turned twelve—an adult according to Islamic custom—Sami Efendi initiated him and served as his first spiritual guide. Sami Efendi was aware that he would very shortly pass from this world, but because Muzaffer was still young and loved him like a father, he protected him from this knowledge. One Friday after Jum'a prayers, he asked Muzaffer, "If you were to die, where would you want to be buried?" Muzaffer, recalling one of the local cemeteries where a famous and saintly Islamic scholar had recently been interred, answered that he would want to be buried there among the tombs of all the scholars.

Sami Efendi countered, "Well, if anything ever happens to me, don't bury me there. There is a spot near a cornfield where I would rather be buried." The saint explained, "You see, I am not a worthy man. I've sinned a great deal, and if Allah chooses to punish me in my grave, I don't want others nearby to be harmed. So bury me near the cornfield." Sheikh Sami made sure Muzaffer understood and told him in which mosque his funeral prayers should be held. The following Tuesday he passed away and these arrangements were carried out in accordance with his directions.[5]

A free translation follows of one of 'Abdul-Rahman Sami Efendi's finest ilahis, describing what transpires in the dervish *meydan* or circle of dhikr, *Meydan Bu Meydan*:

This arena of love is turning,
This circle of lovers is whirling,
Infinitely deepening, spiraling into Reality,
This consciousness is watching,
Whirling in the Timeless Now.

Passing ages of time, opening and closing;
One absolute moment, merged in Eternal Unity;
Being beyond being,
Only one Reality!

In this dervish circle, Perfect Unity;
We live in this pure moment,
O circle of remembrance, where all limitations pass away.
O circle of the lovers! Here, souls merge in the Mystery of Love.

Muzaffer Efendi's family name, Ozak, comes from his mother's side of the family. The Ozaks were sayyids, descended from the Prophet Muhammad through Hazrat 'Ali and Hazrati Fatima. When Muzaffer's maternal grandfather, Captain Ibrahim Agha, fell ill during a voyage to Bulgaria, he was taken to a Halveti lodge at Yanbolu for treatment. There, he met Sheikh Husayn

Efendi and joined that tekke through marriage to the sheikh's daughter. The fruit of that union was Muzaffer Efendi's mother, Hajja Ayesha Ozak Hanim.

Muzaffer Efendi recounted that his mother had originally hoped he would join the army and become a military man in the tradition of his father's side of the family. As the family's resources were meager, this probably seemed to her like a well-paying career. However, a very holy spiritual entity appeared to her in a dream with the message: "Do not make him a soldier of men, but a soldier of God." Muzaffer added: "That holy person followed me all of my life. Whenever I wanted to skip school to play and do mischief, he was always with me, leading me on the right path. Even after my first master died, this holy being taught me hadith and the basis of all the religious knowledge I possess, occupying himself fully with me." This being, Efendi noted, was a non-physical spiritual entity.[6]

According to his secretary, Ibrahim, Muzaffer's mother used to sell books outside the Fatih mosque, dressed in black, as befits a sayyid. When Muzaffer was older, he helped her sell books, thus gaining early experience in his future trade. Often, Muzaffer and his mother gave away their book-selling profits to the needy around them as charity.

In one of his early Turkish works, *Anwar ul-Qulub* (Lights of the Hearts), Muzaffer Efendi speaks of his mother and her passing:

> My beloved mother was a pious woman who resolutely bore many difficulties, passing her worldly life amid troubles and tribulations. May Allah, Whose Glory is Immense, engulf in the flood of His Mercy that blessed woman, who had me educated and trained as a man of religion in spite of nearly insurmountable material difficulties.
>
> A few hours before she passed away, she said to me, "Son,

> Satan appeared before me and wanted my faith. I said to that accursed creature, 'Is such a thing possible—that I should give you my faith?' Shaking his head, Satan answered, 'You are headstrong,' and he went off in a bewildered state." A little later, my mother lifted her witness finger and repeated the testimony of faith (the *kalima at-tawhid: La ilaha illallah, Muhammadun rasulullah*), and in profound tranquility and repose, her mighty soul flew to the world of the Hereafter and she was gone. May the Mercy of Allah be upon her.

Muzaffer later eulogized his mother in a poem, from which we quote a few stanzas:[7]

My eyes always search for you, mother,
Longing fills my heart,
When I think of you I burn with grief,
Your image is always before me,
My heart beats with your love.

For years you soothed my pain,
This miserable time was unkind to you,
Paradise is now your home,
My eyes always search for you, mother,
Longing fills my heart.

You were father and mother to me,
You carried two burdens,
There is no one like you,
My heart beats with your love, mother,
My eyes always search for you.

Mother to orphans and the needy,
You gave this passing life meaning,
You were a perfected woman,
My eyes always search for you, mother,

Longing fills my heart.

"May her grave be filled with light,"
Is the prayer of all who knew you,
Wherever you walked became paradise,
My heart beats with your love,
My eyes always search for you, mother.

May the Truth make Paradise your abode;
May He place you close to the Messenger,
I shall always recite the Fatiha for you.
Mother, longing fills my heart,
When I think of you I burn with grief.

O Ashki! There is no cure,
Nothing is worse than your mother's absence,
Remember her with compassion, pray for her forgiveness,
Your image is always before me, mother,
My heart beats with your love.

During Muzaffer's teen years, following the passing of Sami Efendi, but while his mother was still alive, Muzaffer worked by day to help with the finances and undertook religious studies by night. Though the madrasas were closed during those years, he was able to follow the lectures of Arnavut Husrev Efendi on hadith and Islamic law for eight years and also study with one of the greatest local scholars and saints of the time, Gumuljineli Mustafa Efendi, known as the "Walking Library". Mustafa Efendi taught Muzaffer a wide variety of subjects, such as astronomy, healing, rare hadith, even the art of affecting the weather—such as producing snow.

Mustafa Efendi used to take young Muzaffer to the Fatih Library to see Fahreddin Efendi, who could often be found studying there. Fahreddin had been the active grand-sheikh of the Halveti-Jerrahis until the closing of the tekkes in 1925. Mustafa would encourage Muzaffer to kiss Fahreddin Efendi's hand, and would ask Fahreddin to pray for the boy, that his faith would open and that he would become less rigid and dogmatic in his approach to the shariat. This took place in the 1930's when Muzaffer was a teenager.

Mustafa Efendi used to share a variety of teachings with Muzaffer, and would frequently end the sessions with some parting thought, adding, "Who knows, maybe you'll need this information someday?" During this period, Muzaffer often passed time at a barber shop in Balat, where he would engage in discussions with an assortment of interesting people, one of whom was the deputy to the bishop in the Orthodox Christian Patriarchal Church in nearby Fener.

Muzaffer noticed that often, during his discussions with the priest, a question would arise whose answer had earlier been supplied in his session with Mustafa Efendi. However, a day came when the priest asked him a difficult question which he had not previously encountered. The priest inquired why the Prophet Muhammad was traditionally referred to as the "Seal of the Prophets"(*khatam an-nabiyyin*) but wasn't called the "Seal of the Divine Messengers" (*khatam ar-rasuli*). The question was natural since, in the testimony of faith, the Muslim stresses Muhammad's stature as a *rasul* of Allah—a *rasul* being usually understood as a special prophetic messenger who brings a revealed book and sacred law to a nation or community. Having no ready answer for the priest from his teacher's discourses, Muzaffer "leaned toward his heart" and offered a silent supplication, saying: "O Allah, please do not embarrass me, but allow me to speak the truth concerning this matter." After a long pause he received an answer which he gave to the priest: "It is because every *rasul* (divine messenger) is a *nabi* (prophet), but not every *nabi* has the station of a *rasul*. If Muhammad was called *khatam-ar-rasuli*, this would open the possibility of another *nabi* coming after him. But by calling him *khatam an-nabiyyin*, Allah has precluded the possibility of any further successor." The priest was very satisfied with this answer.[8]

Years later, Muzaffer Efendi recounted how Mustafa Efendi had taught him many alchemical secrets, including the art of turning a sheet of paper into gold. However, the sheet would only stay gold for 48 hours, after which it would revert to its original paper form. Muzaffer's teacher made his students vow not to use any of these methods except in case of dire necessity. Yet, one fellow student could not restrain himself and attempted to use a certain chant which he had been taught in order to attract a young lady acquaintance to fall in love with him.

The young man went into his room, drew a circle of protection around him, as he had been taught, sat down, and began to chant, concentrating on attracting the girl. After a few minutes, he began to feel extraordinarily thirsty, but realized he had brought no water with him; yet, he could not stop the incantation at that point. Then, to his amazement, he saw a large nearly human-sized black cat—evidently a jinn in animal form—appear in the room with him. The dark animal menacingly fixed his gaze upon the student from just outside the circle.

Soon, several more large dark felines appeared in the room, ominously surrounding him, just outside the circle of protection he had drawn. Extremely frightened, and about to expire from thirst, the student feverishly began to reverse the spell, chanting Qur'anic ayats such as, "I take refuge in Allah..." until the dark figures all disappeared and he was able to safely leave the circle and get a drink of water.

When his teacher learned of this, he was quite upset with the student for this blatant abuse of the alchemical knowledge he had received. The young lady, for her part, was duly informed of what had transpired. She related that, just as she was preparing to go to bed on that very snowy night, she began to experience an irresistible urge to go visit the young man. She put on her coat and scarf and started out the door—all the while wondering why she should be so anxious to go see this man in the middle of a blizzard—when suddenly she came to her senses, returned to the house and went to bed. The moment that she returned to the house corresponded to the point at which the student had desperately begun to reverse the spell.[9] The story amply illustrates why Muzaffer's first teacher, Sami Efendi, who penned several manuscripts on spiritual alchemy, decided to destroy these books himself, lest they fall into the wrong hands, and cause harm to someone.

Being a *sakalayn*—one who communicates with and teaches in both the human world and the world of subtle beings such as the jinn plane—Muzaffer Efendi was very much in touch with the unseen realms. In later life, he attained great mastery in dealing with these forces. However, in his youth he was not always prepared for the intensity of these encounters.

He once shared how, as a young man of nineteen, he spent the night with a friend and the mother of the friend sleeping on the floor of an old mosque. The dilapidated structure was scheduled to be demolished the next day and Muzaffer's party intended to remove some fixtures early in the morning.

In the middle of this cold winter night, Muzaffer felt someone crawl under the covers next to him. At first he assumed it was one of the others sleeping near him who wanted to get warm; but he became alarmed when an enormously heavy arm and leg reached out and began to crush him. Turning over, he saw that the entity, who appeared to be a living skeleton with no skin, was trying to climb on top of him. "Many a man," Muzaffer Efendi recounted with a twinkle in his eye, "would have perished of fright on the spot." At the time, young Muzaffer was certainly terrified—enough that he found his throat incapable of emitting even the slightest sound. Struggling frantically, he finally managed to kick his friend, who sprang to his feet and raised the lights. Only then did Muzaffer's voice return enough to utter an *ayat* of protection, at which point the terrifying creature vanished.

"I could tell many such stories that have occurred to people in Turkey," Efendi continued with a mischievous chuckle. Then, tongue-in-cheek, he added: "But you needn't worry about these things happening here in America. Such things don't exist in the United States; they only occur in the East."[10]

Muzaffer Ozak as a young man (photo courtesy of Muzaffer Ergür)

Muzaffer Efendi's profession as a bookseller began in earnest when an old couple who were friends of his family bequeathed him a huge collection of rare Arabic books. The Turkish government was trying to eradicate the use of Arabic script in Turkey, and was promoting books written in the modern European Turkish script. In light of this, the elderly couple decided to get rid of their Arabic books and sought a worthy person to whom they could donate the collection. Muzaffer offered to purchase the books from them, but they refused to take his money. Having no children, they asked in return for their valuable collection only that Muzaffer would see to their burial when they passed away; to this he agreed. It seems that the couple had borrowed money from Muzaffer's father before his untimely demise, but they had been unable to repay the debt during his lifetime, so the gift of the books was considered as repayment.

In Ottoman times, craftsmen and businessmen commonly joined the Ahi Order. This guild tarikat oversaw, protected and insured fair business practice among all the merchants of the city. While in his early twenties, Muzaffer Efendi had accepted an unofficial position as reciter of Qur'an at a small local Ahi mosque near the Covered Bazaar. Apparently, the imam of that mosque was jealous of Muzaffer's popularity with the ladies; so Muzaffer was thankful to be able to leave that mosque and start a small bookstore with the rare books he received. His first booth was a small partitioned area out in the open part of the Bazaar which allowed only room enough for one person to sit and converse with him. Mustafa Efendi, "the Walking Library," could often be seen there making sohbet with Muzaffer. Being on the corpulent side, Mustafa's ample frame more than filled the tiny curtained booth, thus presenting an almost comical silhouette to passers-by.

In his autobiographical accounts, Muzaffer Efendi mentions many of the mosques in which he served over the years. The first was the 'Ali Yaziji Mosque, followed by the Soghan Agha Mosque, and then the Kefeli Mosque in Karagümrük. There, he was instructed in the art of book-dealing by the imam, Shakir Efendi. Around 1938, he was appointed muezzin of the Beyazid Mosque, the beautiful grand mosque next to the booksellers section of the Covered Bazaar, near the University. On Fridays, he would give teachings in the rear area of the Beyazid mosque and preach the Jum'a sermon whenever the imam was absent.

During his time there, he studied the musical art of *ilahi*, *kaside* and *mevlud* with Ismail Hakki Efendi, the hafiz of the Bakirkoy Mosque. Ismail Hakki was the father of Ragib Bey, who in later years selflessly served as Muzaffer Efendi's personal attendent. Muzaffer and the hafiz became very close, and Muzaffer married his relative, Gulsum Hanim, a woman considerably older than himself who was the headmistress of a local school. The union lasted nearly twenty years, but, in spite of Muzaffer's great longing to be a father, the marriage produced no children. Upon marrying Gulsum Hanim, Muzaffer moved into her family's house near the famous Süleymaniye Mosque, a masjid hailed as one of the greatest creations of the Ottoman master architect, Sinan.

Though he had by this time accepted the imamate of the Veznejiler Mosque, he was also invited to serve as honorary imam during the month of Ramadan at the Süleymaniye Mosque, an unofficial post which he maintained over the next twenty-three years. He did not accept payment from the government for his services there, but functioned on a strictly volunteer basis. Later, when the Veznejiler Mosque collapsed, Muzaffer Efendi was appointed imam of a small restored mosque in the Covered Bazaar, known as Jamili Han.[11]

In his early years as an imam, Muzaffer Efendi was very attuned to the shariat and, according to his own later testimony, was more than a little resistant to the mystical aspects of Islam. Yet, however skeptical his rational mind remained, his dream life was rich with mystic symbols. For instance, he dreamed that he met the Prophet Muhammad and Hazrat 'Ali. The holy Prophet asked Muzaffer if his faith was strong enough that he would sacrifice his head for Islam. When he answered in the affirmative, Hazrat 'Ali, the noble Fountain of the Mystics, raised his great sword, *Zulfikar*, and beheaded him. Muzaffer was terrified by the dream, not recognizing its classic mystic symbolism because of his youth. When he told his Qur'an teacher, who had been a fellow exile with Muzaffer's father, the teacher interpreted the dream to mean that Muzaffer would give himself over to the Sufi way and become a sheikh.[12]

Another vivid dream occurred in the early 1940's during the short interval between Muzaffer Efendi's two stints in the Turkish Military. After serving four years during World War II, he received his discharge and returned to reopen his bookstore. Fifteen days later, he dreamed that he was in a dark, totally devastated city just before dawn. The only building left standing was a domed mosque. He entered that building and there, the voice of a departed spirit spoke to him saying: "Of what are you afraid? You will soon come to me."

The next morning, Muzaffer told his wife that he had been called from the tomb in a dream. Surmising that his end might be near, he began preparing and repaying what debts he owed. Later, that day, two men came to his house, asked for his birth certificate and re-inducted him into the military. As it was wartime, he was taken immediately and placed on a train which traveled through the Turkish countryside for two days and nights. On the second night, toward morning, the train stopped and Muzaffer was left off at a station on the outskirts of a ruined village with no electricity. In total darkness, he walked into the devastated town. Looking around, he saw a lame man and inquired as to whether there was a coffee house in the town. The man told him that he was the coffee house owner, and was on his way to open it. Muzaffer Efendi followed him there and drank some tea.

Seeing that the sun was about to rise, Muzaffer asked the shop owner if there was a place nearby where one could make morning prayers. He was taken toward the center of town, where he came upon the precise scene that he had beheld in his dream three nights earlier. He learned that this city, Chekesh, had recently been destroyed by an earthquake. All the buildings were in a rubble except for a domed mosque, which Muzaffer was told contained the tomb of a Halveti saint named Sapet Tanim. Boldly, Muzaffer Efendi opened the door of the mosque, recited some Qur'an and approached the tomb of the *waliyullah*, saying: "You see, my saint, I wasn't afraid. Here I am. You called me in my dream and I have come to you; and because of that, I am going to ask a favor of you. Since you got me back into military service, please make it a comfortable stay of duty." The next day, he reported back to the station and he was asked about his profession. When he informed them that he was a hoja, a religious man, they assigned him to serve as imam of the hospital, a relatively comfortable position.[13]

Muzaffer Efendi's First Hajj

When the war ended, Muzaffer returned to Istanbul and resumed his profession as bookseller and imam of the small mosque in the Bazaar. By this time, he had an indoor bookshop. He had also secured a modest place for himself and his wife to live, with the help of a friend whose father was the curator of the Fatih Library. For years, Efendi had wanted to make the pilgrimage to Mecca and Medina, known as the hajj, but throughout his adult life the Turkish government had forbidden its citizens to travel there. Finally, in 1949, Muzaffer Efendi was approved as one of 2000 Turks who would be permitted to visit the holy cities. It was his first of eleven hajjs.

Traveling alone, on a shoestring budget, Muzaffer took a boat to Jeddah, the port of entry in Saudi Arabia from which one proceeds to the Ka'ba in the holy city of Mecca. Though he had desired to make the voyage as a lone pilgrim, armed with copious reference books on the hajj, Muzaffer—now thirty-three and fairly fluent in Arabic—ended up with a party of rather dependent elderly Turkish men and women, none of whom spoke any Arabic. One of them had served as the royal imam for the final sultan of the Ottoman Empire; but he only knew Arabic in the form of Qur'anic scriptures. The entire party attached themselves to Muzaffer for the duration of the hajj. Rather than the intensely interior solo pilgrimage he had anticipated, Muzaffer experienced the beauty of service and companionship on his first journey to Mecca, and was shown a number of miraculous signs as well. Acting as Arabic translator for his little group, with his rosy cheeks and light complexion, Muzaffer was frequently taken for a Syrian, perhaps from Damascus.

The pilgrimage from Turkey in 1949 was long and extremely hot, taking some forty-six days to accomplish. The conditions in Jeddah were primitive: no running water, flies all over the food in the markets, streets so narrow that no more than two could walk abreast in them. Whereas many millions travel to make the hajj each year in modern times, in 1949, no more than 120,000 pilgrims could be found circling the Ka'ba during the month of hajj (*Dhu'l-Hijjah*), most of them Saudis.

The first of the extraordinary signs that Muzaffer Efendi witnessed on his first hajj occurred on Mt. Arafat. Haydar Bey, an acquaintance of Muzaffer Efendi who owned a factory in Istanbul, had also come on the pilgrimage that year, accompanied by his friend, Haji Abdullah, the imam of the Edirnekapi Mosque in Istanbul. Muzaffer Efendi recounts the story in his *Anwar ul-Qulub*. While standing with the group on Mt. Arafat, Haydar Bey suddenly became ill and surrendered his soul to Allah. As the others gathered around the body, a piece of paper floated down from the sky and landed on the chest of the dead haji. None of them could fathom its origin. Upon examining the message, Haydar Bey's companions were amazed to read the words: "The Mercy of Allah is upon him, and His Mercy is vast." Later, both Muzaffer and Abdullah would report the details of this amazing event to Haydar Bey's son in Istanbul.

When the official rites of hajj were completed, Muzaffer put away his white pilgrim's garments and donned an Arabic burnoose and head covering. He was invited to dine with a couple whom he knew from Istanbul. Around three in the morning, he left their house and proceeded to the Ka'ba. On the way, he stopped and bought ten pieces of flat bread for his companions, which he zipped up in the black leather bag that hung around his neck. Unlike present-day conditions, the nighttime lighting around the Ka'ba was very dim. Muzaffer carefully stepped over and around the crowds of poor and sick people sleeping on the ground near the Ka'ba, making his way toward the holy black shrine in the center of the complex.

Suddenly, from out of the darkness behind Muzaffer Efendi, a voice called out, “Hey, Turk! Turk! Look at me!” At first Muzaffer thought that it couldn’t be himself the man was calling, because he was in near darkness, dressed as an Arab, and there was nothing about his external appearance that would give away his nationality. But when the voice continued, he stopped and turned to look. There, far away in the darkness, was a man with long hair sitting up among the sleepers, waving his hand, motioning Efendi to come over to him. Muzaffer walked back and saw that the man had a dark-complexion and beautiful features, but his nationality was unidentifiable. In a strange Turkish dialect he said, “You came here in great comfort in a boat. It took me four years to come here by foot.” Then pointing to Muzaffer’s bag, he said, “You have ten pieces of bread in your bag. Give me one of them.”

The Ka‘ba by night

Astonished that the man knew the contents of his thick, closed, leather bag, Efendi opened it and gave the man a piece of bread. The man accepted it adding, "You have some *riyals* in your pocket. Give me some of them too." Muzaffer indeed had a pocket full of silver coins. He pulled them out, hoping that the man wouldn't take them all, as it comprised his entire travel budget. "Don't worry; I'm not going to take all of it," the man assured him as he selected one coin to keep. The haji then raised his palms toward heaven and prayed for Muzaffer: "May Allah permit you to come here many times and may He shower you with abundant blessings each time you come."

Muzaffer indeed made hajj ten more times after this and attributed the sheer amount of pilgrimages to Allah's acceptance that night of this God-intoxicated lover's prayer. Muzaffer never went on pilgrimage or made any important decision without some sign of confirmation from Allah. In fact, in later years, he once went so far as to pack his bags to make hajj, but receiving no dream or sign of divine confirmation, he put off going until the very last possible day. That morning at breakfast, his wife casually mentioned that she had received a dream. Upon hearing it, Muzaffer Efendi jumped up and said, "That's the sign I've been waiting for. *Alhamdulillah*!" With that, he kissed her, grabbed his suitcase and hurried off for Saudi Arabia.

To conclude his first hajj in 1949, Muzaffer Efendi traveled to Medina, where the tomb of the Prophet and his daughter Fatima are located. He visited the battlefield of Uhud, where many of the companions of the Prophet were martyred, including the Prophet's uncle, Hamza. Muzaffer wept at the site and his guide stroked his back saying, "I understand why you're weeping. May Allah reward you for those holy tears." That night, Muzaffer dreamed of Hazrati Fatima, but he couldn't see her face. He woke up the next morning in a sad mood, reflecting on the dream and wondering, "Why didn't the beloved Prophet's daughter show me her blessed face?" He did not have to wait long for an answer. On the boat trip back to Istanbul, the splendid beauty of her countenance was revealed to him in a waking vision, shining brightly like the full moon on the horizon. His hajj had been divinely accepted.[14]

The Mysterious Sheikh who Beckoned with his Walking Stick

When Haji Muzaffer Efendi returned from his first pilgrimage to Mecca and Medina he resumed his trade as imam and seller of rare books in the Grand Bazaar. Before long, he received a dream in which a beautiful man, in religious garments, walked toward him. In the dream, Muzaffer was traveling from Fatih to the Beyazid section of Istanbul. Dividing the street were the rails of the tram way. Just beyond them, on the other side of the street, a man approached. He stopped, waved his walking stick, beckoning Muzaffer Efendi to cross the street to his side.

Tahir Efendi (photo courtesy of Muzaffer Ergür)

The next day, Muzaffer Efendi was amazed to see the very man he had encountered in his dream passing in front of his bookstore. Muzaffer did not approach him but held back, waiting to see if the man would seek him out and thus confirm the seeming coincidence. Unbeknownst to Muzaffer, the man was Sheikh Ahmad Tahir ul-Marashi, *türbedar* (tomb-keeper) of the Fatih Mosque, head of the Halveti-Shabani Order in Istanbul, and a specialist in the teachings of Ibn al-'Arabi. As he passed through the bookseller's section of the bazaar that morning, he vaguely glanced toward Muzaffer Efendi's bookstore but did not stop.

A few days later, Muzaffer received another dream involving the same man. This time, he found himself in a small sailboat in the middle of the Bosphorus. A terrible storm raged all about him, a storm which had broken the rudders of the boat and shredded the sails. In the midst of this calamity, someone handed Muzaffer a written note and told him to read and then swallow the message in order to save himself. The messenger then added: "Have no fear; you'll be safe." It was the same man, now dressed, not in a religious gown, but barefooted and wearing a sheikh's turban.

The next morning, Muzaffer again saw the mysterious sheikh from his dreams walk by his bookshop. By now, there was no question in Muzaffer's mind that these dreams carried an important spiritual meaning, yet he could not bring himself to approach the sheikh. For the second time, he remained inside his shop, watching as Tahir Efendi passed by.

The third dream came within a few days. This time Muzaffer dreamed that Tahir Efendi squeezed him so hard he thought his bones would break, then he placed the turban of the Halveti Order on Muzaffer's head. The weight of it was enormous, as if the seven heavens had been placed upon him. The initial embrace was reminiscent of the experience of the Prophet who, upon receiving the first verses of the Qur'an on Mount Hira, was hugged by an angelic being with such force that he thought his ribs would be crushed.

That morning Tahir Efendi again passed by the bookstore, and Muzaffer Efendi again observed him with fascination, but resisted going to him. This time, the sheikh passed about two-hundred steps beyond the shop, halted and turned back toward Muzaffer's bookstore. He walked up, opened the door and put his head in the shop, saying, "You stubborn *mullah* ! I've appeared to you three times now. How long do I have to wait for you, before you start having faith?" Muzaffer rushed to the door, kissed the sheikh's hands and brought him into the shop. He hugged the sheikh and assured him that he had faith in him "right now."

Muzaffer Efendi's bookshop in the Covered Bazaar (photo by the author).

That day, Muzaffer began his spiritual training with Tahir Efendi, studying with him for the next seven years, until his teacher's passing, around 1956. During these years, Tahir Efendi would visit Muzaffer's shop on a daily basis. For hours on end they would sit together, communicating deeply, sometimes through speech, but more often without a word of overt instruction. "I didn't ask anything of him," Muzaffer Efendi recalls, "but he gave heart to heart from his knowledge." He adds: "I began to see everything through his eyes, and began to witness everywhere the Truth and signs of the Truth. I learned what a great treasure is hidden within the human soul, and what secrets are plainly evident, yet normally veiled from our eyes."[15]

Muzaffer Hoja, the well-known imam and religious preacher

of Istanbul had at last entered the mystical path. Speaking about that psychological transition, Muzaffer later recounted,

> I was swimming in the shariat, obeying what is prescribed as lawful and unlawful in the Qur'an. By the time of Jesus, the followers of Moses had stiffened the sacred law into a rigid orthodoxy. Born into the midst of this calcified religious society, Jesus renewed its lifeblood by emphasizing its core inner teachings of the heart. In a similar way, there is a certain heaviness to the shariat, the sacred law of Islam, insofar as it functions to rein in the ignoble tendencies of the lower self. When I entered the mystic path of Islam, this slightly bitter taste of the shariat became sweeter. So that which, taken by itself, seemed bitter to the lower self, has become sweetened by the honey of mysticism on the Sufi way. Through the Halveti path, I was able to pass through this stage. It is one of the greatest gifts I have received from Allah.[16]

During this period of his life, Muzaffer not only embraced the mystic path but also began to blossom as a popular preacher in Istanbul. In 1948, he published his first book, *Musratli Ilmihayi*, a basic Islamic instruction book on how to pray and how to know Allah. As regular imam of the Veznejiler Mosque and guest imam at the Süleymaniye Mosque during Ramadan, Muzaffer Efendi was often called upon to preach and to attend to the spiritual needs of his congregations, including the poor, the sick and the dying.

In *Anwar ul-Qulub*, he recounts a touching episode which took place at the local café across from the mosque where he used to relax and drink tea between prayer times. One regular customer at the café was a drunkard who consistently squandered his money on alcohol while his wife and children went without. One evening, the man became very upset and obscene, smashing his wine bottle in the middle of the street in front of the café. Silently, Muzaffer Efendi walked over and picked up the scattered pieces of glass from the street. Just as Muzaffer went back to sit down, the angry drunk threw his wineglass into the street. As the noble Prophet had encouraged Muslims to pick up anything sharp from the road that might injure another person who subsequently walked there, Efendi patiently walked back out to the street and removed the broken glass a second time.

From left to right: Kemal Evren, Muzaffer Ozak and Safer Dal at a local café (photo courtesy of Muzaffer Ergür)

The drunk was moved by this and asked Efendi if he was the local imam. They conversed and Efendi learned that the man had attended his mosque on one of the feast days. He desperately wanted to straighten up his life, but was too ashamed to go with Efendi to the mosque for prayers and have the congregation see him in this drunken condition. Muzaffer asked him gently, "But aren't you then ashamed to appear before Allah in this condition?" adding that they were both already now in the Divine Presence, not just when they prayed at the mosque. The man agreed that it was so, and went home, weeping bitter tears of contrition. He returned in fresh clothes the next morning for dawn prayers. He asked for Efendi's help in repenting, took *shahada*—embracing Islam—and within a short time stopped drinking altogether and became a solid family man.

Muzaffer Efendi leading dhikrullah (photo courtesy of Muzaffer Ergür)

Muzaffer used to invite people from the congregation over to his home near the Süleymaniye Mosque for fast-breaking meals during Ramadan. Sometimes, if a person was in financial need, he would give them "tooth money," joking that, after inviting them, he owed them payment on account of the tooth workout they had undergone eating at his house. His wife, on the other hand, was not always as enthusiastic as her husband about hosting these crowds at their house. By nature gregarious and good-humored, Muzaffer put people instantly at ease with his interesting stories and witticisms. At the table after dinner, he would lead his guests in chanting *La ilaha illallah*, in the manner of the Sufis. After the government closing of the dervish tekkes in the 1920's, such informal gatherings were the closest most Turkish people came to tasting the mystical side of Islam.

In the early 1950's, Muzaffer Efendi and Gulsum Hanim, his wife of almost twenty years, were divorced on grounds of incompatibility. In 1953, Muzaffer Efendi embarked on his second hajj. Having experienced a period of profound sadness that year, a depressed Muzaffer had prayed to make one more hajj to the holy land and to die there. He embarked on a ship with a number of high government officials, including a minister whom Efendi counted as a close personal friend.

One evening, early in the trip, he spoke with his friend as they camped in Jeddah. Feeling very powerless and discouraged throughout the conversation, Muzaffer retired to his tent to sleep. Upon lying down, he suddenly heard a high-pitched ringing sound in his ears. In a strange way, Muzaffer later recalled, it was like a "celestial telephone call". As soon as the ringing stopped, a voice followed with a message. The voice was neither inward nor outward—nor was he dreaming. It warned: "Your books are burning!" Then a dark-complexioned stranger in desert robes appeared to him and advised him: "You mustn't be so sad; nor should you ask for your death. You will live a long, full, happy life in the service of Islam. So be joyful."

A few minutes later, the minister came over to Efendi's tent and asked if something was wrong. Omitting mention of the apparition he had just witnessed, Muzaffer related how a voice had told him, "Your books are burning." His friend dismissed it as a dream, but ten days later a ship came from Istanbul, bearing a letter for Efendi, informing him that his books in the Custom's Building had burned in a localized fire. Efendi was relieved to learn that the only books burned were those he had recently ordered from Egypt. In another location, he had many rare books, behind which were stored explosive materials. Had this other location caught fire, a substantial section of Istanbul might have gone up in flames.[17]

How Muzaffer Hoja Found his Spiritual Master

In early 1957, Muzaffer's teacher, Tahir Efendi, fell and broke his hip as he was leaving Efendi's bookstore. He survived only three months after his fall and was buried in the cemetery of the Fatih Mosque, next to his own sheikh, Türbedar Efendi. After the funeral, Muzaffer was left without a spiritual mentor; nor had any official rank, such as sheikh, been conferred upon him. He was attracted to teachers in the Rifa'iyya and the Qadiriyya traditions, but was uncertain which Sufi teacher he should choose to further his Sufi studies. Finally, he submitted the matter to divine guidance, performing two rakat of *istikhara* prayers before sleep; then he waited for a dream to see how he should proceed.

That night, he did not dream of either teacher he had considered, but dreamed of the venerable old Halveti-Jerrahi sheikh, Fahreddin Efendi, whom he had met as a teenager at the Fatih Library and had only seen a few times in recent years at local gatherings or at the coffee house. Muzaffer was surprised at the dream; as far as he knew, the Jerrahi tekke in Karagümrük was closed, and he wasn't even sure whether the aged teacher was still actively accepting students.

He pondered the situation for three days, and on the third night, after Friday *isha* prayers, finally resolved to pay a visit to the sheikh, hoping that Fahreddin Efendi would be generous enough to receive him.

Meanwhile, Fahreddin Efendi, now 70, was in the habit of gathering with a few of his students in the local coffee-house. According to Safer (Sefer) Efendi, who was one of them, Fahreddin had heard about Muzaffer's spiritual gatherings at his home near the Süleymaniye mosque, and began to mention him to the others. "I understand Muzaffer Hoja is opening a dhikr at his house," he would remark. "They say he is a sheikh. What do you think?"

"*Eyvallah*, Efendi," they would answer, "That is the rumor we hear also." Safer Efendi adds that Fahreddin brought up the subject so often that everyone became thoroughly fatigued with hearing about it.

Fahreddin Efendi at table, seated at right (photo courtesy of Muzaffer Ergür)

Then one night, in the summer of 1957, as Safer Efendi and a few others were casually gathered at the residence of Fahreddin Efendi, they heard a knock on the door. Safer Efendi went and opened it to find Muzaffer Efendi standing there. "Is Fahreddin Efendi in?' he asked, seeking permission for a visit. He asked Safer Efendi, "Do you know me?" Safer replied, "Certainly, I know Muzaffer Hoja." Safer Efendi had seen him from time to time at the coffee house sitting with his congregation, and also leading prayers at the Qadiri gatherings. Muzaffer then inquired: "Would you please ask the sheikh if he will accept a visit from me?" Safer Efendi stepped back inside, received permission from Fahreddin Efendi, and then brought Muzaffer inside.

Muzaffer Efendi recalls that Fahreddin paid him the honor of standing when he entered. There were several others present and Muzaffer was invited to sit down and have coffee. Out of respect, Muzaffer would have refrained from smoking had not Fahreddin insisted, saying: "Coffee without a cigarette is like sleeping without a blanket in winter." Then he added, "Among ourselves we attach more importance to love than to respect."

Fahreddin Efendi (photo courtesy of Peri Fezier)

Muzaffer began to explain the reason for his visit, who his father was, and where he was an imam, when Fahreddin laughed and said, "Who doesn't know the famous preacher to women?" The implication, beyond the obvious reference to Muzaffer's popularity with the women of the mosque, was that *real* men (or fully realized human beings) wouldn't be prevented from remembering Allah, the Source of Being, at every moment. Catching the spirit of Fahreddin's pointed ribbing, Muzaffer replied, "If I could find some men, I would preach to them too."[18]

Upon hearing Muzaffer's dream, Fahreddin Efendi told him, "Indeed, your dream seems to point to us; but what you have seen is your entitlement. We must seek our permissions as well. Let us submit the matter with *istikhara* and see what message we receive. On Monday you may return and we will see." With that, Muzaffer took his leave.

By Monday, no dream had come to Fahreddin Efendi, so he sent Safer Efendi with a note for Muzaffer saying: "There is as yet no news. *Sabur*—be patient." During the week, Fahreddin dreamed of a saint named Ismail Mashoki. In the same dream, Muzaffer was present in Fahreddin Efendi's house and was given the name *Ashki*, the lover. Fahreddin sent word to Muzaffer that he had received a dream and asked that he come see him on Friday. On Friday, Muzaffer was given the Sufi name Ashki and was accepted as a spiritual student of Fahreddin Efendi. That night, his teacher made a dua for Muzaffer: "*Nam ola jihanda dili agah ile*," meaning, "May he be known throughout the world as one with a wakeful, heedful heart."

Henceforth, Muzaffer Efendi visited Fahreddin several times a week. In his autobiography, Muzaffer speaks very highly of his master as a gifted dream interpreter "whose miracles were well-known." He was an "intelligent...happy man with a great sense of humor" whose "conversation was a delight...Loved and respected by everyone, he was a man who made us taste the love of the Prophet, the mysteries of the saints; a compassionate man and a generous one who protected the poor and bound everyone to himself." He adds that Fahreddin would sometimes joke with him mercilessly, pushing him toward the point of anger. Then he would publicly declare that Muzaffer was invited by Hazrati Pir Nureddin, the founding saint of the Order, and that no one could touch him.[19]

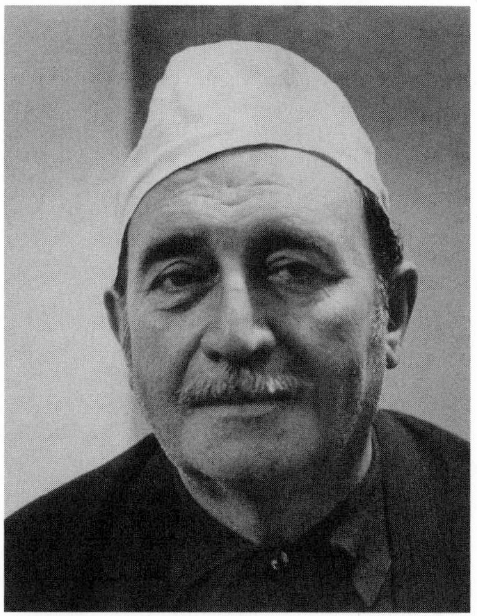

Muzaffer Hoja (photo courtesy of Salik Schwartz)

Already a knowledgeable scholar, seasoned in the mystic way when he came to Fahreddin Efendi, Muzaffer made swift progress in his training. Within six months, Ashki Muzaffereddin received a series of auspicious dreams which signaled his permission to function as a spiritual teacher in the Halveti-Jerrahi tradition of his master.

In Muzaffer's first dream, three men came to his house in order to give him an examination to test his abilities as a prayer leader, or imam. Efendi agreed to be examined and began to chant a sura from the Qur'an in which Moses goes up to Mount Sinai to behold the Divine Countenance, but is told, "You cannot see My Face." Muzaffer Efendi chanted well but could not recall the very end of the sura, so he quickly substituted another similar passage in order to smoothly complete the recitation. Two of the examiners agreed that Efendi had chanted well and had passed the examination but the third examiner objected to his substitution of a secondary passage. Muzaffer countered that he had already passed many previous imam examinations and that according to the rules, it was perfectly acceptable to finish with another passage. At that, the third examiner acquiesced and made it unanimous that Efendi had passed.

Fahreddin Efendi (photo courtesy of Muzaffer Ergür)

The dream came on a Monday morning. Though Muzaffer knew the importance of relaying such a dream to his teacher without delay, because of his busy schedule, he was not able to find time that day to visit Fahreddin Efendi and tell him the dream. That night, he made extra prayers and repetitions of various Divine Names, then fell asleep around four in the morning. He dreamed a "shameful" incestuous dream and awoke feeling extremely upset and angry that his previous night's spiritual efforts had yielded such a revolting dream which seemed to be satanically inspired. Again busy, and deeming the second dream unsuitable to reveal to his teacher, Muzaffer did not make time to visit Fahreddin Efendi on the second day.

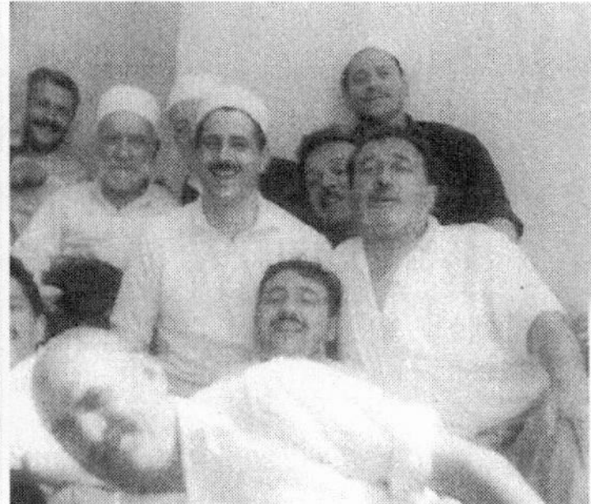

Left photo: Fahreddin Efendi center. Right photo: middle row, left to right: Fahreddin Efendi, Safer Efendi and Muzaffer Efendi (photo courtesy of Muzaffer Ergür)

On the third successive night, Muzaffer dreamed that he went to visit Fahreddin at his residence, but beheld the other students there, all engaged in odd forms of prayer while the Qur'an was recited in startlingly unconventional ways. Some of them were standing up saying, *La ilaha illallah*, then bowing and prostrating. Passing through the house to the garden, Muzaffer encountered his master, who called him over and suddenly lifted him up by his ear and began slapping him hard on his left side as though he were cleaning a dusty rug. He dragged Muzaffer upstairs and showed him a room full of refuse. "Clear the garbage from this room," Fahreddin told him, "and it will be yours." When he awoke that morning, Muzaffer immediately realized that he was being chastised as punishment for his delay in recounting his dreams to his teacher. Unbeknownst to him at the time, the messy room Efendi was shown in the dream belonged to Fahreddin's senior student. A few days later, he would see that actual room and recognize it as the one he had been shown in the dream.

Muzaffer dressed quickly and went straight over to Fahreddin Efendi's residence where a number of other disciples were sitting around with their teacher, having afternoon tea and spiritual conversation. It was a snowy winter day. Muzaffer sat down with them, saying that he had a dream to share. "May it be positive," Fahreddin responded. Muzaffer recounted the first and last of the three dreams, omitting the shameful second one. Fahreddin smiled and said, "Between these two dreams is another dream. You could not have gone from the first one to next one without another dream in between." Muzaffer admitted it was so, but added, "I assumed it was a satanic dream and was embarrassed to tell you."

Fahreddin asked the others to leave the room and listened to the middle dream. Contrary to its shocking surface content, this dream also carried a propitious, unitive meaning in relation to the mystic path. Having heard all three dreams, Fahreddin indicated that the sequence of events now fit and that all the permissions were there for Muzaffer to begin teaching and guiding souls on the mystic way. Years later, during a public talk, Muzaffer Efendi volunteered that his permission to teach came when he and his teacher dreamed the same dream. According to Muzaffer Efendi's family, in 1959 Fahreddin Efendi traveled to Muzaffer's apartment and there conferred on him the authority of acting sheikh and at that time turned over to Muzaffer full responsibility for the community as his successor. When Muzaffer then asked Fahreddin for permission to make a 40 day halvet, the traditional secluded retreat of the order, he was told that he was already spiritually complete without it. Fahreddin Efendi would be the last Jerrahi sheikh to make the full 40 day halvet. However, as we shall see, subsequent events would offer Efendi the opportunity for the period of seclusion he had desired, but in an unexpected way. After this, the elder sheikh went into semi-retirement, yet still remained available for spiritual consult as his health permitted. Muzaffer's relationship with Fahreddin Efendi would last nine years until Fahreddin's passing in 1966.

During his time with Fahreddin Efendi, Muzaffer became well-known and widely sought-after as an interpreter of dreams. However, in time, this ability would inadvertently bring him under suspicion by the secularist government.

Muzaffer Efendi's Detention

Nineteen-sixty was a year of political unrest in Turkey, marked by demonstrations and the closing of the universities in Istanbul. The crisis was diffused by a swift military coup, headed by General Jamal Gursel. The Democratic Party of Prime Minister Menderes which had ruled throughout the 1950's was ousted and a new party, the Committee of National Unity, was created with Gursel at its head. General Gursel took over as Turkey's president (1959-1966) and in 1961 introduced a new Turkish constitution, the fifth new constitution of the century.[20]

During the height of the political unrest, a man came to Muzaffer's bookstore and related a dream to him. Muzaffer Efendi told the man, "This could not possibly be your dream. It is someone else's." The man admitted that the dream actually came to his father, a commander in the Turkish army. The meaning of the dream, Efendi informed him, was that the current Turkish political crisis would soon be resolved by a military coup. When General Gursel's military takeover occurred a short time later, Muzaffer Efendi's prediction became widely known. However, this engendered an unfortunate misunderstanding: the secularist military leaders, apparently suspecting that Muzaffer Efendi obtained his advanced knowledge of the coup through some sort of espionage, issued orders for his arrest. Thus, Muzaffer Efendi came to be numbered among the growing ranks of mullahs who were briefly detained by the military after the coup.

Muzaffer was placed in a crowded cell with a number of other prisoners. When his cellmates asked Efendi why he was there, he told them he had been selling religious books and preaching. "You had followers around you," they responded. "That's probably why they arrested you. But don't worry; you'll be out of here soon." Indeed, most of the arrested mullahs were released within fifteen days. Determined to make the best of the situation,

Muzaffer began to teach Qur'an and the mystical principles of Islam to his fellow detainees. He taught them to make dhikr and had them vigorously chanting *La ilaha illallah* in their cells.

Before long, the prison officials put an end to this by moving Muzaffer Efendi away from the others in a solitary cell. It was a hot summer, and Efendi's metal cell had no windows or ventilation system. Efendi's only connection with the outside world was a small slit in the door used for delivering food. Muzaffer accepted this as a retreat, or *halvet*, passing the long, hot days in prayer, dhikr and silent meditation, enduring many weeks of confinement. Though gradually weakened by these conditions, Efendi, like the prophet Joseph in Egypt, continued to trust in the divine wisdom which had brought him there, and which would also, in due time, free him. He accepted all of this as coming from Allah.

As the story is told, his release came after one of the guards began to notice cool air emanating from Efendi's cell when he delivered the food. He brought his supervisor to confirm the unusual phenomenon. Amazed, both guards reported to the warden that, despite the hot summer temperatures throughout Istanbul, there was a cool breeze, almost like an air-conditioner, flowing from Efendi's cell and cooling him.

Recalling Efendi's reputation as a seer of dreams, the prison officials pondered whether this might be a further miraculous sign of a divine friend or *waliyullah*. As no formal charges had yet been brought against him, they reasoned that it would probably be best not to continue to keep him incarcerated. The next day Efendi was released. No one else had a clue that he was out. In a weakened condition, Muzaffer made his way to a nearby relative's apartment to rest and recuperate. He told her, "No one knows I'm here. I must sleep. I don't want to be disturbed under any circumstances."

The next day, a stranger came to the apartment and knocked

on the door. Efendi's relative opened the door and beheld a humbly-dressed man who asked to see Muzaffer Efendi. She was astonished at the request, since no one knew that Efendi was at her house nor that he was even out of jail. The man explained that he had been divinely guided to this location. He had been a fellow detainee with Efendi and had also just been released and had come here today for the purpose of asking Efendi to accept him as a student on the mystical path.

Muzaffer Efendi was awakened and informed of the visitor's presence. As soon as he emerged from the back room, he recognized the man. His name was Hulki Efendi. Hulki explained that he had come to formally ask to study the mystical path of Islam with him, a request to which Muzaffer consented. Hulki explained that during his long incarceration, he had prayed every day for a spiritual teacher, fervently supplicating: "O Allah! Please send me a spiritual master." Finally, in His infinite compassion, Hulki concluded, Allah had answered his supplications and sent him a spiritual guide. At once incredulous and bemused, Efendi exclaimed, "You silly man! Why did you pray for Allah to send a spiritual master *to you*? Why didn't you pray to first be released and then be guided to one? It's beyond me why you would want to pray your teacher into jail!"

After his recovery, Muzaffer returned home and resumed his life as bookseller, imam, and mystic guide. Muzaffer Efendi was never again arrested. Fahreddin Efendi used to write down his petitions for Muzaffer's protection and leave them at the tomb of Hazrati Pir Nureddin Jerrahi.[21]

Not long after this, on January 23, 1961, Muzaffer Efendi remarried. He was joined in matrimony with Mehlika, a younger woman, later known as Baji Sultan. After having passed over forty years of his life childless, Mehlika would bring joy back into his life; but, sadly, the first few years of this second marriage still did not produce the children he longed for. On the advice of a friend, he visited and made supplications at the tomb of the saint, Telli Baba. A Qadiri sheikh of old, Telli Baba was famous, both during his lifetime and after, for granting intercessory help to those in need, regardless of their religious creed, including those troubled with infertility. Efendi traveled north of Istanbul to make prayers at the small mosque adjoining Telli Baba's tomb. Then he entered the room where the saint is buried. According to the prevailing custom, Telli Baba's sarcophagus is covered in tinsel-like silver threads, to be taken by visiting supplicants and replenished by the many whose prayers are answered by Allah, through the intercession of the saint.

Baji Sultan with Muzaffer Efendi (photo courtesy of Muzaffer Ergür)

In the presence of the tomb, Muzaffer Efendi promised that if, for the sake of Telli Baba, Allah would bequeath him a daughter or son, he would offer 70,000 repetitions of divine unity, *La ilaha illallah*. After a total of twenty-four years of childless marriage, within the space of one short year, Muzaffer Efendi and his wife, Baji Sultan were blessed with a beautiful golden-haired daughter, whom they named Ayşe. After this, Muzaffer would often visit Telli Baba's tomb and recite the opening seven verses of the Qur'an, known as the *Fatiha*, on his behalf. Several years after their daughter's birth, Efendi also prayed for a son, a prayer which again was speedily granted.

After this, Muzaffer Efendi too became known for his ability to help infertile couples become pregnant through the power of his intercessory prayers to Allah. People of all religious backgrounds would seek him out for the efficacy of his supplications to Allah on their behalf.

Safer Efendi and the Passing of Fahreddin Efendi

In early 1966, Fahreddin Efendi's health began to seriously decline. He became bedridden for eight months, confined to the upstairs portion of his residence. Unable to continue meeting with his students, he asked Muzaffer Efendi to take over some of these duties, also depending on Safer Efendi and other senior students. Safer Dal, along with his close friend Kemal Evren, had begun to study with Fahreddin Efendi, beginning around 1952. After Fahreddin's passing, Safer would become Muzaffer's head disciple, and accompany him on his many trips to America.

Fahreddin Efendi and Safer Efendi

Safer Efendi was born in Istanbul on Friday, August 20, 1926 and grew up in the Dervish 'Ali district near Karagümrük. His father, Sadık Ramazan, was a halva seller of Albanian origin and his mother, Ulker Hanım, descended from both Haji Rüstem Oğulları and Emir Sultan, her family coming from the city of Zishtov in Rumeli (present day Bulgaria). Safer married in his early twenties and worked in a number of jobs over the years including employment at the shipyards, as a chicken farmer, and as an assistant for two years at Muzaffer Efendi's bookshop.

Fahreddin Efendi and his wife Valide Sultan (photo courtesy of Muzaffer Ergür)

When Safer Efendi and several other disciples of Fahreddin conceived the idea of opening a hall for wedding receptions, they consulted their teacher, who volunteered his entire savings to finance it. Fahreddin Efendi gave them 10,000 Turkish lira—worth 100 pieces of gold at the time—as well as his blessing and told them he did not mind losing the money if the project failed, but he prayed it would be a success. The Nur Wedding Salon and Yumni Bakery indeed proved to be extremely lucrative and provided ample employment for many years.

By 1966, Fahreddin was bedridden and had to look to his disciples to continue his work. During his prolonged illness, he would drift in and out of sleep most of the day and sometimes sit up in bed. Occasionally, he might say: "O, has the sun set yet? I need water for ablutions," and other such things, but he was too weak to do much. Sometimes he would exclaim, "I'm going now; I'm leaving." One day his wife, Valide Sultan, said to him, "You keep saying you're about to go. With whom will you leave us when you're gone?" She was concerned since they had married later in life and had no biological children to take care of them. Fahreddin Efendi answered her, referring to his devoted disciples, "Look at me, woman; I am leaving you with such children that all will be well for you after I'm gone." Then he added, "There couldn't be anyone closer or more helpful than these, even if they were from our own progeny."

During his active life, Fahreddin Efendi had often given the teaching that, for those believers who accept sickness as a purification, the illness can burn away impurities and sins—or, if they have few sins to purify, the sickness can be an opportunity to raise one's spiritual level. This teaching is based on an hadith of the Prophet. Safer Efendi recalls how one day during this period, in a rather daring mood, he visited his master Fahreddin, who was lying in bed looking weak and very uncomfortable. Safer said to him, "Well, now all of your sins are being erased and the heavenly maidens, the *houris,* are waiting for you in paradise." Fahreddin rolled over and grumbled, "Enough with the *houris* and the erasing of sins! I'm aching all over! Now stop bothering me."

On one of his better days toward the end, Fahreddin Efendi arranged to have Safer Efendi recite the litany of Hazrati Pir Nureddin as soon as he saw his teacher's state change during the moment of his transition to the next world. When Fahreddin

Efendi's final night on earth arrived—on the fifth of Shaban in December of 1966—Valide Sultan asked Safer Efendi and some of the others to stay the night with her husband, who wanted company. When the moment came, there were only two women in the room, along with Safer Efendi and his master. Fahreddin made a weak gesture and his breath began to grow faint. Safer Efendi began chanting the beginning of the litany, but did not finish it. When he looked up, his master had passed and the room had filled with people. They all formed a circle around their teacher and began to chant *La ilaha illallah.*

After this, the body was prepared for burial. Muzaffer Efendi gave the master ablutions while Safer and Kemal poured the water. Amazingly, Fahreddin's body remained warm and flexible when rigor mortis would normally have set in. After the preparations were complete, the body was placed in a casket. In accordance with Fahreddin's last wishes, Safer Efendi placed on each of his master's eyes a small compressed lump of soil from Karbala, the ground upon which the Prophet's grandson, Husayn, had been martyred. When he returned a short time later, Safer was astonished to see that tears of blood for the sake of the martyr of Karbala had accumulated in the casket beneath Fahreddin Efendi's head.

On the day of burial, the casket and body were carried to Fatih mosque, where the final funeral prayers were made.[22] During the procession, Muzaffer Efendi had all of them chanting dhikr publicly in the streets. No one had seen such a procession since Ottoman times. One professor said: "If Muzaffer is leading such funeral processions as this, I am now content to die."

In his *Divan*, Muzaffer Efendi gave thanks for all the spiritual gifts imparted through his sheikh:[23]

My turning is within the turning,
Thanks and praise to Allah.

My vision within radiant lights,
Thanks and praise to Allah.

I took the Sheikh's hand,
I found the way of union,
He brought his servant Home,
Thanks and praise to Allah...

In the circle we cried "Allah,"
And were annihilated in His Glory,
In an instant we reached the Throne,
Thanks and praise to Allah.

Ashki met his Beloved,
He reached the Lotus Tree,
He ascended with his Sheikh,
Thanks and praise to Allah.

After the funeral, a dispute arose over who was to be Fahreddin Efendi's acknowledged spiritual successor. Some observed that Safer Efendi had originally been nominated, but Safer himself deferred to Muzaffer, as did most of the other students. However, there was another advanced disciple to consider who had been with Fahreddin Efendi longer than any of the others. This was Fahreddin Efendi's half-brother, Husameddin Efendi, who was born of the same mother, or "milk mother" as Fahreddin Efendi and had entered the tarikat several decades earlier. Muzaffer Efendi relayed the events as follows: Husameddin Efendi pointed out that Muzaffer was a much more recent arrival and, as Fahreddin Efendi had not sufficiently clarified who his successor should be, Husameddin felt that it was his right to inherit the mantle of his teacher and close relative. Muzaffer Efendi suggested that they all meditate, make *istikhara* prayers, and wait for orders to come from beyond themselves. Husameddin and the others all agreed to this.

Safer Efendi and Muzaffer Efendi (photo courtesy of Muzaffer Ergür)

A week later, the group gathered and Husameddin Efendi said, "Bring the senior disciples in here and close the doors." Then he recounted a dream he had received that week, in which he dreamed he was leading all of the other disciples of Fahreddin Efendi in prayer; however, they were not joining together in proper prayer lines, but were gathering in small groups of three or four. Though the prayers were not going well, Husameddin persisted in trying to lead them. Then Hazrati Pir Nureddin himself appeared and told Husameddin to leave the *mithrab*, where the prayer leader stands. When he hesitated to do so, the pir pulled him back by his collar and put Muzaffer Efendi in his place, thus ending the dream.

Full of emotion, Husameddin said to Muzaffer, "Let me be the first to pledge myself to you as our spiritual leader. From now on, you are not only our teacher, but our very soul!" At this, all of the others agreed to pledge allegiance to Muzaffer. Husameddin also generously transmitted to Muzaffer, over the following months, some of the more advanced divine names which Muzaffer had not yet received at the time of Fahreddin Efendi's passing. During that pivotal week in December of 1966, Muzaffer Efendi also received a dream which directed him to begin teaching and spreading the fruits of the mystical path of Islam in a much more open way than he previously had.[24]

Every saint has his miracle or *karamat.* It is said that the greatest miracle of Ashki Muzaffer was to open up the path of *ashk*—of heartfelt passionate love in the way of mystic Islam—after it had been shrouded for so many years in secrecy and suppression. Through mystic dreams and divine intimations, he was given an abundance of spiritual permissions. Hazrati Pir Nureddin al-Jerrahi, founder of his mystic order, had seven khalifas during his lifetime. Muzaffer counted himself as the eighth khalifa of Hazrati Nureddin[25]—a direct spiritual heir called by the pir beyond the limits of time and space. As a direct representative of the founding pir, Nureddin al-Jerrahi, his mission was to revitalize the path and spread the Way of Mystic Love far and wide, teaching as many souls as possible to affirm the Divine Reality, saying, "*La ilaha illallah.*"

An Extended Pilgrimage to the Holy Sites

In 1967, Muzaffer Efendi led a group of his spiritual followers on a collective hajj to Mecca and Medina. On the way to Saudi Arabia, they traveled through Jerusalem, Jordan and Baghdad, where they visited the tomb of Abdul Qadir Gaylani. Safer Efendi also joined them on this pilgrimage. In Jerusalem, they visited the Masjid al-Aqsa, "the Farthest Mosque," on the Temple Mount, where the Prophet was transported, according to Islamic tradition, and led the other prophets in prayer during his mystical night journey. This was in early 1967, before the famous June Six-Day War during which the Israelis captured the West Bank of Jerusalem from Jordan, along with the Gaza strip, Sinai Peninsula, and Golan Heights from Egypt and Syria.

At the Dome of the Rock in Jerusalem (photo courtesy of Muzaffer Ergür)

Muzaffer Efendi and a party of twelve visited the Masjid al-Aqsa on a Friday, the day of congregational worship in Islam. They were dismayed to find only six other Muslim worshipers in attendance at the noon prayers, including the imam and muezzin. When they left the mosque, a disturbed Muzaffer Efendi told his companions, "If people do not honor something with its true value, Allah will take it from their hands." One of his companions tried to smooth it over, saying that everything would probably be okay. "No!" Muzaffer insisted, "I'm telling you the truth. You'll see that what I'm saying will come to pass!" They did not have to wait long. Right after the group returned to Istanbul from their hajj, the Israelis took possession of the Temple Mount.

Muzaffer Efendi and companions in Baghdad (courtesy of Muzaffer Ergür)

The group traveled on through Amman, Jordan, taking three taxis through the desert to Baghdad. There they found a hotel, changed, and set out for the mosque at the site of Abdul Qadir Gaylani's tomb. Though they seemed to be running late, they walked to the mosque in almost no time, made the evening prayers and stayed for a chanted litany or *usul*. On the way back, they walked and walked until they were tired—some forty-five minutes. They all puzzled over the seeming brevity of the first trip compared to the great length of the return journey to the hotel. Suddenly, the explanation occurred to Muzaffer Efendi. He informed the others that as they had walked from the hotel to the mosque, the saint of Gaylan had transported them there quickly by the miracle of *tayy-i mekan*—the spontaneous traversing of time and place.

I came to Baghdad,
And fell into the torrent of love,
I was infatuated with the rose of
Sultan Abd al-Qadir.

I submitted to his word,
And attached my being to his,
I fell in love with the face of
Sultan Abd al-Qadir.

I uttered Hu at his resurrection,
And tasted the sweetness of his love,
On my heart I engraved the litanies of
Sultan Abd al-Qadir.

I made his rose my crown,
He became a remedy for my pain,
I extracted the secret of
Sultan Abd al-Qadir.

The friends of God stand in ranks,
Everyone moves to bow down,
They circle the house of
Sultan Abd al-Qadir..[26]

While staying in Baghdad, Muzaffer Efendi dreamed that he

was handed a luminous baby boy and told: "This is the child that is going to be born to you, the one you prayed for. You are to name him Muhammad Junayd." Then he was given four dolls. These, Efendi was told, represented his grand-children who would be born through Junayd. Efendi's son, Junayd was born not long after the group returned to Istanbul.

Muzaffer Efendi and Safer Efendi on hajj (courtesy of Muzaffer Ergür)

Efendi wrote down the dream and sent it to his wife in Istanbul, making sure that she was given the name in case something unforseen should happen to him. Baji Sultan wrote back to him and said that on about the same day as his dream occurred, a stranger had knocked on her door. Upon answering it, she was greeted by a man wearing a unusual turban—this, during a time when turbans were forbidden in Turkey. He told her, "My daughter, I'd like to make my ablution." She let him in and furnished him with a towel, with which he made his ablutions. They spoke briefly and, as he prepared to leave, he looked at her, pointed toward her stomach and said, "You are going to have a boy." Thus both of them were informed in advance of her pregnancy, following shortly after Efendi's divine supplications for a son at the tomb of Telli Baba.

From Baghdad, the pilgrims traveled on to the hajj in Mecca. Somehow a dispute over water erupted among the group in the vicinity of the Ka'ba. As a result of these events, Muzaffer scolded Safer Efendi, blaming him in a way that Safer felt was unjustified. Safer Efendi felt wounded by this and even went so far as to consider leaving the group altogether. That night, he dreamed that Fahreddin Efendi came, took his hand and led him to Muzaffer Efendi. Fahreddin kissed Muzaffer's hand, and told Safer Efendi: "You kiss too." Without hesitation, he did so. "Now," said Fahreddin, "Can you stay upset about this matter?" In looking back on the episode, Safer Efendi reflected, "We shouldn't so easily give into the tendencies of the limited lower self, the *nafs al-ammara*. Certainly, it's not an easy job."[27]

Safer Efendi recalled another group pilgrimage in 1976 in which some of them traveled with Muzaffer Efendi through Iraq and Syria to Mecca for the *hajj*. This time, they brought an ample supply of water with them and traveled by bus. On the evening when they came to the Syrian border, where they intended to pass into Iraq, they were made to wait for hours outside a little cabin at the desert checkpoint. Some of them left the bus and waited outside, including Safer Efendi. Suddenly, he saw a beautiful, turbaned man with dark hair, beard, and large, bright eyes coming toward them from out of the desert. The stranger gave his greetings to Safer Efendi, and chatted with him for a few minutes in strangely accented, antiquated Turkish. He asked from which country Safer's party had come, and, learning that they were from Istanbul, made an odd-seeming inquiry as to whether there were mosques and Muslims there. Safer Efendi explained that some of the greatest mosques in the world were in Istanbul and asked the man if he would like to meet their leader, who was inside the bus. When the Arab agreed, Safer Efendi entered the bus, woke up Muzaffer Efendi, and told him about the visitor. Muzaffer arose and exchanged greetings with the man, embracing him warmly. They spoke for a little while; then the man departed.

Safer Efendi (center) with Süleyman Dede

Soon afterwards, the bus was allowed to pull across the border into Iraq, but on the other side of the checkpoint, Iraqi soldiers absolutely refused to process them or let them pass until the next morning. None of them wanted to spend the night there in the desert. Muzaffer Efendi and some of the others pleaded with them in broken Arabic, but it was no use—the soldiers screamed at them angrily, refusing to hear any more requests for the night. Suddenly, a car drove up from the desert, driven by an officer who very much resembled the beautiful Arab they had talked to earlier. The officer approached with a whip in his hand, which he kept striking against the palm of his other hand. "Fill out these people's forms and let them pass through right now!" he ordered the soldiers. The soldiers obediently responded as the man continued his harangue: "All the time you've been refusing you could have had them through, now get moving with it!" Within a very short time, Efendi's people were all back in the bus and being waved on their way.

Weeks after they returned from the hajj, when they were together in the bookstore, Muzaffer Efendi asked Safer Efendi: "Do you know whom that man was that we saw on the Syrian side of the checkpoint—the one who came from the desert and spoke to us at the border? It was the spirit of Abdul Qadir Gaylani, may Allah sanctify his spirit." Then he asked, "Remember the officer who arrived and helped us on the Iraqi side? That was him as well."[28]

Muzaffer Efendi made a number of trips abroad during the 1970's. On one trip to Egypt, he was questioned at the border as to the purpose of his visit. His response was immediate: "To say a *fatiha* for the Pharaoh."

Two intimate perspectives: Efendi's Secretary and Hafiz Ismail

Ibrahim Akkökler was a lawyer and petty officer in the Turkish government who became Efendi's secretary and bookstore assistant. One day, he dreamed that Muzaffer was giving a khutba or sermon on a platform that could be heard around the world. Others, including Muzaffer Efendi, were also receiving such dreams at the time, and dreaming that people from many countries would soon be coming to Efendi. Muzaffer told Ibrahim that his dream was added confirmation that he, Efendi, would soon carry the message of unity and divine love abroad.

Ibrahim Akkökler

As Ibrahim traveled a great deal to supplement his salary, he was inspired to travel around the world saying *Salawats* and *Fatihas* in all of the cities which he visited. Muzaffer Efendi encouraged him to make such a journey, saying that it could be done in the spirit of a halvet, with Ibrahim fasting most of the time. Thus, Ibrahim set out on an itinerary which included Brazil, Africa, Germany, Japan, and Oklahoma, in the United States.

One episode from this tour that struck Ibrahim was his reaction to the city of Berlin. It impressed him as being a rather wild and decadent city, and he noticed that, because of this negative assessment, his heart began to close to the people there. Then Muzaffer Efendi appeared to him in a dream and gave him a hard jolt, signaling that his attitude to the people there was unacceptable. The next day, Ibrahim put on a friendly face and went out into the streets and distributed candy to the people. The whole atmosphere changed and he left the city feeling much better about them. Later, Efendi connected with many beautiful people in Berlin who converted to Islam. "You see," Ibrahim concludes, "We must view everyone as Allah does—with love and mercy."

Muzaffer Efendi in his imam's turban inside his bookstore

After Ibrahim returned, he began to work in Muzaffer Efendi's bookshop, feeding the approximately thirty-five cats around the premises, stocking and selling books, watching over the bookstore in Efendi's absence and acting as Muzaffer's secretary and English translator. Ibrahim recalls a wealth of stories from his days at the bookstore with Efendi.

One day at the bookstore, they received an Islamic book with which they were not familiar. As they perused it, the author's condemnatory tone became quickly apparent. According to the book, almost everyone was an infidel for one reason or another. Ibrahim read a number of passages aloud for Efendi. Hearing nothing positive or uplifting in the book, Efendi said to Ibrahim, "Throw that book in the garbage!"

Muzaffer Efendi

Ibrahim recalls a professor of theology who visited the bookstore and criticized the mystic path of Islam, complaining, for instance, that it was against Islamic practice for Muzaffer Efendi to allow his followers to kiss his hands and knees, as if he were a god. Muzaffer Efendi turned to Ibrahim and said, "Ibrahim, go to the shelf and get volume three of the *Taj ahadith* for me. (The

Taj collection of *ahadith* are a five volume set, which contain, among other things, mystical traditions associated with the holy Prophet.) Muzaffer opened the volume and showed the professor a well-attested hadith which told how the Prophet, out of love for his companions, used to allow them to kiss his hand. The man was genuinely surprised to see this and, after discussing it with Efendi, agreed that, if it were simply a gesture of loving respect, then there was nothing wrong with it

Muzaffer Efendi and companions in front of his bookshop. Ibrahim is at far left (photo courtesy of Muzaffer Ergür)

A more well-known story involved a man whose father was a great *sayyid*, a descendant of the Prophet Muhammad. He used to come to the bookstore and joke with Efendi, asserting that Efendi couldn't do some of the things he was reputed to be able to do, like causing snow to fall in the off-season. The man kept on in this vein until Efendi had enough of his skepticism. Muzaffer Efendi took out a strip of paper, inscribed it with some Arabic calligraphy, folded it up, and had someone deposit it in a tree outside. Within a short time, snowflakes began to fall, despite the fact that it was a warm, clear day. Everyone who witnessed it was amazed.

Efendi turned to the man and said, “Your turn!” When he realized that a light snowfall had actually commenced, the man said in a nervous voice, “Ok. I admit you can do it. Now, make it stop.” Efendi answered, “You wanted it to snow. *You* make it stop!” As he obviously couldn't, Efendi finally had the calligraphy retrieved, removed the ink and uttered a short supplication, whereupon the snow ceased to fall. This was done not simply to amaze, but to bring faith to a closed heart, because the greatest miracle is to open hearts to God.

Finally, Ibrahim recalls a visitor who came into the bookstore in the early 1980s, about a year before Muzaffer Efendi's passing. The man, who was old and very sick as though he had cancer or AIDS, approached Ibrahim and asked to speak with the owner of the bookstore. When he was brought to Efendi, the man asked him: “Do you remember me?” Muzaffer looked closely at him and then answered, “I'm sorry. I don't.” The man said, “Allow me to introduce myself. I was the chief of police years ago when you were arrested and brought into the police station. At the time, I was the one who questioned people and had them locked up. I know I was rough with you then, and now I'm ashamed of what I did. As a man who is about to die, I'm asking for your forgiveness.”

In a sympathetic voice, Muzaffer told the man, “I really don't remember anyone doing anything to harm me. You see, I always consider whatever happens to me, whether good or bad, as coming from Allah. Whatever it was you did, I didn't think it came from you. So please don't worry about it." With that, the old man began to weep. They attempted to console him and sent him on his way, with prayerful wishes on his behalf.

Hafiz Ismail Hakkı Çimen was another intimate of Muzaffer Efendi who was with him in Istanbul on an almost daily basis from the early 1970's until Efendi's passing in 1985. Ismail was born in 1959 in the Eastern part of Turkey in a town named Erzürüm, near Mount Ararat. Although blind, Ismail has always shown great independence of spirit, negotiating the busy streets of Istanbul with amazing ease. At age ten, he left Eastern Turkey and set out alone for Istanbul, experiencing many adventures along the way. Ismail relates that when he first arrived in Istanbul, he spent almost two years living on the streets.

Hafiz Ismail Çimen playing his ney

One of his favorite places was a coffee shop called Koska, in the Aksaray section near Istanbul University and the Covered Bazaar, not far from Muzaffer Efendi's bookstore. There, Ismail would pass the time smoking the shop's water-pipe, drinking coffee and visiting with people. One evening, when he went to pay his tab, the proprietor told him, "You don't need to pay. It's already been taken care of." Ismail asked who had paid for him and was told that the party who had paid had already left, but they would be back again the following night. Ismail went back the next evening, located the one who had paid his bill and thanked him; it was Muzaffer Efendi. Ismail says, "After that, I began to spend as many evenings as I could listening to him in various coffee shops around Istanbul."

According to Ismail, Efendi and his close companions and disciples would gather most evenings at one of the local shops toward midnight, and sit and make conversation until shortly before dawn. Then they would walk over to the mosque for morning prayers and finally go home and catch a few hours' sleep. Young Ismail loved spending time with Muzaffer Efendi and the other beautiful souls around him, but one night he was moved to say, "Efendi, its wonderful that I met you, but somehow it's not enough. One day, I would like to really be close to you." Efendi answered, "Don't worry. One day you will be close to me."

Six years later, on Oct. 14, 1976, Ismail became the official muezzin of the Beyazid mosque, not far from Muzaffer's bookshop. Efendi told Ismail, "Didn't I tell you I was going to get you close to me? Now you are close." Ismail remembers fondly how their relationship became just like father and son—there was about 25 years difference in their ages. Ismail would often go to the bookstore to be with Efendi. Sometimes, when they would travel by car, Efendi would have the driver make a special trip to drop Ismail off at the mosque before he himself was taken to his destination.

Finally one day Ismail said to Efendi, "I would really like to understand why you are treating me like such a special person, when you have so many other good people around you. Who am I to deserve all of this favor?" Efendi answered:

> Let me explain why I treat you like this and perhaps you'll feel more comfortable with it. Today, I am a well-known and respected spiritual teacher, but years ago it was very different. As a young man, things were very difficult; I had little money and was unknown in Istanbul. No one knew me. I wasn't being invited to chant or preach in any of the mosques. But in the Beyazid mosque, there was a blind hafiz named Kadir Efendi. He loved me from the first day I met him and greeted him. Kadir Efendi was being paid to work there as a muezzin two days a week. One day he asked me to fill in for him at the mosque. I chanted for the prayers, and Kadir Efendi turned that day's wages over to me.

Efendi said that this had been a great opportunity and opening for him which he never forgot. He told Ismail, "You came to the mosque, and when I look at you I remember him. That's why I'm helping you."

Until Efendi's passing, Hafiz Ismail spent as much time as he could with Efendi, happily passing most week nights among the other intimate disciples and companions who joined Muzaffer Efendi at his bookstore in the late afternoon for conversation and prayers. This would be followed by a walk to a local restaurant for dinner, further prayers and visits, with the group finally settling in some place like the Bosphorus tea gardens until the morning prayers. Ismail recalls:

> Muzaffer Efendi had a wide circle of friends including some of the most famous singers and hufaz of Turkey. In the 1950's and 1960's, after Turkey joined the Western alliance, these professional singers and chanters of Qur'an began to perform on the radio and tour, reviving and popularizing the ilahis, the mystic hymns of the Sufis. Sometimes Muzaffer Efendi would invite these popular recording artists to perform for his

followers and friends. He invited not only chanters of Qur'an, but secular film and radio celebrities and female singers from contemporary culture. For half a century, no one had wanted to sing the Sufi hymns, but when these popular performers started recording the ilahis and singing them on the radio, everyone started getting enthusiastic about them again.*

Muzaffer Efendi was an incredibly generous person. Nothing could make him happier than to be able to give something to another person. Sometimes at the mosque, people would lose their shoes after leaving them in the shoe rack—they would be sent to Muzaffer Efendi and he would get them more shoes. If someone came to Istanbul and had no money and things weren't working out, people would tell them, "Go to Muzaffer Efendi. He gives whatever you need." It was incredible. He wasn't a rich man, just a humble bookshop owner; so where did all this money come from? Sometimes when people would come and sit around at Muzaffer Efendi's bookshop, Efendi would say, "Why are you just sitting there? Why not buy something or go sell something? We can always use the money to feed people."

In the courtyard around Beyazid mosque he would frequently urge us to buy something from the beggars selling their wares. "Buy some prayer beads, some audio tapes, some tea. Buy something! We have to help these people. We should help them earn a little money so they will have something too." He would go and buy food from the gypsy girls and feed it to the birds that were all around. In this way, everyone benefitted.

Ismail concludes with a remembrance of Efendi during Ramadan:

In 1978, Ramadan fell in the hottest part of the summer, when the days of fasting were longest. The fast began at 4:30 in the morning, and lasted until almost 9:00 at night. As evening

* Sheikha Fariha also recalls that in New Mexico she met an older gentleman, an actor who had been with a contemporary American acting troupe that passed through Istanbul. He said that Muzaffer Efendi invited them to perform their play for his people and they did so.

approached and the congregation was really starving and ready to break the fast, Muzaffer Efendi was sometimes inspired to tease with the people about their hunger.

At the Bayezid mosque, several hufaz would come around 5:30 and chant Qur'an until about 7:00. Then Muzaffer Efendi would give a short talk from under the muezzin's balcony. One evening after a short discourse on Qur'an, Muzaffer Efendi said to the hungry congregation: "Now, let us think about the recipe for making omelettes." (This was followed predictably by groans of protest from the people, but Efendi went on, unperturbed.)

"Now imagine that this is the sound of striking the match to start the fire. (He imitates the sound.) *Cshwoffff!* Now we take out the pan and put it on the fire and add some delicious butter. And now it's melting and sizzling. (He makes a perfect imitation of butter sizzling in the pan.) *Sszszsszsz!* "

The people are drooling and saying, "Enough, Efendi. We are suffering." But he carries on: "Now, let us put this egg in the pan. (He imitates the breaking of the egg into the pan.) And where is that scrumptious sausage?" By the time he finished, there was so much drool on the carpet, they had to clean it up with soap and water.

But when it was finally time to break the fast, Efendi took everyone out and treated them to dinner at one of the most beautiful restaurants in Istanbul. He had been increasing their hunger so he could buy them even more food to satisfy them—huge portions of kebab and all kinds of delicacies. Then in the middle of the dinner, Muzaffer Efendi took his shoes off, climbed up on the table and started snapping his fingers and dancing with joy. When some of them showed surprise, Efendi explained, "This is my happiest day, when I am able to feed all my beloved ones. What else could bring me more joy than this?"

The Call of the West

The connections that led to Efendi's travels to America in the late nineteen-seventies and early eighties were already being formed as early as 1970. One of the first major contacts was Tosun Bayrak, a Turkish-born artist and professor at Fairleigh Dickinson and Cooper Union in New York City.

Sheikh Tosun Bayrak photo (couresty of Salik Schwartz)

Tosun was born in 1926, just a few years after Efendi. His first forty years were steeped in the pursuit of worldly attainment: he was an Olympic heavyweight wrestler in Turkey, a twice published poet in his youth, a political activist, the first diplomatic consol from Turkey to Morocco during the 1950's, recipient of a

Guggenheim fellowship in 1965, and finally an established artist and art history professor in New York City. Yet, after enjoying some years of acclaim as an avant-garde artist, Tosun renounced the art scene when he began to realize the extent of ego-inflation that could accompany artistic fame.

By his own account, the spiritual peril of it was brought home to him one day when he was introduced to an attractive young woman who showered enthusiastic praise upon him and his artwork. Instead of feeling elated and self-important as a result of this praise, Tosun was inwardly disturbed because he saw how eagerly the ego feeds upon such adulation and how easily conceit could accompany artistic fame. Then and there, he resolved to deny the ego this avenue of aggrandizement by discontinuing his career as an artist. Afterwards, Tosun and his wife, Jemila, also an artist, began to direct their energies primarily toward spiritual pursuits.

Haydar and Fariha Friedrich, Muzaffer Efendi, Jemila and Tosun Bayrak at table.

In 1968, Tosun and Jemila traveled to Konya to attend the

Mevlevi ceremonies. During the trip, they met a lady named Munever Ayashli Hanim, who told them about a very special master in Istanbul named Muzaffer Efendi. In 1970, she took them to Efendi, who accepted them as his students. When, after only a few years, Efendi was ready to make Tosun a sheikh, Tosun inquired: why him, a person who had not followed any spiritual pursuits or practices for most of his life? Efendi told him, "By age thirty you had tasted riches, women, and fame as an artist and a wrestler. Now there's nothing to make you turn back and say, 'I missed something.' That's why I'm making you a sheikh."

By 1976, the couple had opened a space in their home in Spring Valley, New York, where they could give Sufi classes in America, with the long distance spiritual support of Muzaffer Efendi. Tosun thus became the first Jerrahi sheikh to live and teach in America, assisted by his wife, who is also a sheikha in the Order. This was the beginning of a process that would soon lead to Efendi's visits to America, where he could openly teach the Sufi path of love in an environment protected by democratic political and religious freedoms.

Jemila Bayrak worked to transcribe many of the hitherto unrecorded ilahis in western musical notation so that the dervishes in America could sing them. Though they experimented with putting a few singable English translations under the Turkish words, the initial results were unsatisfying and the group unanimously elected to keep the hymns in the original Turkish.

Over the years, Tosun would translate and publish a number of fine works on Sufism, including *The Most Beautiful Names*, *Inspirations*, and *What the Seeker Needs*. It was also through the efforts of Tosun, Jemila, and the early Spring Valley community (The Jerrahi Order of America) that Muzaffer Efendi's first trips to the United States were made possible. Beginning in 1978, generous endowments were granted by the Dia Art Foundation, an organization sponsored by Fariha and Haydar Friedrich.

John Bennett with Muzaffer Efendi (courtesy of Muzaffer Ergür)

John G. Bennett, a British student of the famous Armenian philosopher, G. I. Gurdjieff, had also visited Muzaffer Efendi in the late 1960's and in one of his books complimented him on being one of the few true sheikhs he had come across in his travels. Prior to his passing in 1974, Bennet sent a number of his own students to visit Muzaffer in Istanbul. For his own part, Efendi later commented that Bennett did not speak very fluent Turkish and, though they did converse, they never found a suitable translator to assist them in a real in-depth spiritual conversation. Nevertheless, their meeting forged a link that continued in the Bennett-Gurdjieff line. Efendi was aware that both Gurdjieff and Bennett had spent time in Istanbul (then Constantinople) in the early 1920's, before the closing of the tekkes, and that Gurdjieff had visited many of the local Sufis, particularly the Mevlevis, learning and adapting some of their sacred dervish movements for use in his own Gurdjieffain movements. In subsequent years, Muzaffer Efendi and his followers were invited to the Claymont Institute in West Virginia, headed by another direct student of

Gurdjieff, Pierre Elliot. The school at Claymont was an esoteric community established in the Gurdjieff tradition, an American offshoot of Bennett's Sherbourne Institute in England.

Shems Friedlander and Salik Schwartz were two Americans who met Muzaffer Efendi around 1972. They both became his students after an initial attraction to the Mevlevi Order in Konya. The Mevlevis toured America in 1972, attracting many souls with their whirling sama performances. Around this time, Shems traveled to Konya and did research on the Mevlevi order, studying the traditions from its current leaders, such as Süleyman Dede, and producing a beautifully illustrated English book called *The Whirling Dervishes.* After he met Muzaffer Efendi in Konya, Shems turned his attention to the Jerrahis and adapted from Muzaffer Efendi's *Irshad* two books, *Submission: The Sayings of the Prophet Muhammad* and *Ninety-Nine Names of Allah*. In 1987, Shems would pen a set of Jerrahi-inspired dervish essays entitled, *When You Hear Hoofbeats, Think of a Zebra*, and go on to produce several fine films on Sufism in the following decades.

In early 1977, Shems was interviewed on the *In the Spirit* radio show, hosted by his friend, Lex Hixon. Shems described the wonderful sheikh he had met in Istanbul and the Halveti-Jerrahi tradition, which was practically unknown in the United States at the time. "The first time I saw this man make *salat* [prayer]," Shems said of Muzaffer Efendi, "was in the middle of the day in his bookshop. When the *muezzin* intoned the call to prayer, this man got up and rolled his little prayer carpet out on the floor in the bookstore—while everyone was around—and knelt down and prayed. As I watched, a tear came to my eye as I realized that this man was not praying for himself, but was truly praying for the entire world. There was something very special in those moments and in the way he did that."

Hazrat Inayat Khan and his wife, Ora Ray Baker (1926)

Both Shems and Salik had a previous Sufi connection with Pir Vilayat Khan, head of the Sufi Order in the West, who taught meditation and a universalist approach to Sufi mysticism throughout Europe and America. Pir Vilayat's father, Hazrat Inayat Khan, a great Indian musician and murshid, was the first to bring Sufism to Europe and America, during the years 1910-1926. Born into a Muslim family, Hazrat Inayat Khan received his Sufi training in four schools, including the Chisti Order, and emerged with a unitive mystical teaching which drew on the essence of all the world's major religions.

Sheikh Salik Schwartz

Guiding Westerners in the early part of the twentieth century—who tended to be intrigued with the externals of oriental mysticism, yet reluctant to accept the Prophet Muhammad or the rituals of Islam—Inayat Khan simply taught the essential unitive principles of Islam, stressing the acceptance of all the authentic messengers and their teachings. In Sufi parlance, he was teaching from the perspective of universal truth, the level of hakikat. In this way, he gradually sowed the seeds of religious tolerance for future generations, at the same time preparing the ground for Islam and its tarikat in the West. Muzaffer Efendi considered Hazrat Inayat Khan to have been "a very great man" and also had ample respect for his son, Pir Vilayat Khan.

Shems Friedlander accompanied Pir Vilayat to Konya in the early seventies and then brought him to meet Muzaffer Efendi in Istanbul. Later, Pir Vilayat would pay another courtesy visit to Efendi in New York to personally give his permission for his khalif, Salik, to study with Efendi. Muzaffer Efendi said he was honored to accept a khalif of Pir Vilayat. As Salik had for years led the *Dances of Universal Peace* in New York City's huge Cathedral of St. John the Divine, this highly ecumenical Episcopal Church became a natural choice as a location for the Jerrahis to perform their public *dhikr* ceremonies when they visited America.

Muzaffer Efendi with wife Mehlika, son Junayd and daughter Fatma Ayşe

SECTION TWO

Muzaffer Efendi Comes to America

Muzaffer Efendi leading sitting dhikr (photo by James Wentzy)

"I was invited to the Fifth International Festival of Traditional Art in Rennes," Muzaffer Efendi recounts in his introduction to the Turkish version of *The Unveiling of Love.*[1] He attended the festival, accompanied by twenty-two of his followers. The public performance of the Jerrahi dhikr at the French festival stirred great interest and received much acclaim. From Rennes, the group traveled to Paris and Berlin, where the reception was equally enthusiastic. As Muzaffer Efendi describes:

> In the Berlin Grand Opera House we publicly performed the Halveti-Jerrahi Sufi dhikr ceremony. As the traditional ceremonies are full of Turkish tekke music, we played and sang from the mystic hymns of Yunus Emre, Haji Bektash Veli, Eshrefoglu Rumi and other great Sufi masters. The audience was extremely appreciative and clearly enjoyed the performance.
>
> The Opera House was filled to capacity. I later learned that

there were others outside the building, trying to hear the ceremony. Among the audience were people from a number of European countries; some of them knew about Sufism and others among them didn't. As one might anticipate, we began our evening by chanting the affirmation of Divine Unity. Many in the audience intoned the affirmation of Divine Unity, the *tawhid*, *La ilaha illallah*, along with us while those who didn't watched silently with bated breath. After this, when we stood up and formed our circle to perform standing dhikr, I realized with great excitement and admiration that everyone in the audience was joining the *devran* circle, one after another. They looked so thirsty for union; they were longing to quench their thirst.

There are many universities in Europe which have departments of Islamic-Turkish Sufism. These departments research and study Islamic Sufism in depth, and present these teachings to large groups of people, sometimes comparing Sufism to the mystic paths found in the world's other religions. Because of this, the Europeans have become knowledgeable about Sufism and its various mystic orders, but very few of them had ever actually seen the dhikr ceremony. Therefore, they were most grateful to witness a direct demonstration of that precious knowledge about which they had only read in books.

When the Jerrahis began to tour Europe, the people who came to see them were truly astonished and mesmerized by the mystic hymns and by witnessing the dervishes in states of ecstasy. As the crowds tended to applaud wildly at the end, someone had to announce that clapping was inappropriate, since dhikr is a religious ceremony. The people's hearts were overflowing. They were thirsty and didn't want to leave even after we finished and it was announced that the event was over. Many came up to personally thank us. Somehow, they weren't getting satisfied in their churches.

In Rennes, the mayor hosted us with a great banquet. We stayed there three days and three nights. On each subsequent evening the people went deeper and deeper into the dhikr, and were especially enthusiastic in chanting "Allah". People would come and make inquiries—and also test us, which did not escape our attention.

One night, I was asked, "Even though you are a Muslim, you accept Christians into your circle and permit them to make dhikr with you, without discriminating against them in the slightest. Could you explain the meaning of this?" My answer was: "I am a poor servant of Allah—a Muslim sheikh—and I accept everyone into our circle, everyone who says, '*Allah*'. I say '*Allah*' and I encourage them to say '*Allah*'. That's my job." I think this answer satisfied the questioner. As we know, the responsibility of all the prophets and messengers has been to invite people to affirm: "*La ilaha illallah*." And likewise, as the inheritors of those divine messengers, our principal duty is to invite humanity to affirm "*La ilaha illallah*" and experience unity.

Both in Rennes and in Paris I personally witnessed that the people were thirsty for this. The press even ran positive newspaper articles, some of which were reprinted in Turkey's *Dunya* newspaper, with headlines reading: "Dervishes Spellbind Audiences."

Our musicians also played at the Rennes Festival before massive crowds numbering as many as 15,000. There were groups from twenty-five nations there. The dervishes represented Turkey and their religious music, and became the hit of the festival, widely covered by the European press. We were pleased to be able to share with them in the light of unity. Even though they didn't understand the words of our ilahis, the Europeans were spellbound by this music. Just think; if they enjoyed it that much without knowing what we were singing, how much more they would have been uplifted if they had understood the beautiful depth of meaning in the mystic poems we sang, especially those of Hazrat Yunus Emre

We left those sympathetic people of France just like the soul leaves the body—we were that close—and proceeded to America, where we had been invited with divine permission. We were greeted by those Americans whom we had met previously in Istanbul. We felt fortunate to have met them and since that day, have been engaged, so to speak, in a love affair

> with the American people. We were housed at Professor Tosun Bayrak's house. We performed at Columbia University and New York University, preceded by a talk on Sufism and Islam by the honorable Talat Halman. Tosun was most helpful in translating my words and expounding the disciplines of Sufism, inspiring me with great trust in his abilities in this regard.

During the group's stay in France, a film documentary of the Jerrahi dhikr ceremony was created by Pierre-Marie Goulet in conjunction with Peter Brook. Kudsi Ergüner, a Turkish musician who helped with the organization of the Rennes festival, recounts a side trip, organized by Pierre Zuber, in which Muzaffer Efendi and his retinue were taken to visit the Christian monastery of Mont Saint-Michel in northern Brittany. There, they met the monastery abbot who gave a welcoming speech in which he described his own first contact with Islam. This came in the form of an earthenware plate with the name "Allah" in Arabic script inscribed upon it. It was hung on the wall over the bed in which he slept whenever he visited his grandmother's house. He added that, as a child, he was always fearful that the heavy plate might fall on his head during the night.

Before the abbot's words could be translated from French into Turkish, Muzaffer Efendi, who had no knowledge of the French language, stood up and handed Kudsi a wrapped parcel, asking him to present it to the abbot. Everyone was astonished when he added, "It is a big earthenware plate on which 'Allah' is written. Tell him to hang it over his bed. God will protect him." Even the abbot was rendered speechless.[2]

In the meantime, Tosun Baba and his assistant Gül 'Ali had flown over to France to join the group. Before the tour was over, they had secured visas and standby plane tickets for Muzaffer Efendi and some of his disciples to travel on to America.

During this first trip to the United States in March of 1978, only about ten or fifteen people came over with Efendi. The stay lasted ten days, a most memorable week and a half for the American Jerrahi community and the visitors who attended. At the time, there were no more than thirteen people in the Spring Valley community. The first public Halveti-Jerrahi dhikr performance in America was held at Earl Hall at Columbia University in New York on March 11, 1978. Two of the other earliest performances in America were at the Kevorkian Center at N.Y.U. and at Cooper-Union, where Tosun was on the faculty.

John and Dominique de Menil were a socially committed Catholic couple of wide-ranging ecumenical interests who lived in Houston, Texas, where they were well known as generous patrons of the arts and founders of the De Menil collection. In 1971, they built the Rothko Chapel in Houston around a commissioned series of large murals by the artist Mark Rothko. The chapel was founded as an interfaith place of worship and as a refuge for meditation and prayer. Inspired by the 1972 Mevlevi tour of America, the de Menils discussed sponsoring a return trip of the whirling dervishes to America which would include a performance in the Rothko Chapel; however John passed away in 1973 before this dream could be realized.

In the fall of 1977, Dominique made contact through a mutual friend with Tosun Baba, who was recommended as someone who could give advice on how to host the Mevlevis. Dominique arranged a meeting between Tosun, herself and her daughter, Fariha (Phillipa de Menil), in which they discussed the logistics of bringing the Mevlevis to America. After the meeting, as Tosun was leaving, he confided to Fariha: "We've talked about the Mevlevis, but you should meet *my* sheikh." These words, Fariha recalls, conveyed the fragrance of Muzaffer Efendi which inspired her and her then husband, Haydar (Heiner) Friedrich, to sponsor the eminent sheikh and ten of his disciples and musicians on their first trip to America in the spring of 1978. Subsequently, in 1980, Fariha would be invested as a sheikha by

Muzaffer Efendi (along with Lex Hixon) and begin to assume a significant leadership role in the Order, which would increase with time. Fariha recalls that her duties in the early days included leading the women in silent dhikr.

In the summer of 1978, following the Jerrahi's spring visit to America, Fariha and her mother traveled to Turkey to visit Efendi. They were invited to meet with him at Tosun's summer house in Üsküdar. They came bearing gifts of two small earth balls, collected from *The Lightning Field* in New Mexico—an artistic endeavor by Walter de Maria—which were given to Muzaffer Efendi along with a note which implored him: "Please come and transform us." Efendi accepted the earth balls with delight, holding them in his large palms and saying: "This earth comes from the West." When he finally visited the West Coast of the United states two years later, he mentioned the earth balls again and said that now he had reached this destination and stood on the soil from whence they came.

In the Spirit, WBAI

During his initial visit to the U.S., Efendi was interviewed on the radio with Tosun Bayrak serving as his translator. On Sunday afternoon, April 12, 1978, Efendi and his disciples crowded into the WBAI studios in a converted church on East 62nd Street in Manhattan, for a radio interview and live, on-the-air dhikr. The program, whose broadcast signal radiated from the top of the Empire State Building, was called *In the Spirit* and was hosted by Lex Hixon. Tall, with blonde hair, blue eyes, and an open, friendly disposition, Lex was born in California, but had long since relocated to New York's Hudson Valley. He was a Yale graduate who had recently received his Ph.D in World Religions from Columbia University. An ardent universalist and seasoned initiate in several Eastern traditions, including Vedantic Hinduism (Ramakrishna Order) and Vajrayana Buddhism (Gelugpa sect), Lex had just authored his first of many books, *Coming Home*, which was in publication stage at the time. He hosted the *In the Spirit* radio show which had begun in 1971 and would continue to broadcast until 1984, featuring interviews with some of the greatest spiritual teachers of our time, including the Dalai Lama, Mother Teresa, Bawa Muhaiyaddeen, Pir Vilayat Khan, Rabbi Shlomo Carlebach, Reb Zalman Schachter-Shalomi, Jiddu Krishnamurti and many others.

Though Lex looked forward that Sunday morning to meeting and interviewing the noted Sufi master from Istanbul, he was only vaguely aware of the impact the meeting would have on his life. Later, he recalled picking up his guitar the night before and playing passionate flamenco improvisations for hours. The next morning, as he recounted:

> I was running late and hurrying to make the morning radio program, which was from 11:00 till 1:00. I got there just in

time to set up the studio.... It was very chaotic. Sitting in the corner, I saw this gentleman wearing a brown suit and a hat. I sensed that he must be the sheikh, but I didn't have time to go over and meet him. Finally, when everything was all set up, we sat down with the microphones between us. We just had a minute before going on the air, and finally I could look at him for the first time.

Call to prayer over the radio on WBAI in New York

Then, the call to prayer began—which was the way I wanted to begin the program—and tears began to come from his eyes. I was amazed, because as a radio interviewer, you expect a certain amount of detachment when you're having a radio discussion. You don't think that *that* much spiritual emotion will begin to manifest. I only experienced that one other time with a spiritual leader, when I interviewed Rabbi Gadelia Kenek from Jerusalem, who was the Breslover Menek at that time. I asked him to pray and he said, "Well, it will have to be a real prayer." I said,

"Okay, please pray a real prayer." So, as he prayed, tears came out of his eyes too. This great Jewish rabbi and this great Islamic sheikh were the only two, in thirteen years of interviews, that I saw weeping on the radio. The interview still exists on tape. It was a very powerful, intimate contact between two souls.[3]

Sufism on the air with host Lex Hixon (front, right).

The program began with a hafiz beautifully chanting the *adhan* or call to prayer. As Lex later observed, half in jest: the *adhan*, with its signal broadcast from the top of the Empire State Building, temporarily transformed the skyscraper into the world's tallest minaret. The call to prayer was immediately followed by a florid solo recitation of the *Fatiha* in Arabic. Asked about the meaning and significance of the *Fatiha*, as the opening sura of the Qur'an, Muzaffer Efendi gave the following interpretation:

> May the compassion and gifts of Allah be upon all humanity. All thanks, praise and love is for Allah alone, the Creator and Owner of the whole Universe. Allah is the Compassionate and Beneficent, Who showers His love upon the entire creation, and extends His Divine Compassion and Mercy to His servants in the Hereafter. Allah is the Owner and Sovereign of the Day of Requital. Everything we possess and all that we are in this world are divine gifts which He has distributed; and His sovereignty extends to the Hereafter. O Allah, through Whom all these qualities shine forth, we supplicate You, we love You, and we hold You in awe. We ask Your aid and Your help in order to serve You. If You don't aid us and accept us, how can we pray

to You? May You keep our feet firm on Your straight path, and keep us among those who enter Your Paradise. Keep us on the straight path, and please do not let us be among those who earn Your displeasure. Amin. Accept our prayer. May You keep us with You, and never turn us away; and may You keep our hearts illumined with Your Love.

By way of context for the live dhikr performance, Lex further inquired about the meaning and practice of dhikr. Efendi responded:

One must seek and find one's Lord through remembrance (*dhikr*). All success in life comes from remembering one's Divine Source. By nature, humanity is created as the beloved of God and the most supreme of all His creation. Humans who forget their Lord fall below what is proper even to animals. The heart is the core of every human being, and the heart, by nature, is the Divine Abode. Allah, Who cannot be contained in all the heavenly or earthly realms, dwells in your heart. The heart that is united with Divine Truth is well established and full of beauty. The heart that is empty of Divine Truth is a receptacle open to base influences. Therefore, one should strive to purify and cleanse the heart so that it may be honored as the house of the Lord. The King cannot be invited to a squalid house. Beautify your heart so that Allah may enter it. The way the heart is cleansed is through *dhikr*, the remembrance of one's Divine Source.

Dhikr not only profits the one who remembers Allah, but also helps awaken those who have forgotten Allah. All existence, from the tiniest speck of dust to the furthest corner of the heavens, is a reminder of Allah. The entire creation remembers Him and makes *dhikr*, each creature in their own way. The one whose ears are truly open, listens and perceives this cosmic remembrance. Through remembrance, the veils are lifted and Allah becomes plainly visible all around us. Wherever we look, we behold His beautiful Divine Countenance. *Dhikr* is the key to these secrets. When you remember Allah, Allah will remember you.

Following Efendi's explanation, Lex asked him if everyone listening could, in some way, join in with the *dhikr* that was about to be performed, or if the practice had any esoteric restrictions. Efendi answered: "*Dhikr* can be done by oneself or in community. All the creation is engaged in the continuous remembrance of Allah. However, some are consciously participating, while others are not aware that they are remembering Allah with every breath and movement. Those with love in their hearts find joy in *dhikr*, and their love increases. The blowing of the wind, the rustling of the leaves, the gurgling of the water, the subtle movement of the fishes—these are all various ways of repeating the name of the Lord—for those who have eyes to see this splendor and ears to hear this music."

In Muzaffer's personal account, he recalls the program and the deep feelings it stirred in him:

> The program began with the *Adhan-i Muhammadi* and readings from the *Qur'an-i Karim* After explaining the meanings of these, we went on to speak about *dhikr* and divine unity (*tawhid*). At one point, the interviewer interrupted our explanation to say: "The lovers in America are expecting a real experience of dhikr. Words are not enough. Could Efendi repeat the most basic dhikr for us?" After we agreed to his request, he announced to the radio audience: "All the lovers who are listening to our interview, please take your telephones off the hook and lock your doors, because a dhikr is going to be offered." I couldn't hold back my tears and began to weep. How could I have done otherwise? Millions of Americans were listening over the radio, expecting to hear our repetition of divine unity. I started repeating *La ilaha illallah*, and was fervently joined by my dervishes, including the older American lovers.
>
> At that point, I felt as though the skies of America were echoing with *tawhid* and the entire creation was listening to our affirmation of divine unity. The whole earth and sky and

everything in between—the known and unknown, the seen and unseen—were being bathed and infused with divine light and wisdom through the light of unity.

After our enthusiasm and joy had reached its peak, we paused and the announcer issued an interesting word of caution, reminding us that the Arabic words of the *tawhid* might be a little difficult for Americans to pronounce. In order for them to learn these precious words of unity correctly, he requested that I slowly articulate it in my own voice, one syllable at a time. This *fakir* realized that his warning was rightly placed and began to pronounce it slowly, in this way making it easier for them.

Kemal Evren, Safer Dal, Muzaffer Ozak and Tosun Bayrak singing ilahis

The Americans who heard us over the radio flooded the radio station with calls. Those who were outside New York, but heard about the program and our visit, would subsequently come to see us in New York from Canada, Washington, California, Alaska, Texas and from various other places whose names I didn't even know. For instance one man, Mr. Hardy, traveled 27 hours by train to hear this poor one speak, which astonished me. A respected teacher came and brought many of his students from the Washington D.C. area. This great response was an occasion in my humble life to treasure and cherish. Those who came to attend our gatherings and listen to our teaching—asking questions about divine unity and so forth—turned our discourses into rains of divine mercy and our gatherings into gardens from paradise.

I observed individually that each of these people were lovers of Allah Most High. In countenance, in heart and in form, they were very pure, clean, and beautiful. What they had inside could be seen in their faces. Without exception, they were all asking about the True Beloved, and longing to hear our teachings about Allah and the Path of Love.

I want to be very clear about this. I've hardly ever experienced the degree of love and goodness that I encountered in America in any of the Islamic countries I've visited. I utter this admission in the belief that I am simply repaying them; it is my duty to tell this.

After the Sunday morning radio program on April 12, Tosun Baba invited everyone to join Efendi back at the Spring Valley tekke. Lex Hixon also joined them for the momentous final six days of Efendi's stay, which Lex later compared to the six days of the creation of the world. Here is how Efendi described the extraordinary honeymoon atmosphere that prevailed during this time:

Once *dhikr* started, there was hardly an eye that didn't weep, a tongue that didn't express the love of Truth, or heart that wasn't moved by Divine Love. These American lovers made *tawhid* the litany of their tongue and completely forgot about eating and drinking. The air they breathed and the water they drank was completely saturated with the love of Allah. I am not exaggerating this. They weren't eating, drinking or sleeping. They just wanted to talk about Allah and continuously opened up new conversations in this vein. The divine love simply made them forget their physiological needs. They almost became like angels in that respect, and like children in the way they listened and absorbed what was said.

At one point, I decided to test their wisdom and asked them, "What is it that Allah Most High cannot see?" One of them named Lex replied: "There is nothing that Allah cannot see or know, so this could not possibly be the case. But if there is anything that Allah overlooks, perhaps it would be the faults of some of his servants." In some sense, he meant to say that Allah covers for the shortcomings of His servants. Actually, the answer that this fakir was going for was that Allah Most High does not see dreams. Allah would never dream because His Essence neither sleeps nor slumbers. But since I wasn't expecting this other answer, I was deepened in my interest and love for the one who gave it.

Together, from midnight to three in the morning, we all made *dhikr*, *tawhid* and the *sohbet* of Truth. When I would remind them that the time for sleep and rest had come, they would say: "Doesn't Efendi love us, that he wants to sleep?" In reality, as I reminded them, we will one day soon enter into a very long sleep from which we will wake up only on the Day of Judgment. They responded: "Since we know that Efendi is only going to be with us a few days, we would gladly sacrifice our sleep for these few precious moments in his presence." With such an answer they would overrule me so that I couldn't say anything else about resting. Finally after about two hours of sleep, we would rise for the morning prayers and—I swear to God as my witness—I would find some of them awake still affirming the divine unity on their prayer beads.

In a 1989 *New Dimensions* radio interview, Lex Hixon recalled his own experience on the evening of the April 12 radio broadcast:

I went to the tekke in Spring Valley, New York; we all did dhikr together and it became very late. Efendi asked me if I wanted to spend the night and I agreed. He clapped his hands in the manner of an Oriental sultan and one of his dervishes brought me a pair of Efendi's own pajamas. They were silky,

> with a rich, golden-brown color. I thought it a little peculiar, but the height of hospitality, so I changed into the pajamas. Then Efendi brought me into his own bedroom and I slept in the bed of his attendant, right next to his. We woke up very early in the morning at dawn for prayers. We had only gone to sleep a couple of hours before.
>
> As I opened my eyes, Efendi was looking at me and, again, tears were coming out of his eyes. So I realized that it wasn't necessarily the call to prayer that made him weep during the show; it was apparently something that he saw in me. He recognized—let us say—an old friend or someone who would carry his spirit or transmission into the modern world. When you feel that kind of love directed toward you, there's no way to respond but with love in return.

Lex's concluding comment undoubtedly echoes the experience of many souls who met Efendi and felt completely embraced by his love. In Lex's own case, there seemed to be a special chemistry almost as between a father and a spiritual son, a relationship that was shown to Efendi in a dream in which he and Baji Sultan seemed to be Lex's spiritual parents. Lex took hand within three days at Spring Valley and was given the Islamic name *Nur al-Anwar* by Efendi. That evening, he dreamed that flames were coming forth out of his head, which Efendi interpreted as divine inspiration—burning with the fire of love for Allah. Within two years Nur would receive the green and gold turban of the Order from Efendi, along with Fariha Friedrich and Gül 'Ali, a principal baba at the Spring Valley community.

Though strongly drawn to Muzaffer Efendi and the Islamic mystical teachings of unity, Nur quietly continued his involvement with other forms of spirituality, a propensity which Efendi generously allowed, while remaining personally convinced of the completeness of Islam, with all its mystic depths. As Nur's wife, Sheila Hixon, expressed it: "Lex felt a calling to experience the divine through all of the sacred traditions, but having not previously encountered Islamic Sufism or the intensity of love that Muzaffer Efendi directed toward him, Lex became intrigued by it and strongly attracted to the tradition. His previous experience with Bawa Muhayideen had not exposed him to any overtly Islamic teaching. Lex didn't like to think of it as converting or changing his religion in the sense of renouncing the other paths, but was drawn to the universality of Islam, and in time developed a strong commitment to represent and spread this noble tradition."

Nur Lex Hixon with Muzaffer Efendi (photo: Saskia Friedrich)

Concerning this, Nur recalls a conversation which he had with Efendi during one of the sheikh's early trips to America:

> When my sheikh, Muzaffer Efendi, first came to our house in New York City, he looked around and saw the Buddha statues and various icons and could see at a glance that I was a spiritually pluralistic person. He asked me: "What is your experience of these different traditions? Tell me your real experience. Don't give me an intellectual explanation." So I thought about it and gave him an answer which spontaneously came to my

> mind: "The religions are like a vast tree, and there are different branches coming out of this one tree. Some people feel comfortable in only one branch, but I feel comfortable in several branches." He answered: "That's very precise. That's exactly the way it is. But I prefer to stay inside the trunk of the tree."[4]

Muzaffer Efendi and his Turkish disciples returned to Istanbul in late April of 1978. Ramadan fell in July and August of that year and many of Efendi's Western followers were invited to come experience that holy month with Efendi in Istanbul.

In his book, *Heart of the Koran*, Nur described one of his own experiences from that trip, saying:

> I was sitting with Sheikh Muzaffer one late afternoon in the ancient Beyazid Mosque of Istanbul...We were enjoying together the poignant beauty of a *hafiz*, an Islamic cantor, singing the Holy Qur'an from memory, verses which he had repeated since childhood and which had become as natural to him as his own breathing. Gazing into the great domed space, radiant and peaceful, surrounded by this living revelation in pure sound, I was granted the vision of a translucent emerald mosque, above even the highest heaven. There were no human figures visible, only a vast Qur'an whose letters radiated light and whose pages turned gracefully as it spontaneously chanted itself. Later the sheikh confirmed to me that this had been an authentic mystical experience, not simply the product of creative imagination.[5]

Salik Schwartz recalls that Efendi looked after all of those who came to Istanbul and even made sure that they visited the tourist attractions, however briefly. Salik relates how once he was riding in a car with Efendi, who ordered the driver to pull up at the famous Blue Mosque in Sultanahmet, then instructed Salik to go spend a little time in the mosque and then return. When Salik got back in the car, Efendi told him, "Your friends in America will want to know if you visited the famous sites of

Istanbul such as the Blue Mosque. Now you can tell them yes."

Nur also recounted to the author how, on another day, he was riding in the car with Muzaffer Efendi, who offered to have the driver stop by the Blue Mosque. Nur recalled feeling that he was really happy just to be with his sheikh without stopping, so he declined, saying, "Efendi, you're my Blue Mosque." Efendi smiled, seemingly satisfied with this response, and told the driver to keep going.

The interior of the Blue Mosque Sultanahmet Camii (photo by the author)

Nur also recalled another car ride with Efendi during which he began to recite his Sufi practice, saying, "Allah . . . Allah . . . Allah . . ." Before long Efendi stopped him, saying: "What if I tried to get your attention and said, 'Nur,' but just as you started to respond, 'Yes, here I am,' I just kept repeating, 'Nur . . . Nur . . . Nur' over and over? Sometimes you have to stop repeating and go beyond the name to the *named*—in order to discover the Essence."

Upon his return to Istanbul from his first American visit in the spring, Muzaffer Efendi had begun writing a book, designed especially for American readers, which he dedicated to Nur Lex Hixon. On his next trip to America, Efendi would bring along the manuscript, which he entitled *The Unveiling of Love*. Tosun Baba located an excellent translator, Muhtar Holland, and procured his services in translating the book. Within a year, it would be published in both America and Turkey, the versions differing only in language and the content of the introduction. Upon the completion of *The Unveiling of Love*, Muhtar would be commissioned to translate an edition of Efendi's massive Turkish work, *Irshad*, a collection of stories and teachings on many aspects of Islam and Sufism. However, a series of significant delays would cause this translation to be published only after Efendi's passing in 1985.

During the winter of 1978, Efendi developed severe prostate problems and had to undergo a serious operation, which he barely survived. By spring, he was well enough to travel again and a second trip was scheduled to the United States. Beginning on March 22, 1979, the trip was scheduled as a more extensive three week tour of the Northeastern United States for which Muzaffer Efendi would be able to bring thirty of his Turkish followers and perform the dhikr ceremony in a number of major American cities.

Efendi was anxious to return to America. Compared to the totalitarian regimes that controlled many of the Eastern countries, Efendi felt that America's founding principles of democratic freedom were very much in keeping with authentic Islamic ideals. He told New York newspaper reporter Roberta Goldstein, "When

I am in your country, I see light and clarity in the faces of the people. I have gone to the Balkan countries to preach, but there the people have little joy, and only look down at the ground in front of them when they walk. Here, the people look straight ahead, and a sense of purpose is within them." He also told Rochester reporter Susan McNamara[6]: "I am very appreciative of the attachment America has for their God, from the government to the people. All the coins read, 'In God we trust.' I pray and bless your country. Your country is working for humanity and that is good. I pray the name of America will be written in gold for the pages of history.

Nur Lex Hixon and Muzaffer Efendi making joyful music (photo courtesy of Salik Schwartz)

The Second American Tour

The American itinerary in the Spring of 1979 included two public dhikrs in Manhattan; one at Cooper Union and the other at the Cathedral of St. John the Divine. The tour included performances at the University of Pennsylvania in Philadelphia and the Smithsonian Institute in Washington D.C. The final three performances took place in Ann Arbor, Michigan, Toronto, Ontario (at the World Symposium on Humanity) and Rochester, New York.

The public dhikr at Cooper-Union included a separate women's circle

During this visit, the author had the pleasure of meeting Muzaffer Efendi at the Claymont Institute, a Gurdjieff School directed by Pierre Elliot in Charlestown, West Virginia. I had an immediate favorable impression of the sheikh and felt a very powerful presence emanating from his ample frame. Efendi was received with great respect as one might honor a padishah from the old world; yet he immediately put everyone at ease with his down-to-earth sense of humor. Muzaffer Efendi's son and wife, Junayd and Baji Sultan, had also accompanied him on this trip as well as several dozen male and female disciples from Istanbul. After a huge banquet of lamb, exotic breads and various Turkish specialties, followed by coffee, cigarettes and a closing prayer, everyone retired to the main hall, a converted gymnasium. There, the Claymont students performed their sacred movements for Efendi and everyone else who had come for the weekend.

After a lengthy break, the whole community joined Efendi

and the dervishes for a full dhikr ceremony, replete with a Mevlevi dervish turning in the center of the circle. This dervish was Jelaluddin Loras, the son of the sheikh of Konya, who attended Claymont for the course that year. (A month later, the Mevlevis would also visit Claymont and perform their noble turning sama, led by Jelaluddin's father, Süleyman Dede.) During the standing dhikr, three or four rows of men moved clockwise in concentric circles around Efendi and his musicians, while the women, in accordance with Turkish custom, made standing dhikr in rows next to the men. The dhikr lasted several hours, but seemed far too short.

Sometime after midnight, we reconvened in the main hall for more coffee, tea, cigarettes, and questions with Efendi. Tosun Baba was translating. One of the women asked if it would have been permissible for the women to form their own dhikr circle like the men. Efendi apologized for not having thought to suggest it beforehand, saying that they were used to making dhikr where there wasn't enough room for two circles. At Cooper Union, a few weeks prior, they had formed two dhikr circles in their public performance. Many times, he added, the men make their dhikr in rows like the women did. In Turkey, except for the Alawis and Bektashis, who mix men and women, the sexes are usually kept separate in deference to the shariat. "Actually in Turkey, I would be considered very liberal in my views on this issue, "Efendi said, "but here I am considered very conservative. What is most important is to experience oneself in the presence of Allah in whatever way one does dhikr, whether standing, sitting or even lying down."

Late the next evening, a few of us, mostly musicians and course members, were invited to an intimate gathering with two of Efendi's Turkish musicians, who played *ney* and *kemenche*. The improvisations of the two master musicians, regulars on the Istanbul Radio, were truly sublime. When they finished, we thanked them profusely and they, in turn, humbly thanked us, the listeners, for our great receptivity, without which, they insisted, such depths of feeling could not have been expressed in their playing.

On Saturday, as on Sunday morning, we were treated to Sufi stories by Efendi for hours on end, tirelessly translated by Tosun Baba. One of the most memorable stories was the classic tale of the pauper who met his double in a Turkish bath:

> A man from a far away place came to a town in which he was stranger. He was tired and dirty and wanted to go to a Turkish bath, a *hammam*. He was a poor man, with no property and little money. There was a man selling sweets in front of the bathhouse and the man bought a little piece of candy in order to satisfy his hunger and sweeten his mouth. He ate the candy, then entered the Turkish bath. As he was poor, he undressed in the public section of the bath. He put on an old, torn loin cloth and entered the bath. He sat in the center under the dome, the public place where one sits down to sweat, and saw that there was nobody else in the huge bath area except him.
>
> After a while the door opened and a big man with an incense burner in his hand entered, spreading the beautiful scent of perfume into the bath. Following him were other attendants with towels, soaps and more perfumes. Behind them came a thin man, covered by a most beautiful silken embroidered loin cloth, with other attendants following him. As they were passing by him, the poor man noticed that the man in the silken loin cloth, who was obviously very important and rich, looked exactly like him—the same nose, the same eyes, same hair, same body, and the same age. The entourage passed on by and entered into a chamber which was reserved for the rich.
>
> After a while, the attendants, who washed and perfumed the rich man, left him quietly in this private chamber. As there were now just two of them in the whole bath, the poor man, being very curious, decided to go and see and speak with this man who had such an amazing resemblance to him. He waited for

a while, then got up and entered the private chambers. To his surprise, he found that the rich man laying on the table had expired, apparently unbeknownst to his attendants. It occurred to the poor man that if he would just unwrap his own tattered loin cloth and put it around the dead man, then put on the rich man's silken loin cloth and move the corpse into the public section where he had been sitting, he could seat himself in the private section and be taken for the rich man; and so he did this.

After a while, the attendants came back and massaged him and wrapped him in soft, expensive towels. As the attendants were leaving, they saw the poor dead man lying in the public section and, to avoid offending their master, carried the man out and dumped his body out of sight. The poor man, posing as his rich counterpart, now emerged and entered the chamber where he could change back into his clothes. The attendants dressed him in silk and furs. He put his hand in his pants pockets and found they contained gold coins. To avoid giving himself away, the man avoided speaking to his attendants. Soon, they came and said, "Your carriage is waiting for you. Would you like to go to the palace?" And he nodded his head and said yes and climbed in the carriage and embarked on the journey to his palace, enjoying his new-found wealth and station, but nervous about not knowing exactly who he was supposed to be.

When he arrived at his palace, his servants asked him if he would like to go to the women's section, or his private quarters. He shook his head no to the women's section and nodded yes to his quarters in the men's section. They escorted him there and brought him food. He looked around and saw that he was surrounded by great riches. He sat there, thinking that he mustn't go to the women's section for fear that his wife would know he was an imposter. He was desperately trying to figure out: Who am I? Where am I? What is my identity? Physically, I resemble this man—but who was he and what was his position? (You see all men are like that. A man dies, his house is sold and another man who will also die, buys the house. One president follows another, but each in turn will die. Each has their rank, title and trappings of their office, but none of them know deeply who they really are.)

Before long, a carriage came with an invitation to visit the Sultan. When the man looked at the paper, he could see from the content of the invitation that he was the Minister of Foreign Affairs for the Sultan. The man realized that he must escape, because surely the Sultan would see through his ploy and know his identity. (The Sultan, of course, represents God.) So the man filled his pockets with diamonds and other small valuables from the palace, jumped out the window and started running. Some people saw him and chased him, but he escaped by ducking into a mosque and hiding among the coffins in a dark, seldom-used section of the mosque cemetery.

He climbed in a coffin and slept until nightfall, waiting until it was safe to emerge Sometime after dark, he was startled awake by the sound of thieves going through the caskets looking for valuables. The man began to shake with fear until he rattled the coffin. This alerted the robbers, who were at first taken by surprise, then realized that this man knew of their unlawful activities and must be stopped. The man leaped out of the coffin and ran for his life, closely pursued by the robbers who chased him up the stairs of the minaret, round and around the circular balcony. Finally, they came at him from both sides, caught him and started beating him. He struggled and broke away from the robbers, then plunged off the minaret, landing and hitting his head with a thud on a hard marble surface.

Then he woke up and realized that he had fallen asleep in the Turkish bath and two of the bath attendants had knocked him onto the floor and were hitting him, saying, "Get out of here, you loafer! You paid a penny and have stayed here and slept the whole day, now get out! It's time for closing." All this was in a dream. The candy he had eaten as he entered the bath contained a little opium which made him fall asleep and dream.

This is how life is. Both the faithful and the unfaithful dream. If a person knows who he is, there is no problem, but the one who does not know, who, like the man in the story, doesn't know himself or what he is supposed to do in life, is liable to be dragged off to jail because of it. Like this pauper who posed as a rich man, we ourselves do not know who we are. We should ask ourselves: "Who am I? What is my position and purpose here in a human body?" The Prophet, may his noble soul be blest, says: "All men are asleep and wake up when they die." Those who die before death and awaken to who they are now, do not have to wait until their physical death to learn who they are. By dying before death we mean that we return to our origin, our Divine Essence... A fish swam over to the head fish and asked,"What is water?" When the fisherman takes that fish out of the sea, then the fish will know.

Questions, answers, and more stories with Efendi

Efendi also spoke about conscience, saying: "Like Adam, when he was about to eat the fruit and trembled and sweated, we all have warning bells that signal us when we are about to do wrong. Even if this wrong action is pleasurable, if we feel hesitancy and experience warning signals, we should definitely avoid it. If we persist in doing it, there is a curse that comes after overriding the warning four or five times: the warning disappears and we begin to think our wrongs to be right."

After Efendi had shared these and many other stories, the time finally came for him and his troupe to leave West Virginia and travel to the nation's capital where they would perform at the Smithsonian Institute Auditorium before returning to New York. Almost all the guests and students from Claymont drove up to Washington D.C. as well.

For the public performance, the men wore various colors of *haydariyya* vests over their white robes, and the women wore bright, full-length dresses with multicolored head-scarves. After a brief introduction, the performance commenced with a ritual entrance, with each dervish entering and kissing the sheikh's hand, then forming a line in which everyone in turn exchanged hand kisses, a sign of honoring the divine light within each soul. As the auditorium stage was small, it was not possible to offer the by-now traditional invitation to everyone in the audience to join the circles of the dervishes during the standing dhikr. However, everyone was invited to another room after the performance to ask the sheikh any questions they might have.

When everyone had settled in, Efendi began with a story about a Bektashi dervish. The Bektashis are very unorthodox dervishes who are not observant of Islamic prayers and other rituals. In the story, someone had offered to pay a Bektashi 100 dollars just to do his prayer. The Bektashi agreed, took the money and made a few rak'at of salat. The other man said, "But you did not make your ablution first." The Bektashi answered: "I won't do that for less than 200 dollars!" Efendi concluded with a chuckle, "After two hours of saying 'Hayy, Hayy,' I won't answer any questions until I get some coffee." As laughter filled the room, a couple of Smithsonian personnel jumped up and went out to find coffee and water.

Efendi and some of the others began to smoke. The next question from the audience was about cigarettes and alcohol in Islam. They received one of Efendi's famous tongue-in-cheek replies: "I'm against it." Amidst further laughter, Tosun explained: "Efendi says just because he is using tobacco he is not going to say that it is recommended. However, he does feel there is some good in it. First of all, if someone smokes, the thieves won't come to their house at night." Amidst laughter beginning with the Turks in the audience, we heard Efendi continue in Turkish, punctuated by comical gestures and ludicrous imitations of someone with a hacking cough—*uhuh, uhuh!* "Tosun translated: "That's because the smoker is up all night coughing and can't sleep. He says: also the smoker has a cane for a friend. When he gets old, he can't breath and has to walk carrying a cane. Also, a cigarette is better than a bad friend."

"As for drinking," Efendi concluded, "we don't think this is a good idea in Islam." Then he added: "Actually you should drink wine, but not the wine you buy in a liquor store. You should drink the wine of Jesus—meaning the wine of Divine Love which is the sustenance of the Sufis."

Someone asked about taking advantage of opportunities. Efendi quoted a hadith to the effect that there are five things for which to be grateful before the end of one's life. You should be thankful for your health before illness and infirmity come upon you. You should give thanks for what you have before you lose it; for leisure time before you no longer have any; for youth before old age comes; and for life before death comes. Then Efendi turned and said something apparently humorous to Tosun Baba, which he passed on to us: "I made Efendi promise not to ask for coffee or tea. He says: Did I also make the rest of you promise not to offer him any as well?" Just about that time, amidst renewed laughter, some coffee was finally brought to Efendi and Tosun.

As far as we could tell, the sheikh knew not a word of English. Yet, when asked how old he was, Efendi surprised us by answering directly in his slightly raspy bass voice: "Young!" Chortling, he added in Turkish that he was sixty-three.

Having stepped out of the audience of the dhikr ceremony a little bit early, my wife and I had found seats very near the front center of the room where the question and answers were held. Toward the end of the session, as Efendi listened to a more lengthy question, I realized that his glance had fallen upon me for what seemed like a long time. As our eyes met, my whole being opened in a mixture of wonder and acceptance. It was one of the most loving gazes I ever exchanged.

A few minutes later my wife asked what turned out to be the final question. Though we are now the parents of a wonderful, grown daughter, at the time we were, by choice, childless after six years of marriage, feeling that the world was not such a good place to raise children. With this in mind, my wife asked Efendi: "How important is having children to our spiritual growth?" Efendi's answer was brief and direct: "Because you feel the greatest of love. You feel the greatest compassion—that of motherhood. That's the taste you will have." The answer planted within us a seed of hope and longing to experience this unconditional love, a gift that would bear fruit within a few years' time.

Efendi looked at his watch and asked if the audience would grant permission for them to start their drive back to New York. He quoted the hadith of the Prophet: "You will be together with the ones you love in Paradise," and affirmed that there would be no separation between any of us, even after our departure, because of the love and sympathy we have shared between us. We all rose and a few people kissed Efendi's hand as he exited the room. It was the last time I would see him in the flesh. However, Efendi would soon begin to appear in my dreams.

A few days later, I dreamed that I came before Efendi outdoors and kissed his hand. He then offered me a piece of spiritual instruction, something to the effect of: "Accept nothing from outside yourself," or "Do not look to any exterior source for the fulfillment of your needs." I sent the dream in a letter to Efendi, care of Tosun Baba at Spring Valley and received a kind return letter offering Efendi's salaams. It was only later that I came across an almost identical saying in both a hadith of the Prophet and an extra-canonical saying of Jesus from the *Doctrine of Addai*. The Muhammadan saying translates approximately: "Do not seek knowledge outside yourself;" while the saying of Christ reads: "Accept not anything from any man, and possess nothing in this world."

During Efendi's stay in New York in 1979, Tosun Baba secured space in a carpet shop called the *Nur Oriental Gallery* where visitors and dervishes could come and meet with Efendi in Manhattan in addition to the Spring Valley location in upstate New York. Another frequent meeting place for Efendi in the city was on 7 East 82nd Street, at the time the home of Haydar and Fariha Friedrich. Many of Nur's listeners from WBAI, as well as distinguished guests such as the Turkish intellectual, Talat Halman, and Hopi elder, Thomas Banyancya, dropped by to visit Efendi there. As a further treat for the public, the musicians from Turkey would often come and present a concert of the ilahis and kasides for the visitors.

Fariha recalls that during this trip, while Efendi was staying in the Spring Valley tekke, he took an afternoon nap and, upon waking, related that he had been visited in his sleep by many, many souls. She adds, "This was, in a way, a kind of prefiguring of all the people who were going to come and meet him in all of his travels in New York and elsewhere."

On April 1,1979, Muzaffer Efendi was again invited to be interviewed by Nur Lex Hixon on his radio program. This time, the emphasis was on reading from the Qur'an and singing ilahis as well as *sohbet* from the sheikh about the mission of the Prophet Muhammad. Inspired by the daily recitations of the Qur'an which he had heard during his trip to Istanbul last Ramadan, Nur had begun to pen some provisional free translations of the Qur'an in which he strove to avoid the usual stiltedness of literal translations of the meaning of Qur'an into English. In producing a series of lovingly-worded interpretive meditations on Qur'anic passages Nur sought to evoke in the English-speaking listener the same florid sense of beauty and profundity which the Arabic-speaking listener might experience upon hearing the Qur'an chanted in its original language.

During the course of the program, Efendi pointed out that the Qur'an, in its original celestial prototype, is not in any earthly language, nor is it a mere 6,666 verses. Rather, it is an infinite ocean of Divine Knowledge and Truth, of which the words of the historical Arabic revelation are but a small part. The true Torah, Psalms and Gospel are also revealed from this inexhaustible Fount of Wisdom, sometimes referred to as the Mother of the Book (*Umm al-kitab*).

Nur's versions would eventually be published as *Heart of the Koran* in 1988 and would go through several subsequent editions. Both Sheikh Bawa Muhaiyaddeen and Muzaffer Efendi offered their blessings on the early manuscript, Efendi by briefly placing it upon his own head and uttering a prayer and Bawa Muhaiyaddeen by sleeping with the manuscript under his pillow. Upon hearing some of the English passages translated back in to Turkish by Çinar Kologlu, Efendi observed that, considering the exacting standards of Arabic translation, Nur's expansive versions were more like meditations or reflections on the meaning of the Qur'an, rather than exact word for word translations. They were later published as "meditations on the Qur'an," the book becoming a modern spiritual classic.

On the radio program of April, 1979, the show started with a Turkish hafiz chanting from the Qur'an. Here is the translation from the beginning of *Surat al-Mulk* (Sura 67—*The Sovereignty*) which Nur offered on the show:

In the Holy Name of Allah Who is Infinite Compassion,
The spontaneous reverence and praise of all beings
flows to Allah Alone,
In Whose Mysterious Hand of power lies the kingdom of Being,
universe after universe.
Allah is the Living Power behind every cell and every atom,
every thought and every action.
Allah has created the veils of death and life in order to test your
souls, to show forth the nature of your deeds and intentions.
Yet, Allah, Who is thus All-Powerful, having created seven
planes of Being to test the soul, is also All-Forgiving.
The illumined soul never perceives the slightest imperfection
in this vast Kingdom of the All-Merciful One.
Gaze upon the expanse of Being!
Can you see the slightest split or fragmentation there?
Gaze again and again into this Kingdom of Allah,
These Earths and Heavens,
And your gaze will come back to you, weary and dazzled
by Beauty and Perfection.

Later in the show, the dervishes sang an ilahi by Yunus Emre, which Tosun Baba translated for the listeners. Then Nur requested one of Efendi's own ilahis, and revealed to the audience that Efendi was a famous poet in Turkey, writing under the Sufi name *Ashki*, the one who is always in love. The dervishes sang a hymn by Ashki Muzaffer, entitled *Bülbüller Sazda* An approximate English rendering of the hymn, realized from existing translations by Nur Lex Hixon in collaboration with the author, follows:

The nightingale at dawn, sings as the heart of the rose,
Joining with the song all creation knows,
Breathing with every step, *Alhamdulillah*,
Chanting with everystep, *All Praises are Flowing to Allah.*

Creatures moving everywhere think they're going here and there,
One way they cannot flee brings them to Reality,
Whether or not one knows each step belongs to the Beloved,
Each step within the Beloved, *Alhamdulillah*

Ashki faces death before this life passes by,
To *be* and only *Be*, "Die before you die."
Give thanks with Every breath, *Alhamdulillah*,
Give thanks with every step, *All Praises are Flowing to Allah.*

Truth has led me on the path of the Halveti
To the Seal of Founding Pirs, Nureddin Jerrahi.
The way of passionate love, *Alhamdulillah*,
Transformed by Divine Love, *All Praises are flowing to Allah.*

After the dervishes had sung the *ilahi* on the radio, Efendi offered his own extended explanation of the experience which lay behind the words of the hymn:

> One spring, when I was staying in the city of Bursa, I woke up early before sunrise to make my morning prayers. I entered the rose gardens of Bursa, hoping to hear the nightingales, who can often be heard singing in these gardens. As it was a beautiful spring morning, the nightingales were singing their love for the roses. Like every beloved, the rose flirted with the

nightingale. The beloved ones do not always give themselves so easily to the lover, as evidenced by the love between the servant and the Creator. Then I said to the universe, "Stop, and give thanks to Allah for this beauty." By observing this worldly situation I realized that we can only fully give thanks when we see the truth. Our expression of thanks is prayer to the Provider of Truth. That is why there is this repetition of the chorus, "All grace comes from Allah and all praises are due Allah."

But our gratitude has to go beyond words. We must show our thanks in action. How do we give thanks for beauty? By keeping our hearts pure. How do we express gratitude for our possessions? By distributing some of those gifts which Allah has given us. How do we express our thanks for Love, the greatest gift which Allah has given us? By singing our love of Allah. So I have expressed with this humble poem my thanks to Allah for the love which he has put into my heart.

At the time of the morning prayer, before the sun rises, the curtain lifts between the lover of Allah and his Creator. During these early hours of the morning there are thousands of secrets which we may come to know. Should we sleep at that beautiful time when all these gifts are being offered? Wherever you find yourself, send your blessings and thanks to Allah.

Going out onto the streets of Bursa, I observed people rushing in all directions, some going to the mosque, some going to their jobs, and the children going to their schools—at the same time, I was aware of the birds singing. Then, I came to understand the mystery that every single sound and voice in this universe is mentioning, remembering, and invoking the name of Allah. As I watched and listened, I became aware that every breath, inhaled and exhaled, was thanking Allah; and I saw that no matter where people thought they were running, they were all running toward Allah. Everyone, everywhere, at all times, wherever they might think they are running—to their jobs, to their homes, *to* someone, or *from* someone—they are all running toward Allah.

Then I remembered that I had received the light which enabled me to see this from one of the 42 branches of the

> Halveti, the Mystic Path of the Jerrahi. This was the fork in the road where I entered the true path. And what is this wisdom, if not the one single wisdom coming from the One Source of Truth? And all thanks, grace and love is due to Allah.
>
> Finally, I always remember Allah and I always remember death, because to truly *Be* in this world, one must "die before one dies." This is one of the noble sayings of the Prophet Muhammad, may peace and blessings be upon him: "Die before death." I was constantly contemplating this passing away that precedes physical death, so that I might truly *Be*. And finally, I have been made able to speak the truth, and I am thankful for all the gifts which Allah has given me. *Alhamdulillah.*

This time, the radio show ended with a long prayer by Muzaffer Efendi and an invitation to the listeners to attend the free public dhikr at the Cathedral of St. John the Divine. Everyone was invited to join in the Divine remembrance and taste this beautiful wine of love, regardless of their spiritual path. Efendi promised that each person, whether they simply watched and listened or actively joined the dervish circle, would feel something of the transformative power of divine grace which manifests during the dhikr. The merit of simply attending such a gathering of lovers who repeat the names of Allah, Efendi informed the listeners, is spelled out in the *ahadith*, or traditions of the Prophet Muhammad, may peace and blessing always be upon him.

Here is Efendi's concluding prayer from the radio interview:

> O the most beautiful of the beautiful, Allah,
> O Allah, who loves beauty, grant us your love.
> Please grant to our hearts the light of Your love.
> Give happiness and joy to our faces and let us taste
> Your love. Show us Your beautiful countenance.
> Everything that exists and is visible to us is nothing but
> Your face.
> Please lift the veils from Your face, so that we may truly
> see Your countenance.
> Let us come to You. Let us find You. Let us meet You.

Let us be with You and let us love one another, O You
who give what You wish to whomever You wish and
remove what You wish from whomever You wish.
You are the victorious. You are the owner of the kingdom.
You remember those who remember You.
You love those who love You.
You run to those who walk to You and bestow whatever
You wish.
You do not allow us, Your humble servants, to be destitute,
just as we generously provide for those who come to us.
You are the Sovereign of sovereigns, the Merciful, the
Compassionate, the Forgiving, the Most High,
the Beautiful.
Would you turn away those who come to Your door?
Of course not! We come to Your door with our heads bowed.
Please unite us in love, and eliminate our anger
and animosity.
Transform our animosity into love and kindness—
You are the only One who can do this.
The hands that are open to You in supplication, the tongues
which mention Your name, the hearts that love You—
You will not leave them empty.
We come to Your door; we bend our heads and open
our palms in prayer.
O Beloved! O goal of everything! O Allah, grant us Your love
and the pleasure of Your love!
May You place the crown of love on our heads.
May you give the medicine of love to our hearts and
establish our hearts as the throne of Your love.
Please never remove Your love from our hearts—it is our
food, our sustenance—we cannot live without it!
Keep us near You, O Lord, and accept our prayer;
You would not send us away from Your door
empty-handed. Amin.

An Evening of Dhikr at the Cathedral of St. John the Divine

In the following pages, we invite the reader to journey in the imagination to the Cathedral of St. John the Divine, at 112th St. and Amsterdam in the upper East side of New York City, where a diverse cross-section of humanity has gathered for a public dhikr ceremony with the Halveti-Jerrahi Order of dervishes. Through descriptive imagery, may we participate in the spirit of remembrance and breathe the rose-fragrance of union, as might be experienced in an evening of dervish dhikr.

Cathedral of St. John the Divine (Photo by James Wentzy)

This evening, Muzaffer Efendi is leading a public dhikr, featuring musicians from Istanbul accompanying Eastern and Western dervishes in a performance at the Church of St. John the Divine, a magnificent cathedral which is able to accommodate as many as ten thousand people. The broad universal spirit of this historic cathedral is apparent not only at its altar, which features both cross and Jewish menorah, but also among its rear columns, where stands a colorful Native American totem pole. The atmosphere inside the cathedral is electric with expectation, as the audience has an invitation not only to watch but also to participate in the dhikr by joining the dervish circle during the standing portion of the ceremony.

The musicians, seated in chairs near the massive wooden podium, have finished performing an opening set of Turkish *ilahis*, or mystic hymns. The dervishes, dressed in white caps and robes underneath dark sleeveless vests, called *haydariyya*, have taken their places, kneeling on a circle of white sheepskins beneath the huge dome at the center of the cathedral's great nave. At the head of the circle, Muzaffer Efendi, kneels upon the blue sheepskin of the Order, symbol of divine unity and guidance. Two pure white candles burn behind him on the dark stone floor. He is flanked by two red sheepskins, the color of divine majesty, upon which kneel his two senior dervishes. The women, beautifully adorned in rich eastern attire, with elegant head scarfs, kneel on a row of sheep-skins next to the circle of men, following the traditional Islamic etiquette.

The sheikh has pronounced the opening invocation, inviting the divine presence of Allah, flowing through the founder of the order, Hazrati Pir Nureddin Jerrahi, as well as other saints, prophets, angels, and especially the Seal of Prophecy, Sayyidina Muhammad Mustafa (may the peace and blessings of Allah continually be upon him). The dervishes have concluded the singing of the opening hymn to the Prophet, who is hailed as the guiding light, the dawning sun and the full moon of truth. They have chanted the *tawhid*, the mystic words of unity: *La ilaha illallah*, affirming that Nothing exists apart from the One Source of Being. The Divine name of majesty, *Allah*, has also been chanted, as well as the name of Essence, *Hu*, followed by a slow solo hymn. The melodious words of the *durak* reflect the wisdom of the Qur'an, which reveals that when no one is left on earth to call out "*Allah, Allah*," then only the Essential face of Divinity will remain. Mystically, this points to the lover's disappearance within the Beloved even before the physical end of time, as one, in the words of the Prophet, "dies before dying".

What follows, as the dervishes stand up from their kneeling position, mystically represents the resurrection into Eternal Life (*al-Hayy*), where the dervish soul rises out of the dark world of the conventional self into the luminous consciousness of Paradise, feeling and seeing the Divine everywhere. This reflects the station of experience mentioned in the Holy Qur'an (2:115): "Wherever you turn, whether to the East or to the West, there is the One Essential Face of Allah, the All-Knowing, the All-Encompassing."

Having completed the sitting portion of the dhikr, Muzaffer Efendi makes a powerful gesture of striking the floor with the palms of both of his large hands. The dervishes bow to the floor and then immediately stand up; the sheepskins are quickly gathered and removed. The next sound heard is that of mature dervish voices rising in praise, reverberating spaciously off the vast, vaulted stone walls of the sanctuary singing a stately, time-honored Turkish hymn by Yunus Emre, the great mystic poet of the 14th century, an ilahi whose words compare the Love of Allah to a vast and limitless ocean. "*Bu Aşk Bir...*"

This great love is Your most wonderful mystery.
Whenever we behold your great love shining, we are amazed!
Deep meeting of our longing souls with Allah Most Sublime;
We enter breathlessly Your Palace of Unity and are amazed!
O Allah's beauty is truly infinite beauty raining down,
Our palms are opening, Your vast light descending;
We are amazed!

When the hymn is completed, the sheikh pronounces the blessings upon the noble Messenger of Allah. The dervishes, still standing in place, join hands in the circle and begin to move to the left, now slowly intoning the glorious name of Divine Essence, *HU*, its sound prolonged with each inward and outward breath of remembrance. Above this deep drone of *HU*, another hymn of Hazrat Yunus is heard, an ilahi which reflects upon the majestic, yet intimate nearness of the Ultimate Source of Being, "*Ay Sultanim...*"

O Sultan of Love, You are nearer than near and even
nearer than that,
O Life, Who else could I see but You?
Who else could I be but you? Pure Presence, without horizon,
Essence, without division. O my Sultan! nearer than my
central life vein,
You hold all secrets. I live in You as your prophets live.

At certain moments, the sheikh's robust voice is heard ringing out above the voices of the singers, calling out to the Beloved, "*Allah!*" As the rhythm speeds up, the hymn seamlessly flows into another one, "*Hu Bir Allah*," extolling the Unity of that One whose vast Being fills the whole creation with Divine Presence, leaving no existence outside of Itself. As the last verse of the hymn draws to a close, Efendi cries out and the melody slows down, pregnant with divine intention and conscious awareness. The melody finishes, yet lingers vibrantly in the air as if echoing the response of the unseen beings who, at such gatherings, also remember Allah on high.

The next sound heard is the deeply penetrating rhythmic pulsation of the breath as the dervishes begin to chant *Hayy*, the divine name of the Everliving Source and Breath of Life. The sound of *Hayy, Hayy, Hayy* reaches deep into the heart, stimulating and exhilarating the inner life-force of all who hear it. Even the hidden cells and whirling atoms of the body begin to consciously partake of the remembrance, chanting *Hayy! O Life that never dies!* The dervishes who say *hayy* are like the lovers mentioned in a noble tradition by the Rasulullah, who, when they begin to remember Allah, resemble the trees ecstatically swaying in the breeze of Divine Nearness. A Mevlevi dervish, among those in the center of the dhikr circle dons his *sikke*, the tall traditional tombstone-like head-covering, bows low and begins to whirl, his crossed arms unfurling like a flower reaching toward the Beloved.

Photo: James Wentzy

Suddenly a mystic poem of love is heard, its entrance soaring vibrantly above the strong, rhythmic undercurrent of *Hayy.* The sound of this intricate Turkish melodic improvisation echoes majestically throughout the cathedral, mysteriously evoking the soul's memory of other ancient, timeless experiences within Allah's great Citadel of Divine Remembrance. This sound embodies the muezzin's cry from the minaret of love, the heart's plaintive prayer of supplication born of longing for the Beloved Friend, and the joy of the martyr who is empowered to sacrifice all for the sake of Truth. A sense of Divine response descends upon the gathering as the dervishes reenter with a jubilant hymn of victory: "*Serveri ser Bülendemiz, Hazreti Pir Efendimiz...*"

Prince of the most pure, souls of ecstacy,
Hazreti Pir, Our sublime Efendi.
From him is streaming Divine Attraction,
Our noble Master of the Mystic Path. Whirling with love,
Chalice of love, he gave the world his inspiring love.
Allah, Allah! Allah, Allah! The Supreme Truth alone exists!

As this stirring melody comes to a close, the dervish in the center of the meydan finishes his whirling, bows and rejoins the circle of dervishes. Muzaffer Efendi now changes the *esma* to "*YA ALLAH! Hayy, Hayy, YA ALLAH!*" and all join in this robust affirmation of the living name of Divine Majesty. The echoing footsteps of the dervishes, as they strongly and rhythmically intone *Ya Allah!* are marshaled in a cadence of power which emphasizes their divine calling as true warriors of the spirit, metaphorically bearing the bright sword of love which is used, not against others, but in the inner jihad of spiritual mastery. As these soldiers of love march on toward the goal of union with Ultimate Truth, the pitch begins to rise as does the spiritual passion and fiery intensity of their call, "*Ya Allah!*" which reverberates in every direction. The growing sound of a sustained string instrument, a *kemenche*, is heard below the chant, supporting its ringing tonality. Suddenly, it pierces through the chant, resounding like the great horn of the archangel *Israfil*, fervently announcing the end of the conventional world and the resurrection of all that is real. Cascading in brocades of oriental ornamentation, the celestial sound of the instrument summons all souls to awaken and encourages the spirit to soar and dive freely on the wings of the heavenly buraq, over transfigured palaces and landscapes of light.

Photo: James Wentzy

A hafiz takes up the momentum, melodiously crying out, "*Medet Ya Rasulullah, Ya Muhammad Mustafa, olsun sana canim feda...*" Accompanied by the percussive sound of bendirs, the dervishes settle into a profound and deeply resonant chant, *Hayy,*

Hayy, HAAY—as the Messenger of Allah is remembered and invoked in a poetic ode of love. The circle has come closer and is swaying in place, arms around one another. From the center, Muzaffer Efendi begins to call out in a powerful voice invoking the attribute of Divine Mercy. Each time the name is invoked it cuts through like a lightening flash from the very Source of Revelation: *ALLAH!... RAHMAN!... RAHMAN!... RAHIM!...* Now the circle begins to move again, and a further triumphal dervish melody emerges from the inner circle of zakirs, a compelling and stirring *ilahi* which celebrates the merciful aspects of the All-Powerful Source and Goal of creation, whose vast waves of Divine Love powerfully emanated through the heart of the 17th century qutb who founded the Jerrahi order: "*Allah, Allah, Hüve Rabbüna Rahmenin...*"

Photo: James Wentzy

Allah, Allah, Lord of Countless Universes, Infinite Mercy,
Allah, Allah, Lord of Countless Universes, have Mercy,
Through the brilliant light of our holy sheikh, Nureddin Jerrahi.

Noble pir, O Nureddin, the cloak of prophecy is yours,
O Seal of love.
Lost in your embrace, the beauty of your gaze,
lifts our lives into the Truth, Aman, Ya Hu.

The audience has joined the circle at the signal of the sheikh, now swelling into numerous concentric circles of humanity, recreating in New York city something of the powerful, swirling vortex of *hajj* pilgrims circling the black Ka'ba shrine at Mecca, only the white shrouds of the Hijaz are replaced with apparel of every kind: lovers of God in multicolored Jewish yarmulkes, turbans, suits, and street clothes, circling around, not a stone house of Allah in Arabia, but the living human heart of an illuminated Sufi master and saint. The sound of *Ya Hayy* echoes ecstatically from every wall as the dervishes now begin to sing the well-known ilahi, "*Ben Dervişem Diyene...*"

All the Holy Messengers, Beautiful with Allah's beauty,
Shining as the mirror of Truth. HAQQ! La ilaha illallah.

After this, only the subdued sound of *hayy* and the footsteps of those in the dervish circle are heard. A lone voice, intoning the traditional Arabic benediction upon the Messenger of Allah, breaks through in a florid, yet peaceful surge of melodic expression: "*As-salatu as-salaamu 'alieki ya Rasulullah...*"

The circle, having stopped, now begins to move again, this time to the right, accompanied by another exquisite melody, "*Yandım Yakıldım Ben Nar-ı aşka...*"

I burst into the flames of love.
I became drunk on the mystery of love.
True dervish lovers, circling the great Efendi.
Banquet of love in the paradise of love.

Then Muzaffer Efendi initiates a strong rhythmic chant, which is picked up by the circle: *ANT'L HADI, ANT'L HAQQ, LEYSE-L HADI ILLAHU.* ("You are the Guiding, You are True. Nothing exists apart from You.") Both the women and the men can be heard chanting these words along with bendir accompaniment, layered over the ilahi melody of the singers As the concentric circles of dervishes and friends from the public continue to turn, swirling in circumambulation around the sheikh and his musicians in the center of the dhikr circle, a clear sense of heightened energy and ecstasy emerges, together with a feeling of effortless motion, as the participants lose themselves in the beautiful flow of divine action which is taking place. Like the calm in the eye of the storm of love, Efendi is at times very still, eyes closed in divine intimacy, radiating subtle energies outward in every direction. Now he becomes highly animated, changing the underlying chant, which, while maintaining its rhythmic momentum, changes words, and becomes a litany of oneness: *ALLAH, WAHID, AHAD, SAMAD*; then it becomes simply *HAYY, HAYY, HU—*. This continues for sometime, until the circle comes to a halt and the dervishes sing in place a collective hymn known as "Tejelli."

Photo: James Wentzy

> *This unveiling of the radiance of the Only Beloved has intoxicated and bewildered me. In the subtle mystery of "Ana'l-Haqq"—"I am the Absolute Truth"—lies the secret of my soul, a revelation which I cannot conceal. Perhaps you imagine that I am the poet Eshrefoglu Rumi of Iznik, but I am not from Iznik nor from Rum. Ah! In truth, I am that One Eternal "I" Who has appeared in the human form.*

The dervishes now sing the final melodic benediction, "*La ilaha illallah, Muhammad ar-Rasulullah, Salallahu 'aleihi wa salimu teslimen, Hu, Hu, Hu...*" as the hafiz melodically intones: "And bless and give peace to the most noble light of all the prophets and messengers; and praise be to Allah, Lord of the Worlds!"

Efendi now calls out and collectively the dervishes respond, with arms folded across their chests and feet crossed: "*Allahu Akbar, Allahu Akbar, La ilaha illallah...*" When this is finished, an ayat of Qur'an (39:75) is chanted by the hafiz: "And you shall see the angels circling the mystic Throne of Allah on every side, singing glory and praise to their Lord. Their evaluation will be just, and everywhere, their cry will resound: *Alhamdulillah-i Rabbi'l Alamin!*"

The final petitions of the ceremony commence as the dervishes together begin to intone a dronelike field of sound, composed of bee-like murmuring repetitions of the Name of Majesty, *Allah*, while the powerful voice of Muzaffer Efendi rises above them in fervent prayer. He invokes the Oneness of Allah and the secret souls of the saints, martyrs and mystic poles, and especially Hazrati Pir Nureddin Jerrahi, closing with the name of Divine Essence. "*Bi-ismi zatik...*" and all join in with the response, "*YA ALLAH HU—!*"

From the silence, Efendi sends peace to one and all: "*As-salaamu 'aleikum!*"

The men and women dervishes, with hands over their hearts, bow, replying in the traditional Islamic manner, "*Wa'leikum salaam wa rahmatullah-i wa barakatuhu!*" And with these words, the ceremony of dhikr draws to a close.

While the dervish ceremonies at St. John's left a powerful impression on most of the visitors who attended them, they were also memorable occasions for the sheikh himself, as we know from his written testimony. Here are a few of Muzaffer Efendi's own recollections from the first dhikr at St. John's:[7]

> We were invited to make dhikr at the Cathedral of St. John the Divine in New York, which we accepted without any hesitation. At the appointed time, we went to the cathedral and found a large crowd waiting for us. The head priest of the cathedral received us with great respect and showed us a room where we could change into our religious clothing. During the repetition of divine unity in the dhikr ceremony, my dervishes went into a state of ecstasy. This also had a profound effect on the audience and many of them began to repeat *La ilaha illallah* along with us. During the standing dhikr, we made a second, outer circle so that the visitors could also participate in our dhikr. These people plunged into the circle of dhikr and joined in the chants, stirred by divine attraction.
>
> The dome of the cathedral is even higher than St. Sophia's mosque in Istanbul. Chanting and circling below this great expanse, we had the feeling that our dhikr was ascending directly to Allah in great waves. All those present were surrounded by the divine love and caught up in the divine attraction. You could even hear some of the audience singing in English along with our Turkish ilahis. As the dhikr continued, the cathedral actually began to vibrate. I myself witnessed that some of the pictures on the wall were shaking as if they were going to come down.

During a sohbet later that week, Efendi mentioned how the cathedral had actually been shaking during the *Bedevi topu*, when everyone was most fervently chanting and bounding in place, as though the cathedral itself were joining in the dhikr. He said it brought to his mind a story in which Nasruddin Hoja stayed at a very old, creaky hotel. After sitting in his room for a while, listening to the old building creaking and groaning, he finally sought out the owner of the hotel. "This building is making strange creaking noises. It must be very old and decrepit," he said. "No, no, no!" answered the proprietor, "It's a perfectly sound building. The noises you are hearing are the hotel making dhirkullah—remembering Allah." Nasruddin answered, "Well that's what I'm afraid of! Suppose, during its worship, it decides to prostrate!"

Returning to Efendi's narrative concerning the events at St. John's and other public dhikrs, we learn that while the majority of those who attended were profoundly moved by the experience of dhikr, there were others who had less positive reactions to the ceremony:

> After the ceremony ended and I had offered a supplication, we sat down to receive questions from the people. An American said that he had perceived the scent of roses during the dhikr and wondered what that symbolized. This poor one responded that the rose represents the Rasulullah while the tulip represents divine unity.

Then, in the midst of these questions by the American lovers, two young Turks, whom I would guess were graduates of Imam Hatep Islamic High School, asked whether the ladies joining in the *dhikrullah* with the men was approved in Islam. I told them that the Qur'an al-Karim didn't come down in one sitting, but came verse by verse over twenty-three years. One of them responded, "Okay, now we understand what you're trying to do. This dhikr is an innovation—an alteration of accepted traditional Islamic practice—and the music and chanting in a circle is religiously forbidden! With such novelties you can't hope to add to Islam." In other words they were saying: it is a wrong approach to try to attract people into pure Islam with non-Islamic innovations. They were implying that I was laying a faulty foundation.

I asked them if they would recite some suras from the Qur'an for us. One of them agreed and recited *Sura Kawthar* nicely in a traditional musical mode. But then he added, "I'm answering you in a style that I learned from a cassette from your shop." Now, by implication, he was questioning my knowledge and authority in Islam, as if to say, "I know you. You're just a bookstore owner." Now, I was happy to see how sincerely he was trying to defend his religion, but I informed him that in our religion, it is not music per se, but lewd, sexually-provocative music and dance that is considered unlawful. The man claimed he saw no difference between them—a strange argument coming from someone who had just chanted from the Qur'an using a musical scale.

Then a third person from their party chimed in with a more blaming attitude, saying: "There is hypocrisy in this dhikr that you're doing." I told him that every action is judged according to its intention, and shared a tradition of the Prophet which says: "Remember Allah, make dhikr very, very often. In spite of those who blame you, continue to remember Allah." The third friend continued: "I've seen dhikr in Turkey as well, but not the way you did it." I responded: "There are a lot of things you haven't seen and don't know. Just because you haven't seen them or don't know of them doesn't mean they don't exist!"

Then still another one of them joined in the criticism and then they got up and left. As they parted, I beseeched them: “Please do not exclude us from your prayers,” and sent them on their way with our best wishes.

It was obvious that all of us in this exchange were from the motherland. Although I don’t doubt their complete faith in Islam, I did take exception to the bitterness they displayed to us in their public critique. If they didn’t agree, at least they could have been more gracious and less openly hostile to us. After all, Rasulullah said, “If you don’t love one another, you can’t have true faith. And if you don’t love me more than anything else, then your faith will never reach maturity.”

Although we were received warmly at most of our performances, at one convention center, some Jehovah’s Witnesses came and began to broadcast their own limited ideas about the religion. One of the American lovers, thinking that I was broken-hearted and frustrated with them because of their comments, yelled out in a loud voice—and in Turkish—”In America, there are many lovers of Allah, but there are also some crazy people as well.” Then he pointed at them.

At Columbia University, another group of Turks confronted us, this group subscribing to the “left-wing” belief system. They were discussing logic, rationality and the intellect. I told them that “rationalizing” was invented by Shaitan. They said, “O, now you’ve made us Shaitan!” I found it hard to believe they couldn’t distinguish between the quality and its source, and took from my statement that rationalizations were invented by Shaitan that I was calling anyone who rationalized Shaitan himself. When they kept conversing in Turkish, I suggested that we translate for the majority of Americans who were listening, but they walked out instead.

How difficult it is to convince such people of the truth! The limitations of rational logic are obvious, insofar as the mind seeks to justify its own benefit. But such people don’t realize this. On the other hand, passionate and expansive divine love are beyond the intelligence of the mind and can’t be self-serving. The rationalists just don’t have concepts for some of these

> subjects. While we certainly wish and pray for illumination to come to these souls, the sad truth is that our people, whether from the left or right sides, have turned their backs on these truths. Some have done so through narrow-mindedness, others from their own jealousy, or lack of talent in learning the deeper truths. This is what lies at the base of all the conflicts we see in Turkey today.
>
> I have relayed these events so that the readers can judge for themselves. It is with some pain that I admit that, though some of the Turks, especially from the region of Kırım, have received us graciously and with love, most of my own countrymen residing in America—many of them my religious compatriots—have publicly slandered me, while so many Europeans and Americans have received us with great friendship in the name of Allah.

After nearly a month in America, Efendi and his retinue returned to Istanbul in mid-April, 1979. The next trip took place in the spring of the following year, 1980. This time, they were scheduled to travel across the United States to several cities in California as well as Houston, Texas, where they performed their dhikr ceremony in Rothko Chapel and were hosted in the home of Fariha's mother, Dominique de Menil.

On this trip, Efendi invited the distinguished ney player and musicologist, Kudsi Ergüner, to join the tour. Descended from a line of Turkish musicians, Kudsi played ney on the Mevlevi tours of America during the early 1970s, also traveling to Afghanistan with Madame DeSalzmann to play ney in Peter Brook's film on Gurdjieff, "Meetings with Remarkable Men." In 1978, Kudsi had been instrumental in bringing the Jerrahis to Rennes, from whence they traveled on to America for their first ten-day visit. The 1980 tour was his only American tour with Sheikh Muzaffer and the Jerrahi musicians.

It was during the 1980 trip that psychology professor, Dr. Robert Frager of San Francisco, met Muzaffer Efendi and became involved in the Jerrahi Order. He would in time become a sheikh and be known in dervish circles as Ragip Baba. He would also gain professional distinction as the founding president of the Institute of Transpersonal Psychology in California. In the mid-nineteen-eighties he would collect and edit a number of Efendi's recorded sohbets, mostly from 1980 and 1981 West Coast talks, and publish them under the title, *Love is the Wine*. In the introduction to that book, Ragip Baba describes the powerful first impressions he had of the sheikh:

> The moment he glanced at me time seemed to stand still. It felt as if he instantly knew all about me, as if all the data of my life was read and analyzed as if in a high-speed computer in a fraction of a second. . . . I felt a great blend of power and wisdom on the one hand, and a deep love and compassion on the other. The power that radiated from him would have almost been unbearable if it wasn't for the equally strong love he radiated as well. He had the powerful frame of a Turkish wrestler. His hands were huge, the largest I've ever seen. His voice was a deep, rolling bass, the richest and deepest voice I've heard outside an opera house. His face was mobile. One moment he would appear stern and grave, the next he became the quintessential comic storyteller. His eyes were clear and piercing—sometimes fierce like a hawk's, and sometimes loving and twinkling with humor.[8]

The original back cover of *Love is the Wine* was graced with a beautiful black and white photograph by Shems Friedlander. It showed Muzaffer Efendi in his Turkish street clothes, sitting on the deck of a boat, enjoying coffee and a cigar. The picture captured the spirit of one who clearly enjoyed being a human being while at the same time nobly embodying and radiating the divine presence. In the mid-nineteen-nineties, the photograph was replaced with a different photo, a head shot of Efendi, without the tobacco. The publishers had complied when a number of Muslim institutes had expressed interest in using the book for Muslim studies, provided the picture with the cigar could be replaced with another photograph of the sheikh. (We may note that one year before his passing, Efendi did give up the use of tobacco.)

Another American who published a description of his impressions of Muzaffer Efendi and his spiritual community was television host, Lou Rogers, who did 18 television interviews with Efendi in New York City and also took hand as his dervish. He writes of his first encounter with Efendi and the Jerrahi dervishes:

> What struck me most immediately that first evening was the intuitive understanding that this was a community of men and women who sought with all their being to reflect the great love and caring which is to be found in any true spiritual community. And I, as an untutored outsider, felt myself submerged in a sea of love that radiated from the presence of the Sheikh, and as candles lit one by one from a central flame, the same presence could palpably be felt in all his companions, in sometimes greater, sometimes lesser degrees.... To describe Efendi as a spiritual teacher simply fails to do justice to the immense fullness of being one encountered in him. To begin with, one felt safe in his presence. . . . One felt oneself finally to be in safe harbor, spiritually sheltered from the vicissitudes of life, in the presence of one who knew. And of that there was no doubt. Sheikh Muzaffer was like the Sphinx rising majestically in the bare and barren desert, its gaze fixed on eternity while all about it, century after endless century, the affairs of men continued in their aimless and puny fashion. In the presence of the eternal, time loses all meaning, and in just that manner, one felt protected in the presence of the Sheikh, like children in a certain way, safely ensconced under the watchful eye of a loving and powerful father.[9]

Muzaffer Efendi's sohbets in America

A classic phonograph record of the Halveti-Jerrahi dhikr, called *Journey to the Lord of Power*, was released in 1980, followed the next year by an audio cassette of mystic hymns and musical poetry by some of the Turkish musicians, entitled *Calling Out to Allah*. A video featuring an interview and dhikr ceremony was filmed during the California tour at Claremont College, hosted by Lew Ayres. In the film, the congenial white-haired interviewer sits on a couch with a turbaned Muzaffer Efendi and his translator, Tosun Baba, asking simple, mature questions of the sheikh, a dialogue which is interspersed with occasional shots of the Jerrahi dhikr. At the end of the interview, Efendi compliments the moderator on the quality of his questions, his beautiful demeanor and sympathetic heart. What follows are a few excerpts from the interview:

> Q: What is Sufism?
>
> A: To put it in simple terms, *tasawwuf* or Sufism is the cleansing and purification of the heart, and excluding from one's heart everything except Truth, which is an attribute of God.
>
> Q: And is Sufism the Religion of Love, as well as of Truth?
>
> A: That is true without a doubt. *Tasawwuf* is finding God in one's heart and achieving union with Love. Sufism is seeking and finding union with God. Love becomes both a means and an end, uniting one with Divine Love.
>
> Q: Is God more than Love?
>
> A: Love is but one of God's attributes.
>
> Q: Is dhikr an exclusive ceremony for the dervishes?
>
> A: Dhikr means remembrance, remembrance of God through self-remembrance. It is given by God to all of his creatures. We believe that the entire creation is remembering God at all times. In the case of the dervish, he is conscious of calling on God, while the rest of the creation, including some humans, may not be aware of this. But by the very beating of

their hearts and their every breath, they too remember God and testify to His Divine Power. When you place an iron sword into a fire, what happens to it? It becomes fire. So when you put the coarse iron of our bodies into the fire of God's love, it turns into Divine Love, and when we emerge from that fire, we return to servanthood and again become coarse. The body makes us visible. The soul can see without the body, but we ourselves can't be seen without the flesh. This world is the field of the hereafter. Whatever we sow here, we will reap in the hereafter. So we try to teach and learn: where we came from, why we came, and where we are going. In order to establish and properly understand these values, we must learn service (*hizmet*), and teach others Whom we serve and how to serve.

Tosun Bayrak (left) translates for Muzaffer Efendi's interview with Lew Ayres (right) at Claremont College

Q: You are quoted in one of your tracts as saying: "We are tracing the creation of the universe, its breakdown and its destruction, and finally its joy." Must the world be destroyed?

A: Everything that is born, dies. Everything which is built up, perishes. Everything which is gathered together, disperses. Every creation has to end. There is a realm which transcends

> the visible world. There is a transformed condition which still exists even after something has passed away.
>
> Q: Is that the joy?
>
> A: Yes. There is another life which is much dearer. We have lessons of birth and death continually in front of our eyes. We need the blessing of seeing this, which is one of the greatest blessings. A funeral procession was passing and someone asked, "What was the cause of his death"? A wise man answered, "He died from having been born."
>
> Q: Do Sufis consider life after death more important than the life here and now?
>
> A: Yes, because the present life is temporal while the next life is eternal.

Efendi would supply other interesting definitions of Sufism during the tour. At Stanford University, Muzaffer Efendi offered his broadest definition, when asked by a student, "What is Sufism?" answering simply, "People...men and women." When asked if this meant everyone, Efendi replied with a smile, "Yes, but some know that they are Sufis and some don't. Not only people but also the mineral, vegetable and animal world, and the angels—all are Sufis. But animals, for instance, don't know they are Sufis. If you make a horse, a donkey, or a cow pull a heavy load uphill, they will huff and puff and say, 'hu, hu, hu'; but they won't know what they are saying. Even the ones who insist they aren't Sufis, with their very breathing say, 'hu, hu,' all the while denying that they are Sufis. This is because all of God's creation—everything in the universe—calls upon Allah. Not everyone can perceive this, but some are able to hear—to hear how all creation is remembering its creator."

Back in New York, when asked, "What is a Sufi?" he replied: "A Sufi is one who knows this world and is not fooled by it. Likewise, the Sufi knows the next world and attempts to fool no one." Asked on another occasion about the mystic path, Muzaffer Efendi replied: "The path of Sufism is that your soul (essence) and body would be one and the same. This means that your inside would be as your outside—that you would not appear outwardly human while inwardly displaying attributes proper to an animal."[10]

Efendi was then asked how he became a sheikh. He smiled and said, "I was born one from my mother's womb." He went on to recount his three dreams of Tahir Efendi and subsequent tutelage with Fahreddin Efendi, but prefaced these remarks by explaining: "In the universe of souls (*alam-i arwah*), in accordance with divine wisdom, Allah placed all professions on auction. From tyrants to kings to beggars, all livelihoods were put up for auction before the souls came to this world, though most of us don't remember it. So there, in the universe of souls, Allah asked, 'Who wants to be a sheikh in the Jerrahi tradition in such and such a year?' I answered, 'I do.' Then after desiring this in the universe of souls, I came into this world. Actually, it is much easier to become a sheikh than to become an authentic human being."[11]

At Harvard, Efendi was asked why he came to America. "First of all I was invited," he answered with a smile. "I wasn't offered any money: I came for free. My own budget wouldn't have permitted me to come if I hadn't been invited and financed. But beyond that, the purpose of my visit is in accord with the Holy Qur'an, in which Allah says: 'Travel around the world.' Because if one travels, one learns more about others and a greater connection and understanding is built up between people. One can listen to the opinions of others about America, but there is always distortion in that. To really know, it is best to actually come here and meet the people. From what I have seen of America, the people are warm-hearted and seeking knowledge. They also have knowledge and will certainly receive wisdom. . . . My impression of you is that you are like beautiful, pure oil lamps. Allah has made you out of this beautiful crystal and filled it with clear oil and a wick. All that you need is a hand to light the match. The quality of the Americans that impresses me most is the value you give to human beings here. Look at me." Efendi laughed. "I'm a man of no value and yet you honor me by coming and listening to me and asking questions."[12]

At Harvard, Muzaffer Efendi was asked about the closing of the Sufi Orders in Turkey in 1925, and its aftermath. Efendi replied:[13]

> The universe is a Sufi lodge, and everything in this universe, alive or inert, is continuously remembering its Divine Source. All the stars, suns, and moons in the sky are oil lamps in this house of dervishes; and we are the people of this universal house of dervishes—Christians, Muslims, Jews, etc.
>
> A revolution took place in Turkey. Religion, or *shariat* is for the general public; the *tarikat*—the path of Hazrat 'Ali—is the particular mystical nucleus of the religion; but not everyone understands this. It is the business of the pure, the sincere. The change that occurred was from a kingdom, the Ottoman Empire, to a republic. Some of the sheikhs and dervishes, perhaps due to traditionalism, were attached to the empire which had decayed and crumbled; so this nucleus was abandoned—but nobody outlawed the general orthodox part of the religion. Still, a social movement cannot tear the love from people's hearts. The same love and attachment to one's particular path naturally persisted and each dervish continued with his own private prayers and spiritual work—though they did not necessarily continue to come together at some particular time of the week.
>
> A society is comprised of many people who have a common goal and who understand and respect one another; but tens of thousands of people who disagree, misunderstand each another, and pursue different goals is not a society. The Turkish government passed certain laws and took certain measures—but there was never an outright ban on religion. You were free to practice whatever faith you followed. Even countries like Soviet Russia could not make religion disappear entirely. Material forces can

> be easily manipulated; you can coerce people, forbid things and impose a political vision; but it is very difficult in spiritual matters. You can post policemen to prevent outward activities, but how are they going to prevent interior actions?
>
> The effect of the revolution continued until 1946. Then Turkey decided to westernize—introducing "democracy." In our own particular case, we have never gotten involved in politics. Everyone in Turkey knows about the laws that exist, but some of the rulings are not really enforced.

On another occasion, a fellow spiritual teacher, Sheikh Fadhlalla Haeri, asked Muzaffer Efendi about "what happened after the almost complete destruction of the Sufi Orders in Turkey by Kemal Ataturk." Efendi paused, smiled and said simply, 'You look upon it as destruction. We look upon it as slightly excessive grooming.' Then he continued, 'It is like chopping a grapevine to the ground. If he had chopped a little, the branches would have grown only a few meters away, but because he cut the whole grapevine to the ground, it will now grow all over the place. It is only a matter of time. Allah says in the Qur'an, 'They want to extinguish the light of Allah with their utterances, but Allah will not consent to this, for He has willed to spread His Light in all its fullness, however hateful this may be to all who deny the truth.' (Qur`an 9:32)."[14] It was precisely this natural process which encouraged and perhaps hastened the transmission of authentic Islamic mysticism to America in the later years of the twentieth century.

Inevitably, during the public question sessions with Efendi, questions would arise about Islam and how it relates with other religions. At one gathering Efendi was asked to comment on anthropomorphic conceptions of God. He explained that Allah is totally formless and transcendent according to the Islamic conception. "Sometimes I see pictures purporting to represent God as an old man with a long, white beard and feel there is something untoward in the intention there, since Allah doesn't age or have human limbs." Then he added: "As long as you believe in Allah—even if you see Him in that shape—that's fine, because Allah appears as you imagine Him to be. If you think of God as merciful or generous, you will find Him to be merciful or generous. If you think of God as punishing and a torturer, you will find Him that way. There is a hadith of the Prophet in which Allah reveals, "I appear to my servants as they expect Me to appear."

Someone at the University of Maryland asked: "Can a Jew or Christian become a Sufi?" Efendi answered:

> Yes, of course. You also believe in the holy books sent to you by the same God. We (Muslims) believe in what Jews and Christians believe and like what you like in your scriptures, namely: we confirm the Torah; we love Jesus and the Virgin Mary; and we accept the scriptures of the Jews or Christians, regardless of whether their followers confirm our Prophet and scripture. Yes, according to your understanding, you can be a Sufi. We see the 72 nations and tribes as one, and all the prophets as one. If someone doesn't see them as one, they are cross-eyed.
>
> There was a sheikh who had a single bottle of medicine which he asked his dervish to retrieve from the cabinet. The dervish, seeing two bottles there, asked, "Which one?". The sheikh realized that his dervish was cross-eyed and answered, "Break one of them and bring me the other." The surprised dervish came back confessing that both bottles had broken when he smashed only one of them.

In California, Efendi commented further on Jesus, saying:

> According to Islam, Jesus, upon him be peace, is known as *Ruh Allah*, the Spirit of God. In most sects of Chrisitanity, Jesus is described as the son of God. But which is higher, one's son or one's spirit? Also in Islam, the Virgin Mary is considered a prophet because Gabriel came to her [and vouchsafed the

> divine revelation to her]. So today, the door of ignorance on this matter is closed—because the old crusader notion that Islam doesn't accept Jesus Christ or honor Virgin Mary can no longer be maintained. Rather, they are held in extremely high regard, beyond what most Chrisitians realize. Islam contains Christianity and Judaism, so there is no question of Muslims abandoning them.

When another questioner inquired about the Islamic concept of the *Mehdi* (*Mahdi*) who is to expected come, and his relation to Jesus, Efendi responded by presenting the spiritualized meaning of this belief:

> In your body, the Mehdi is your heart. According to the Islamic tradition, the Mehdi is going to come from the progeny of the Prophet, peace and blessings be upon him, and his name will be Muhammad Mehdi. Then Christ is going to come as well and together they will fight against *Dajjal*, the tyrant. The way we understand it, the heart—in the region of the human soul, or *ruhu insani*—is the Mehdi. The center of the heart, or *fu'ad*, is the Christ, and these two will come together and crush the head of the nafs, the ego, whose energies are concentrated below one's waist.
>
> Indeed, it is a prophecy that before the last day of the world a Mehdi will come, Jesus will come, and ad-Dajjal, a tyrant, will come; the first two will make war against the tyrant, and win just before the Day of Resurrection. That will come—but what is it to you? What is important for you is to see that in you is the Mehdi, the Christ, and the Dajjal. Let these two get together and vanquish that tyrant.[15]

A further interesting comment on the Virgin Mary came during a televised ecumenical dialogue which included Efendi and a Christian bishop. Efendi asked the bishop why Christians make the sign of the cross? When the bishop gave the usual answer about its connection with the crucifix, Efendi shared another reason which he said he had found in a very ancient manuscript in the Süleymaniye library, relating it to the time during Mary's pregnancy when people were pressuring her as to why she was carrying a baby without knowing who the father was. Having been instructed by Allah to maintain a vow of silence and to only use sign language if necessary, she touched each side of her shoulders, meaning, "The angels on my left and on my right bear witness...." Then she touched her stomach, followed by her forehead, indicating that the two angels witness "that the child within is 'written on my forehead'"–meaning it is her destiny. The bishop was moved by this answer and took off his ring and gave it to Efendi, saying, "Accept this as a token of my appreciation of something I learned from you."[16]

Efendi also received questions about Eastern religions and their relation to Sufism. In one question and answer session, he was asked, "There is a great deal of emphasis in Sufism and Jewish mysticism on prophets and prophecy, while in contrast, the Far Eastern teachings such as Hinduism, Zen and Tibetan Buddhism, stress not prophecy but transcendence—in the sense of searching after God in oneself. Could that be seen as an essential difference between these two arenas of spirituality?"[17]

Muzaffer Efendi answered:

> Between Adam and the Prophet Muhammad, there were 224,000 prophets. Who knows? Perhaps Buddha and Confucius were among them. The people in the East would have also had divine contact through their messengers, but their religions later became distorted. These are just my beliefs. Abraham came and built the Ka'ba as a temple without images in honor of the One God. But, you see, almost immediately after he passed away, pilgrims came and filled the holy place with idols. That is an example of what has happened many times in history with prophets. Couldn't Buddha's religion have deviated like that? But that aside, the existence of messengers and prophets

> helps facilitate the connection between humanity and its Divine Source. Perhaps someone could find Reality without the guidance of a prophet or teacher. It would just take them longer.
>
> After all, what is *nirvana* but *fana fi'llah* (losing one's self in Divine Reality)? But in our system of Islamic Sufism, there is another step beyond losing one's self in Allah. It is called *baqa*, in which one who has found union through *losing* the self in Allah, *finds* the self in Allah and *emerges* as Allah, living by divine subsistence. There's nothing to be amazed about. All of the mysteries of Allah are contained in the human being, who is higher than the angels—because Allah, who does not fit in the space of this world or in the heavens, fits into the human heart. This was revealed to the Prophet David and preserved in a hadith of the Prophet. It applies to every human being, regardless of whether they're Buddhist or Muslim.

Except for an occasional hint of the type quoted above, Efendi rarely gave teachings above the third level in public. Another glimpse of the deeper teachings was recorded during this time in an off-the-air conversation between Sheikh Nur and Efendi, speaking through a translator. The discussion centered on some teaching the sheikh had given concerning the attributes of paradise. When Nur asked Efendi whether the mystic friends of Allah, the *evliya* or saints, had a direct experience of these states of paradise while living on earth, Efendi answered that, as there were no intermediaries involved, it was direct. Then he offered this further elucidation:

> The intimates of Allah *are* the spirit of paradise... Their body is paradise, their soul (the master) the spirit of paradise. Such teachings are difficult to explain. The more advanced teachings are rarely given to the world since they are easily misunderstood by those unfamiliar with the verities of mysticism. Therefore, in my books I generally write material suitable only for the initial stages on the path.

> In reality, Allah is not outside nor inside of His creation, including humanity. The understanding of Allah is not given to humans. The scale of minds could not support the weight of it. One cannot assign a place (*makam*) to Allah's existence. We have a beginning and an end, but Allah, being infinite, has no such boundaries. Yet the Divine Artist created His art, Adam (humanity), in order to reveal His existence—so that the Divine Truth (*Haqq*) might know itself (*tejelli*). If we weren't already the Divine Truth, the Truth could not be known. In actuality, one *can* know the Artist through His Art, since the creation itself comes from the Night of Divine Essence."[18]

Asked by Nur, on another occasion,[19] about the special gift and mission of Nureddin Jerrahi, Efendi answered:

> *Ashk, ashk, ashk ilahi.* (Love, love, Divine love.) He has studied and received the knowledge of utmost sacred love. Through teaching, he has shared this great love with the world, which leads to knowing, discovering and *becoming* Truth. Our Pir has lost and found himself in Divine Truth, becoming existent in Allah through love. That is his miracle. We have an *ilahi* which we sing in his honor: 'Hazrati Nureddin, the leader of love.' You can see the miracle of Hazrati Pir if you look around during our gatherings. All our hearts are united. Though many have come from far away—some from other cultures and other races—we have come together as one vast heart. Haven't we heard the echoes in the churches of all the people who have come together and chanted and sung the name of Allah? Even for millions of dollars, one could not buy such great love.

Fariha recalls another evening during the early days at Spring Valley, when Sheikh Nur was sitting next to Muzaffer Efendi as he discoursed on *ashk* and on the flames of passionate love. Suddenly, a fire truck raced by outside with its sirens blaring. Nur joked, "Efendi, they're coming to put out this fire." Efendi exchanged a look with Nur and said, "They can never put out this fire!"

During the spring trip of 1980, Muzaffer Efendi was interviewed several times on the *In the Spirit* radio show. During one program,[20] Nur Lex Hixon was joined by another radio host, Mary Houston, who happened to meet and talk with Efendi in the elevator and was spontaneously invited on the show to continue her interesting line of questions. On the air, she inquired of the sheikh why, in one's meditations, a person might one day feel great love while at other times they couldn't reach that level with the same intensity.

Muzaffer Efendi answered that this had to do with the intake of food on every level, including impressions that one receives and even the air one breathes. "All of these have an influence on whether one is quickly accepted into the presence of Allah or is turned away. There is also the question of another's feelings toward one. The eye of jealousy that falls upon one can certainly affect one. In this respect, there are two basic types of glance: the eye of love, mercy and compassion and the eye of envy, arrogance and hypocrisy. Some by nature have poisonous eyes. . . . The only defense against this is the protection of Allah and His mercy which you receive with your prayers and closeness to Him. As for the food we eat, one might assume that relatively minor things like a bite of food, a word, or an impression wouldn't affect one; but they are like a seed thrown into the soil and in one's system, which can grow. For instance, just encountering a beautiful person or friend for a few minutes can make one's whole day bright."

Then Muzaffer Efendi recounted a story:

> There lies in Istanbul, between Beyazid and Fatih, the tomb of a saint by the name of Sheikh Vefa. This sheikh had a five or six year old son who used to play out in the street in front of his house. As there was no running water in certain sections of Istanbul in those days, water-carriers used to deliver water to

people's houses in animal skins. The child of the sheikh used to take a nail and run up to the water-carriers and poke a hole in their water-bags and try to suck the water out where it would leak. The water-carriers were quite annoyed with such behavior but for some time hesitated to inform the child's father, because the moral responsibility of the children falls upon their parents and it was poor manners to complain to a sheikh. But finally one of the water-carriers lost patience with the child's behavior and reported it to the sheikh.

Sheikh Vefa asked how long this had been going on. The water-carrier answered that it had begun only recently, since the boy had been allowed to go out in the streets to play. The sheikh asked them why they hadn't come to him about this sooner and arranged to compensate them in full for any loss of income and aggravation they had sustained as a result of his son's actions. Then he called in his wife, the child's mother, and told her, "Please think very carefully and tell me if there is anything you might have done which was displeasing to Allah, prior to the time our son began to play in the street." At first she could think of nothing, but then remembered something further in the past.

"When I was pregnant with our son, I went to visit our neighbor," she explained. "When the hostess had left the room, I saw a lemon on the table and, being pregnant, began to crave it. However, I was embarrassed to ask for it, so I just poked it with a needle and sucked a drop from it, then put it back so no one would realize that I had touched it."

The sheikh said, "Thank God, we have discovered the problem. You see, my wife, it is the same act, the same imagery that our son is playing out, sucking water without permission, as you did with the lemon." She asked him, "What can be done about it?" The sheikh replied, "You have to go back to our neighbor and explain what you did with her lemon, ask her forgiveness and offer her whatever price she wants for that drop of lemon." The wife found the woman and explained the situation. The neighbor said, "What is a drop of lemon worth? I would have certainly offered it to you at the time had I realized you wanted it. Of course you are forgiven."

You see, the sheikh did not call the child and reprimand him, saying, "Why have you been sticking nails in the water-skins?" The next day, though the child had the same nail in his hand and all the water-carriers were passing in front of him, he didn't touch any of them. Instead, he busied himself drawing a picture in the dirt with his nail. This shows how some actions are not necessarily the fault of a child, but are a reflection of what the parents have done.

There was a man who visited Hazrati 'Abdullah Mubarak seeking advice about the bad state of his child. The sheikh asked him: "Did you ever wish bad upon your son, that he should be punished? Has such a thought ever flashed through your mind?" When the man admitted that it was so, the sheikh told him, "Well, now you're seeing the result of it."

Mary asked Efendi: "If one sees a situation of this kind and there's no one living to go fix the situation, what can be done?" He responded: "If one can't locate the source of the trouble, this increases the pain and suffering of the situation. If you find the source of it, that's the mercy of Allah. They asked Hazrat Imam al-Azam: 'How can we know if our sustenance is lawful?' He answered: 'It's very easy. Watch where you spend it.' So you can seek in this manner. Watch where it came from and where it went. Or: What did I do yesterday? If you find the connection, it means the mercy of Allah has already come to you. Having discovered it, you have to turn to your Creator and ask forgiveness. Not just ask in words—it's a contract you sign that it won't happen again. Then your heart will open."

"Try it!" Efendi concluded with a laugh. "If it doesn't work, you can come back here and say this sheikh is a liar."

On another occasion, Efendi reiterated, by means of a story, the importance of guarding oneself from money obtained through questionable or unlawful means. There was a hidden saint, a Malami sheikh and breadmaker, who lived in Bursa during the time of Sultan Beyazid. His name was Somanju Baba, meaning the *father baker.* At the recommendation of Emir Sultan, a great saint of the time, Somanju Baba was called upon to preach to the congregation at the opening of the Grand Mosque at Bursa. There, he gave an inspired interpretation of the Fatiha (the opening Sura of the Qur'an), unfolding seven mysterious levels of its meaning. Even Mulla Fanari, the Sheikh-al-Islam who was in attendance, could not comprehend the high teaching about the seventh level given in the sermon. So the Sheikh al-Islam afterwards sought out Somanju Baba to learn its meaning. At first, the sheikh, as a condition before teaching him the seventh level interpretation, set the stipulation that the finely dressed and impressively turbaned Sheikh al-Islam, the religious head of the empire, should ride through the streets of bursa parading himself on a lowly donkey. When Mulla Fanari replied in all earnestness that he could not do this in front of the people without gaining a reputation for mentally instability, the sheikh relented, saying he had already shown sufficient humility by coming and sitting as a humble student among his dervishes. Then, through his spiritual glance, he conferred on Mulla Fanari the understanding and permission to write an interpretation of Sura Fatiha, including the seventh level. (Mulla Fanari would later write a great commentary on the Fatiha called *Futihat-i Ayniye.*)

The Sheikh al-Islam, full of gratefulness at this blessing, removed a bag of gold from his pocket and laid it at the feet of the sheikh, saying, "My master, please be kind enough to distribute this gold among your poor dervishes." Somanju Baba stopped him: "I'm sorry, but my dervishes cannot spend or eat from that money, because if they ate from food bought with that money, their spiritual evolution would cease." Mulla Fanari tried to defend himself, saying, "Master, you may think this money is from my state salary, but it is not. It is from the revenue of my parent's farm which has been in the family for a long time. The money is definitely lawful (*halal*)."

"So you think it is lawful?" said the sheikh. "Will you permit me to test it?" When Mulla Fanari agreed, the sheikh opened the bag, removed a gold coin, and instructed one of his dervishes to go to the market and buy some good, fresh straw for the purpose of feeding his donkey. When the dervish returned, the straw was set before the sheikh's donkey. He sniffed at it warily, then turned around and urinated on it.

Detail from a 17th century Ottoman engraving

The sheikh turned to Mulla Fanari. "Sir. You said this money was lawful, but as you can see my donkey pisses on it. How can I give this money to my dervishes when even my donkey won't eat food bought with it?"

The Path of Mystic Love begins with Adam

Photo: James Wentzy

On March 21, 1980, Muzaffer Efendi preached his Friday Jum'a sermon on the air at WBAI, complete with *adhan* and Friday prayers. At the time, the broadcast reached what was probably the largest American radio audience ever to hear an Islamic Friday sermon in America. The sermon is notable for its mystic presentation of the Prophet Muhammad, the *Nur Muhammad* (the first Light of creation) and the Prophet Adam, peace be upon them. The mystical teachings on the Nur Muhammad date as far back as the commentaries of Tabari, around the time of Junayd of Baghdad in the ninth century. We will give a few excerpts from the sermon followed by a further clarification of the mystic significance of Adam, from Efendi's discourse later in the week. Muzaffer Efendi began his sermon:

Muzaffer Efendi preaching a Friday sermon at Masjid al-Farah on 155 Mercer Street in New York

Allah Most High is with the pure, with the believers—those who long to enter his paradise and enjoy His good pleasure—and with the lovers of Allah. For those of you who are listening today for the truth and for the pleasure of Allah—those whose hearts are trembling with love for Allah, whose bodies are vibrating in love, through every cell—I will preach today about the *Khatim an-Nabiyyin*, the Seal of Prophecy, the light of the heavens and the earth, Muhammad, may the fullest divine blessings and peace be upon him. The words we use to communicate about our Prophet will be but a drop from the Ocean of Reality and a glimmer of the Light of Paradise. If the heavens and earth were paper and if all the oceans were ink, and if all the trees in the forests were pens, and they were to attempt to write the attributes of Muhammad, the ink would be exhausted, the pen would be broken, and the paper used up, because the whole creation would be incapable of writing the attributes of the Prophet. . . .

Allah Most High Himself has revealed: "I was a hidden treasure and wished to be known. Therefore I created the universe." His treasure was Hazrati Muhammad Mustafa (*salallahu 'aleihi wa salaam*). Allah has created from His own infinite light the first light of creation, saying, "Be, Muhammad!" Thus the light of Ahmad, the *Nur Muhammad*, was created and spoke saying, "*La ilaha illallah*. Nothing exists except Allah." The Divine Source of all creation, seen and unseen, responded: "And My messenger is Muhammad." Allah also gave the promise at that time that whoever sincerely says, "*La ilaha illallah; Muhammad ar-Rasulullah*," would be protected from the fire and would enter Paradise.

This first Light of Creation, the Muhammad of Light, is also called the first light and the first soul. From this light, Allah Most High has created everything that exists: His heavens, His throne, His paradise, His hell, His angels and the wisdom and light of all His holy messengers. Thus, Adam became the father of our flesh and Muhammad became the father of our souls. In the Holy Qur'an we read that Allah taught the Divine names and the names of all things to Adam, upon him be peace; thus, he became the source of worldly knowledge. Adam knew the *Sifaat Allah*—the Divine attributes or manifestations—but the vast soul of the Prophet Muhammad knew the very Essence of the Creator, and in time would bring that understanding to earth through the person of the historical Muhammad of Arabia. . . . During the time of our Prophet's presence upon the planet, someone asked him, "O Rasulullah, when did you become a prophet?" The noble Muhammad answered, "I was a prophet before Adam was between water and clay."

In paradise, Adam begged his Creator to give him the gift of love. Allah Most High answered him: "O Adam, one cannot experience love in paradise, because love necessitates both happiness and tears. To be able to experience tears of separation and know the joy of reunion, you would have to leave paradise." Then Adam ate from the forbidden tree and left paradise. Then he wept for 300 years, begging for Divine mercy. Finally, after 300 years, he received forgiveness upon uttering these words: "O Allah, the Creator of All, forgive me for the sake of Muhammad, who will be of my progeny." . . . Adam had seen the name Muhammad at the moment Allah blew the Divine breath into his body...the Light of Muhammad which has been the fountain of all the Prophets, including Abraham, Moses and Jesus, each of whom spoke of one to come after them. . . .

As the moon and all the planets gather their light from the sun, all the noble prophets sent by our Creator receive their light from the light of the final Prophet. . . . He is the most beautiful of the beautiful, the Beloved of Allah, the one who gave the news that a black slave would enter paradise while some members of his own family would not. He is the Imam of the believers, the Sultan of all lovers . . . . For his sake, may Allah give guidance and intelligence to humanity. May Allah wipe the tears of those eyes who cry for his sake and may Allah allow all the lovers to arrive at their true destinations. *Amin. Walhamdulillah-i Rabbi'l Alamin.*

A week or so later, at a dinner in San Francisco, the subject of Adam and the path of love resurfaced during a discussion between Efendi and one of the dinner guests who was a Christian priest. Efendi began by pointing out: "The reason that Adam and Eve were taken away from paradise was because Adam wished to know love. Part of love involves suffering and tears, possibilities which are not inherent in paradise since that realm is pure, continuous joy and satisfaction. That is why Allah removed them from paradise."

Questioner: Wasn't there an issue of disobedience?

Answer: Certainly Adam disobeyed. However, according to our faith, the prophets and messengers don't have their own will. Adam wasn't operating by his own will either. He didn't sin by his own will—he was *made* to sin so that he would be taken from paradise.

Q: Wasn't he made to sin by Satan?

A: Shaitan was only an instrument. The devil cannot act on his own either. If Allah doesn't want someone to sin and the devil is able to override that and make them sin anyway, we would have to consider the devil to be stronger than Allah.

Q: Well, we believe that man possesses a completely spiritual will and that he's free to make choices.

A: Yes, of course man has a will, but it is limited in scope. For ordinary people, that will can be likened to someone who is flying on an airplane to New York. He is free to change seats and move around the plane as it travels, but that's about the extent of his freedom on the airplane.

Q: But he freely chose to board the airplane.

A: I'm just using this as a metaphor. Consider that the world is an airplane and that you did not come here by your own will. The question is: did you come to this world by your own free will or were you brought here?

Q: I came here as a result of my parent's will.

A: Ah, but is every parent who wishes for a child able to conceive? It doesn't always happen does it? You see, not everything you wish for or will occurs.

Q: True.

A: Because if everything we willed came to pass, there would be no real difference in us and God—no power greater than us.

Q: But the question of results aside, we *are* able to make choices.

A: Certainly, I'm not denying that—in fact it would be a sin to deny it, as it is one of the greatest gifts that has been given to us. The point is that our will is relatively small. When the Greater Will comes, then what you understand, will, and even think will disappear. Hitler went into World War II, thinking he would be victorious. Had he foreseen his defeat, he probably would have proceeded differently. Allah gives us the right to freely make choices, but the Greater Will, the destiny, is in His hand. When Abraham came to Nimrod, Nimrod asked him to explain the nature of God. Abraham answered, "Allah is the One Who gives life and takes away life." Nimrod responded, "I can also give life and take away life. Watch." He had two prisoners who had been given the death sentence brought before him. He pardoned one and had the other one slain on the spot. "You see, I have granted life and I have taken away life." Seeing that Nimrod didn't truly understand what it meant to give and take life, Abraham said to him: "Allah is the One Who makes the sun rise in the East and set in the West. If you think you can do that, you're welcome to try!" So if man has absolute free will, why doesn't he make the sun rise and set?

Q: Yes, I follow your point.

A: This holds true even in small matters. A person cannot pronounce the letter *B* without using both lips. You cannot pronounce it with the sound of the throat alone. The very structure of the body—which is the Creator's Will—prohibits us from producing this sound except by using the lips. I'm simply trying to clarify the difference in two understandings of the same thing. We consider that Adam did indeed sin, *but* he was *made* to sin. You see, Allah created Adam after His own holy character, investing him with the Divine Attributes, and we are all his children. If Adam and the rest of the human race had been intrinsically sinful, the whole of the universe, with its paradises and hells would not have been created for humanity. Don't you see how great Adam was? From his progeny comes the Virgin Mary, and from her comes Jesus, peace be upon them. Bad produces bad and good produces good. Allah has created everything in the heavens and various worlds, for the benefit of the humans who inhabit them. In a hadith of the Prophet, Allah says to the Prophet David: "O David, I have created the whole creation for humanity and I have created humanity for Myself." Man is great—and I mean woman as well; there is no difference. The word *great* is insufficient. The human being is the jewel of the universe.

Some days later, the same theme resurfaced during one of Efendi's sohbets with the dervishes in Spring Valley, New York.

Efendi was asked: "Could it be said that Adam began the path of love?" Efendi answered:

> Yes. You see, it is only Shaitan who lacks the capacity to love. Whoever lacks love is suffering under shaitanic influence. We must see, however, that love manifests itself in the character of a given human being according to that person's level. For example, at the lowest level, the *nafs al-ammara*, one's animal qualities predominate, accompanied by all the desires, needs and attachments associated with this world. Love is like a glass, where the water assumes the shape of the container into which it is poured. When love conforms to the shape of the *nafs al-ammara*, it manifests primarily as sexual desire. If the cup is the *insan-i kamil*, the perfect human being, then the humanity manifests itself in the shape of perfection, producing perfect love.
>
> Love is like the rain; if it descends on excrement it produces a foul odor. If love descends on rose petals, the sweet scent of perfume arises. That is why love has been represented in Sufi poetry as wine, the sheikh as the distributer of wine, and the dervish tekke as a tavern. The cup is the being of the student. That is the language of Sufism. But the ones who don't know this language imagine that the poet is describing a bartender making alcoholic drinks. But we don't find fault with them either, because they are simply seeing the world according to the color of their own eyeglasses. If you are wearing green sunglasses, you see everything as green, though it is not actually green.
>
> There was a donkey owned by a villager in Kaisery who was so finicky that he would not eat yellow straw. The owner, being an intelligent man, procured a pair of large green spectacles, put them over the eyes of the donkey, and the animal began to eat the yellow straw with great relish! The man also had a cat who wouldn't eat the bread when it got dry, so he put a drop of milk on the cat's nose, and the cat also began to eat with a great appetite!
>
> Many people are like that as well. That's why we need to

be able to distinguish between animal love, human love and Divine love. Please do not misunderstand me: the relationship between a husband and wife is not animal love, because there is the holy touch of procreation bringing forth children into the world. When a husband and wife make love, Allah looks upon them with kindness and joy. Isn't the purpose of this natural act to be an instrument of Allah's creative power? After all, the first duty of a human being is to know God, to find God, and to be one with God. Thus we are given that potential. I hope you have the taste of what I have been discussing, because it is definitely worth tasting.

Question: Efendi, earlier you mentioned the *Insan-i Kamil*. What is the spiritual state of this perfect human being?

Answer: The soul of the one who actively rejects faith is like a dark prison, while the state of the *Insan-i Kamil* is one of being surrounded by fresh air and cool water. It is possible to enter into that state, but if one were to remain continuously in that very high state of union and ecstasy, it would destroy one. It is necessary for the pendulum to swing back. Even though the pendulum swings in the opposite direction of union and the states for which we strive, that too is a blessing. For instance, the perfect human, like Adam, is made to sin, but that sin is automatically forgiven. The perfect human is very conscious of this state and would, like Adam, accept the blame himself. But it was just a case of having to go away from the object of attainment in order to experience it—in order to taste love and to come to earth in order to better appreciate paradise.

The sign of the swing of the pendulum was when Rasulullah entered Mecca and asked Hazrat 'Ali to stand upon his shoulders inside the Ka'ba in order to destroy one of the idols in a high place. When 'Ali protested, he was told, "You could not bear the weight if I climbed on your shoulders." Rasulullah used to say to his wife, "O Ayesha, make me speak." He is asking his wife to bring him more into this world. Then he turns to Hazrat Bilal and asks him to chant Qur'an, to be brought back to the other swing of the pendulum.

He mentions that, "Between me and my creator, I reach such a state that there are no intermediaries—no angels, nor Michael, nor Gabriel. It is a state totally beyond description." The Prophet goes from *'abd*, the state of servanthood, to eating and sleeping with his wife; then he reaches a state of union beyond which even Gabriel cannot reach. When that state of union occurs, Allah is closer than the iris is to the white of your eye.

Even in our own humble cases, we try and try to reach Allah, but the heart only seems to get harder—or one gets depressed. Then, all of a sudden, in the middle of your job, or talking to someone, you find yourself in that state. It is just another sign that we have very little to do with this. The same thing happens to us in the dhikr ceremony. One day you lose yourself in great joy, and experience great love in your heart. Another day, you are jumping up and down, sweating and getting tired and wondering when the dhikr will be over. That's your servanthood. It is absolutely normal—and necessary. Please keep that in mind. But even a bystander who knows nothing about dhikr can profit from it, because if one or two go into ecstatic states during the ceremony, the rest will feel it, including those simply watching it. It is according to how Allah spreads His mercy.

Q: Efendi, you mentioned shaitan. Where is he—within or without?

A: Shaitan is the materialization of the divine attribute *Muzhill*—the One who leaves one in ignorance and misguidance. It exists in one's blood, circulated in the veins, and is called *khannas.* The one outside of you is called *Shaitan*. The essence of *khannas* is the *nafs al-ammara*, the ego or self that ties you to the world and your desires. They are the same, or close friends; *Iblis* (Satan) from the outside, and *khannas* from the inside. If you can, save yourself from them. For that, there is only one way: to take refuge in Allah. Otherwise, no one on their own can be victorious over this strong power, which is itself an attribute of Allah. If you take refuge in Allah, the other runs away.

Q: Does Allah manifest this quality in human beings in order that they would take refuge in Allah?

A: Yes, of course. To oppose Shaitan is to go towards Allah. The devil is like the salt in food. The food can be very bland without a little salt. Without the salt of the devil, you wouldn't need judges, lawyers or policemen. Think if everyone in an orchestra played the same notes. If the whole world was orthodox that's how it would be—a monotonous sameness. But when the Shaitan is put in, it creates variety. May Allah keep us on the proper side. Just as we feed the *khannas* in our blood with food every day, Allah also feeds it, but could withdraw it at any time if He so desired. One of the prophets was able to catch and imprison the devil, but after he had accomplished this, there was no taste in living in the whole world. The baker wouldn't open his shop; the butcher wouldn't cut his lamb, and the tailor quit selling his clothing. Why? Because all ambition was gone.

Believe me, things are perfect the way they are.

Q: Efendi, in a previous talk you stated that when Adam left paradise, he cried for 300 years. Why so long?

A: Because he had eaten from the forbidden tree. Now, to the human way of thinking, this eating from the forbidden tree was an arrogant act of sin. But in reality, it was according to the will of Allah. . . . One has to understand the cycle: Adam wanted to love, but because of love's association with tears, pain and suffering, it was not possible to experience love in paradise, which is a place of peace and tranquility. Therefore the forbidden tree was created, so that Adam could eat from it, quit paradise and come to earth in order to taste love. Part of love is separation and unification; so, being separated from paradise, Adam entered the realm of love which manifested itself in tears. One cannot taste love in separation nor enjoy the satisfactions of love while already in the state of union. So a change was necessary. What appeared as a sinful act of disobedience on Adam's part was really an act of God.

Allah had already taught Adam the divine names. In short, Allah had given Adam the Divine Wisdom, which is our potential. Adam knew perfectly well that what had occurred was not his own action, but again, as a human being—and as a lesson to us—he assumed responsibility for this fault, though there was no fault there. If one knew the taste of love's tears, one would not only weep for 300 years but for eternity. What pleasure there is in love's tears! No real lover would ever desire the total satisfaction and resolution of his or her love. Why would one want everything over and resolved? In the separation, one can continue to enjoy the sweet anticipation of union. That is why he wept for 300 years—it was really too little.

Q: When we, like Adam, ask to return to Allah again, will He accept us as well?

A: Of course, there will be acceptance. There is no proper prayer which Allah will not accept. Allah is generous—the giver of gifts. But there is a reason why some of one's prayers may seem to go unanswered. It is a sign of divine mercy and love for you because, while you may think you are praying for what is best for you, Allah alone knows what is truly good for you. So He grants not necessarily what you think you should have, but what you truly need. Also, Allah sometimes delays the realization of your prayers until the hereafter.

In our limitation, we cannot always see what is best for us and may be attracted to things which could harm us in the long run. Sometimes Allah will grant the prayer of one who asks with a lack of understanding, but the answer to such a prayer is not a blessing but a curse. Someone who is childless may ask for a child, but when the child is born it becomes a nuisance and causes great hardships and suffering for them.

There is also a question of appropriate time and place. The prayers are accepted if you are loved by Allah and are worthy of His care and mercy. It is filtered through His judgment. Allah is the only One Who knows what is best for you, and in His compassion for you, He gives only if it is good for you and if not, delays it, even to the hereafter, or withholds it altogether. Even if Allah withholds, it is certainly an answer to your prayer. Therefore it is wise when you pray for things, either spiritual or material, to always add, "If it is good for me."[22]

Later, at another talk, Efendi went on to say:

When Allah created Adam, he asked him to look to his right where he saw three beautiful lights. Adam inquired and learned that they were: *mind* (located in the head), *modesty* (located in the eyes), and *compassion* (located in the heart). Then Allah asked Adam to look to his left, where he saw three ugly dark areas. He asked and found that they were: *arrogance*, located in the head (when intelligence goes, arrogance takes its place), *greed*, located in the eyes (when modesty leaves, greed enters), and *hatred and jealousy*, located in the heart (when the light of compassion leaves the heart, these take its place).

The *nafs*, or ego, is located in the heart, but its attributes are in the eyes and head. Different attributes of the *nafs* might be in your stomach, genitals, and so on. So when one works on the *nafs*—to change its attributes, to purify it, and unite it with

Truth—then one turns this mental arrogance into modesty, and so forth; but all of these attributes are connected, as with a rope, to the human heart. When the nafs is trained, when the limited self is transformed, only Truth is left in the heart (the state of *fana fi'llah*); but when Truth is not in your heart, then the world fills it instead. One must work with sincerity of heart to change the heart's darkness into light. . . . If you are trying to change your being, knocking on God's door for mercy and compassion, do you think you will be deprived of that? But in three days you can't expect it to happen. Even the flu doesn't pass that quickly. One must work. God won't deprive the one who works.[22]

A Hajj to Mecca & Medina and the Opening of Masjid al-Farah

Toward the end of April, Sheikh Muzaffer and his Turkish disciples returned to Istanbul. The month of hajj in 1980 began in late September. Efendi invited many of his followers, especially the Western ones who had not previously made hajj, to join him in making the pilgrimage. It was his eleventh hajj and would be his final one. During the remaining four years of his life, Muzaffer Efendi directed much of his energy into making biannual spring and fall trips to America. By November of 1984, Efendi had visited the United States a total of 13 times, totaling even more visits than he had made to Mecca and Medina on pilgrimage.

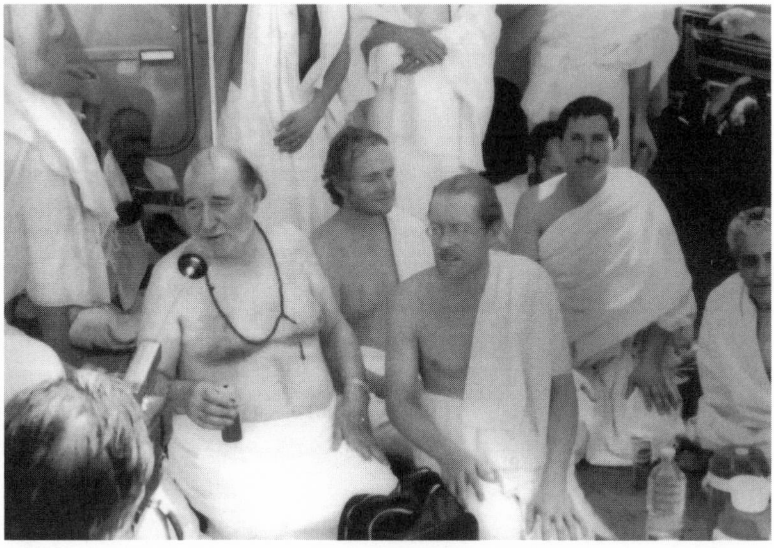

On Hajj at Mount Arafat (1980)

Efendi considered the 1980 hajj an important trip. Nur recalled how one day, he was sitting with a few Turkish brothers in the presence of Efendi when the sheikh suddenly announced, "Nur and I will make hajj together." The others politely agreed, saying,

"*Insha'llah;*" but Efendi interjected, "No! Not *insha'llah*. We *will* make the hajj together!" Indeed that fall, Nur and a number of other American disciples accompanied Efendi on his last hajj. Tosun Baba also brought many of his disciples as well.

In late September, Efendi boarded a plane for America and, from New York, personally accompanied his Western students to Jeddah, Saudi Arabia. During the hajj, Efendi offered many fervent prayers for his spiritual disciples at the tomb of Rasulullah in the green-domed Grand Mosque of Medina, as well as on Mount Arafat and at the Ka'ba in Mecca. The blessings still continue to flow from those divine supplications.

Fariha recalls that Muzaffer Efendi sang a lot during this hajj. He would sit and sing kasides and ilahis at length and just seemed to be immersed in a state of divine love, of *ashk*. At Mina, the men and women were divided into separate adjacent tents. Afterwards, Nur told Fariha how Efendi had explained, in the men's tent, about the four rivers of paradise and how, on one level of meaning, each river corresponded to one of the four bodily fluids. Efendi related that the four rivers of paradise mentioned in the Qur'an can be interpreted as the secretions of the eye, of the nose, of the ear, and of the mouth, clearly pointing to the body as the paradise vessel. Sura 47:15 of the Qur'an speaks allegorically of these rivers, which are promised to the righteous, as rivers of unpolluted water, of pure milk, of delicious wine, and of clear honey, brimming with every kind of fruit and forgiveness.

The group of hajjis spent the day of Arafat at the foot of the mountain and there, Fariha recalls, an extraordinary moment occurred when one of the hufaz in the party recited the 1000 names of Allah which the angel Gabriel had recited over the Prophet Muhammad before going into battle—a recitation which was to give him complete immunity or perfect protection. She remembers that, during the chanting, they all stood under a low tent canopy while Nur held up a staff near the center to help raise the roof. At the *tawwaf*—circling the Ka'ba—there was such a crush that all the male dervishes formed a chain around the women in the group, providing a sort of moving vessel of protection.

In those days, the men and women were not completely separated from each other as they are today in the Masjid an-Nabi, the Prophet's Mosque in Medina. So early one morning, around two or three A.M., Fariha and Haydar accompanied Efendi to the Prophet's mosque to pray at the tomb of the Prophet. Later that day they learned that, at the same time, Nur, who had remained at the hotel in order to sleep, had an important revelatory dream encounter with the Prophet Muhammad, which he subsequently recounted in his book, *Heart of the Qur'an*.

One of the things Sheikh Nur said he vividly remembered about the hajj was Efendi's enthusiastic chanting of the names of the twelve imams on the bus, and the delighted look on the bus driver's face, who happened to be a Shi'ite.

Fariha also recalls another Sufi pilgrimage in which she and some of the other American disciples accompanied Efendi to Konya, Turkey for the Urs of Jelaluddin Rumi on December 17, the date on which Rumi's "wedding" or passing into the Beloved is annually commemorated with a ceremony performed by the whirling dervishes. During the trip, a sheikh came from Scotland saying he had come to Konya especially to meet Muzaffer Efendi because he wanted to meet the *qutb*, or spiritual pole, of his time. He met Efendi, treating him with great deference, but Efendi did not really encourage him as to whether he considered himself a *qutb*. In fact, he told several stories including one where he effaced himself by saying "when the last *qutb* died and they were throwing out the turban, I ducked and let it whiz by." Yet, according to Muzaffer Efendi's son, Junayd, Efendi revealed that he did receive what was apparently a qutb-level dream in which "the banner of the West" was divinely granted to him.

The most memorable moment that Fariha recalls from this trip came just after they all visited Mevlana's tomb. Fariha remembers:

> I stayed back and everyone else left. I just wanted to bask in the radiance of Mevlana. Then when I came out the door, on the walkway, I saw Muzaffer Efendi in such an extraordinary state; clearly he was in *wejd*, in ecstasy. He was greeting each person, kissing the hands of the people coming from Mevlana's tomb. Instantly, I saw him as Mevlana. He just seemed to embody the qualities that were at the tomb and was greeting the visitors. It was extraordinary. He wasn't bowing formally to the visitors; it was more like you are going to meet the most precious friend you've ever seen. I watched him greet several people then I moved on.

Entreating love in your presence, Melvana,
If I drink a cup from your hand,
If with one glance you strip me of all but God,
If I become drunk and ecstatic, Mevlana.

Your holy tomb is the Kaaba of lovers,
Your fragrant dust is the remedy for pain,
If I whirl in a circle,
And fly beyond the spheres, Mevlana.

Those who come in need are made whole,
As the soul finds its lover it becomes the beloved,
Lover and beloved enter Paradise,
If I come, I too would choose my beloved, Mevlana.

You have your book, though you are not a Messenger,
You address yourself to all mankind,
You rush to the sad and to the oppressed,
By your grace, if I reveal your secret, Melvana.

Beloved servant of Allah,
You found Truth's Path through Muhammad's love,
You drank your fill from Ali's hand,
If you give me one drop, I shall shower it, Mevlana...[23]

Another American tour in mid-October followed the 1980 hajj. By this time Tosun Bayrak had procured new property in Chestnut Ridge, New York, for the purpose of building a larger permanent mosque which would serve as the principal tekke in upstate New York for the Jerrahi Order of America. After a long series of delays, the larger mosque was finally completed and dedicated in early 1990.

The mosque in Chestnut Ridge (photo by the author)

As many of Efendi's students lived in the metropolitan area of New York, the need for a tekke in downtown Manhattan gradually became evident. Such a place would also provide Efendi a large centrally located base from which he could receive people, teach and reside. One chilly spring day in 1980, Haydar and Fariha Friedrich brought Efendi and several others to a spacious three-story building at 155 Mercer Street in the Soho district of Manhattan. The building, listed on New York City's historical register, was built in 1854 as a volunteer firehouse. It's social hall, open to the locals as a kind of coffee house, had been visited by Walt Whitman and Ralph Waldo Emerson in December of 1855, during one of Emerson's visits to the city.

Interior of Masjid al-Farah on Mercer St. in New York City

By 1980, the building was owned by the Dia Art Foundation and was being offered for use as a downtown masjid for Muzaffer Efendi. Efendi approved of the idea, and soon a team of fine craftsmen from Turkey were commissioned to build the *mithrab* and *minbar* as the building was prepared for use as a Manhattan Jerrahi Tekke. The result was a beautiful and spacious Eastern-inspired interior, replete with rich oriental carpets, special green track-lighting fixtures by Dan Flavin, and abundant Arabic calligraphy. Efendi named the mosque *Masjid al-Farah*, the Mosque of Divine Ease. The name also carries connotations of a sacred wedding and mystic union.

By the fall of 1980, when Efendi returned to America, the Masjid al-Farah was ready for use as a tekke. Now Muzaffer Efendi began to divide his time in New York between Manhattan and Spring Valley. For the duration of several trips to America between 1981 and 1982, Efendi lived at Masjid al-Farah. By 1980, Ragip Frager had also formed a Jerrahi study group in California which hosted Efendi when he traveled to the West Coast, spreading the network of support even further.

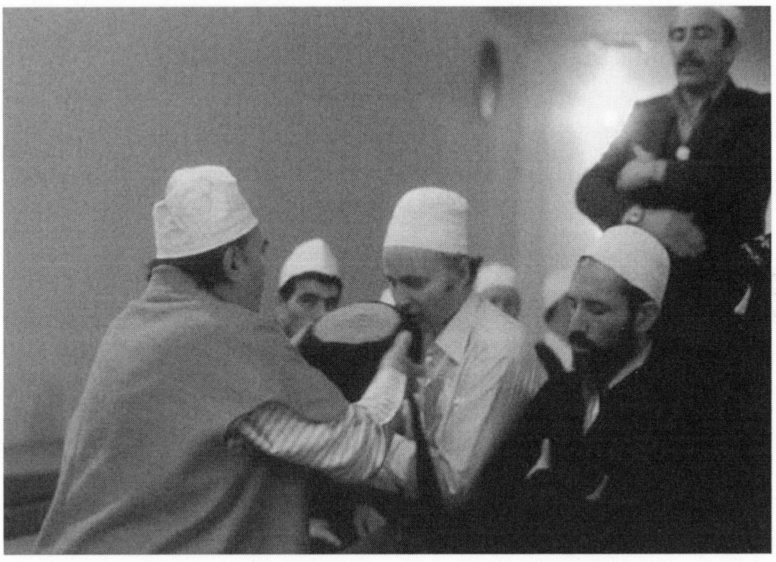

Nur, Gul Ali, and Fariha receiving the turban in 1980

During the fall of 1980 at the Masjid al-Farah, Muzaffer Efendi ceremoniously appointed his first American khalifas by placing the turban of the Order on their heads: Gül 'Ali Gordon, Nur Lex Hixon, and Fariha Friedrich. Gül 'Ali and Nur were called up first, then Fariha. Efendi placed his own turban on each of them briefly during the ceremony and prayed over Nur: "May all that has entered into me enter into Nur." In late 1981, he would bestow the green and gold turban upon two more American khalifas: Shems Friedlander and Salik Schwartz. While Gül Baba assisted the senior sheikh, Tosun Baba, at Spring Valley, the other khalifas shared teaching responsibilities at the Masjid al-Farah during Efendi's absence.

Tosun Baba originally offered some teaching at the new masjid, but as he was already responsible for the Spring Valley tekke, he encouraged the other, newer khalifas to take over these duties. Ragip Baba relates how he was visiting with Tosun Baba at Tosun's house when the phone began to ring. It was Sheikh Nur asking Tosun if he would call Efendi in Turkey and convey his readiness to assume responsibility for the new masjid. Tosun gladly made the call and Efendi happily gave his approval.

Thus Sheikh Nur began to teach and lead dhikr on Thursday nights on a regular basis. Sheikha Fariha also offered guidance for many of the women, while Salik Baba and Shems Baba began to lead music and the Jerrahi litany on other week nights. Somewhat later, Hafiz Ihsan, a knowledgeable Turkish imam affiliated with the Jerrahi Order, began to serve at the masjid as well.

As Sheikh Nur explained to the author, Muzaffer Efendi indicated during Nur's initial trip to Istanbul, that he wanted Nur to assume teaching responsibilities in the Order, but at the time Nur felt conflicted and not inwardly prepared to become a sheikh. In the end, he cut his visit short and hurriedly flew back to the United States on the Night of Power, almost like Jonah desperately trying to escape from his calling. Although saddened by this, Efendi offered no rebuke and even indicated that it is a good sign when one is not too eager to assume such power. By 1980, with time and reflection, Nur was ready.

In one of his talks in America, Muzaffer Efendi revealed that when he was first invited to come teach in the United States, he was himself reticent about all that this entailed:

> Actually, I was reluctant to come to America. You know how it is when a father leaves his family even for a short while and his children cry and lament. I have thousands of children in Turkey and each time I leave for America they lament. We started out several years ago going to a symposium in France where we were invited. Some of the American lovers who loved me came to France and asked me to come to America. I knew they wanted me to come even before this, but I created all sorts of obstacles to coming. As you know, to travel to another country one needs a visa from one's county of origin, but I purposely didn't get my visa in Turkey to come to America. But strangely enough, and almost against international law, they were able to procure our visas while we were in Paris; so I came to this country for 15 days. That's when I had my first contact with Americans in their own country, though many of them had come and visited me previously in Istanbul. My impression of the Americans was so favorable and I found them to be so warm-hearted, hospitable, and such intense spiritual seekers that I really fell in love with them. They obviously attached themselves to me as well, so now they just push and pull me here and there and I have no say in it. Wherever they take me, I go. . . .
>
> When I first went to Paris and got my visa to go to America, the people in France warned me not to go, saying if I went there the Americans would steal me from them. At first I was shocked by what they said but now I have to agree with them—the Americans stole me away! I have very many spiritual children but I also have two biological children, a boy of 11 and a daughter of 14. I had to leave them there with others while I came here with my wife. It's not easy for me to be here. But you see, I come here and they feed me well, give me plenty of tea and coffee and a comfortable bed—so I have found my comfort![24]

With the opening of a second major Jerrahi tekke in America, it became clear that there existed no single model to define how an American dervish community might best be organized. Tosun Baba, while making a few adaptations to Western culture, was primarily drawn to run the rural Spring Valley tekke in accordance with traditional Turkish-Islamic precedents—an approach which has worked well for many of his long-time students. Social responsibility has also become a hallmark of the community at Spring Valley/Chestnut Ridge, with the group repeatedly showing its commitment to divine service by raising funds for aid and disaster relief in war-torn countries such as Bosnia, Iraq, Palestine, as well as orphanages for the victims of the great 2004 tsunami disaster in Indonesia. Over the years, Tosun has also utilized his translation skills to publish a number of solid interpretive translations of classical Sufi works.

At Masjid al-Farah in downtown Manhattan, Sheikh Nur employed a different leadership style, in keeping with his Western training and his background in a variety of mystical traditions which also stressed divine union. While many seekers of traditional-style Islamic Sufi training were drawn to Spring Valley, there was a sizable contingent of Western seekers from various religious backgrounds who had little initial interest in converting to Islam; yet they found themselves attracted to the power of dhikr, the mystical teachings of unity, and to the presence of Muzaffer Efendi. When such persons came to Masjid al-Farah in search of further instruction, Sheikh Nur encouraged them to join the Order and receive the blessings and protections of Islam, with the freedom to learn and participate to whatever extent they were comfortable. This reflected Nur's understanding of Efendi's own open approach to the tarikat in the West ("Whether Jew or Christian... according to your understanding, you can be a Sufi.") and worked well for many Western newcomers who might not otherwise have stayed long enough to develop a deeper interest and involvement with the Islamic path. Nur also encouraged a more active teaching role for the women, citing the precedent of several honored wives of the Prophet who taught in Medina.

Years later, in a 1989 interview on New Dimensions Radio, Nur explained the approach he pursued:

> My sheikh actually gave me the responsibility to express [Islam] in the culture in whatever way I was inspired to do it. He never gave me any limits or guidelines other than his intense love of Islam, his intense love of the Prophet of Islam, the Beloved Muhammad, and his intense love for Allah, for God … . So, for instance, in our Order in New York City...I accept and initiate into our Order people who are Jews or Christians or Buddhists. They don't have to become Muslims. This is a rare thing among the Sufi Orders. Only occasionally, under certain cultural conditions has this happened, and then maybe either privately or secretly. So in America, because of the pluralistic climate, because of, let's say, even the democratic protections that we have against religious persecution—all of these things have come together to make it possible for Jews, Christians, Muslims and Buddhists to come together in an ancient dervish order and be legitimate members of that Order and actually begin to transcend their limited self in the...formal practice of the Order. I wouldn't necessarily call that "American Sufism," but the United States of America does present a pluralistic and protected environment for the most mature expressions to come forward in any of these great traditions.

As he communicated it to the author, Nur also saw in the example of Pir Nureddin Jerrahi's Order, a parallel to this principal of universality on the tarikat level. All of the great turuq of Pir Nureddin's time had brought together their permissions and united them under the Jerrahi banner, creating in some sense a universal tarikat in which all the orders were united. Just as, from the perspective of the mystics, we are not separate selves, neither is there any true separation between pirs, saints and prophets, other than the false barriers people attempt to place between them. In keeping with Islamic belief, Nur saw Abraham *Khalilullah*, the noble friend of God, as the father of true religion, standing at the head of this unitive tradition. In his own words:

> The magnificent patriarch Abraham, the embodiment of true generosity and hospitality whose tent is open in all directions, is spiritual father to the Jewish, Christian and Islamic nations, which are his seed multiplied into galaxies of souls, according to the Divine Promise. Embodying the fundamental religion of humanity, the religion of unity, the Prophet Abraham, upon him be abundant and beautiful peace, is the *hanifa*, the upright one. Even before the Divine Revelation of Torah, Psalms, Gospels, and Qur'an, he demonstrates the original nobility of the human being in direct communion with Truth, without images or mediators....
>
> The beloved Muhammad, the final fruition of the evolution of humanity's understanding, the final link in the lineage of revelatory Light, calls the spirituality innate to the human soul the *hanifiyya*, the way of Abraham. This station of maturity is wisely tolerant of all levels and dimensions of religious understanding, manifest through Prophets who, as the Qur'an discloses, have been sent as Divine Signs to every nation without exception, demonstrating a clear path to the One Reality. This loving tolerance of *hanifiyya* takes as its symbol the Tent of Abraham, open to spiritual travelers from all directions, full of the abundant Generosity of Allah poured out to all seekers of truth without exception. These lovers become friends as well as expressions of Truth, to all precious human beings ...[accepting] all human beings as who they truly are ... May humanity as a whole become conscious of the *hanifiyya*, allowing ineffable harmony to blossom among apparently diverse cultures, sciences, and great religious traditions.[25]

Addressing Western concerns about Islam

With each trip to America, Muzaffer Efendi continued to be interviewed on the radio, thus reaching a wider audience than the immediate dervish community and those who attended the public dhikr ceremonies. During these twilight years of the cold war between the United States and the Soviet Union, the Iranian hostage crisis of 1979 generated a wave of anti-Islamic sentiment in the United States. The crisis came about in 1979 when the Shah of Iran, Mohammad Reza Pahlavi, a U.S supported secularist dictator, became too ill to rule and the Iranian people took to the streets in a massive popular rebellion against him and his brutal secret police force. When the dying Shah fled to the West, where he hoped to receive medical treatment, the anti-Western Shiʿite cleric, Ayatollah Khomeini, who had been exiled by the Shah, returned from France by popular demand to rule in the Shah's place, vowing to reinstate traditional Islamic values.

Because of the people's great anger toward the Shah and the Americans who had supported him, the revolution turned ugly, with the seizing of the American Embassy in Tehran and the parading of some of the blindfolded hostages through the streets, accompanied by chants of hatred for America—"the great Satan" and "enemy of Islam"—and its president, Jimmy Carter, who refused Iranian hostage demands to return the dying Shah to stand trial in Iran. The hostage crisis was not resolved until more than a year later in January 1981, six months after the Shah's passing in Egypt, the last country in which he took asylum.

When Efendi was asked on the radio and on college campuses for his assessment of Khomeini as an Islamic spiritual leader, he answered quite frankly that he did not agree with Khomeini's approach nor his rhetoric, which demonized the American people in the name of Islam. When asked at Rice University, Efendi responded simply, "Indeed, he is a faithful Muslim and a spiritual leader, yet one following a misguided path."[26]

Discussing it among the dervishes at the Spring Valley tekke, Efendi mentioned the historical situation in Islam where the Prophet's enemies tried to murder him and to torture his family and followers. They attacked the faithful on the battlefield, mutilated the corpses of some of the Muslim martyrs, and finally cannibalized the liver of the Prophet's beloved uncle, Hamza, after he fell in battle. Even in that extreme case, Efendi noted, the Prophet didn't give in to the impulse to take revenge, but exercised patience with his enemies. Efendi continued:

> In my interpretation, I am in agreement with the feelings of many a scholar, wise man and general that our hearts are aching and we are extremely saddened with this current situation. Who are those people [the American hostages] that are being tortured by Khomeini's followers? They are but minor officials of a peaceful government who have been paid to do office jobs there. What is the meaning of torturing and tyrannizing these poor people? When a building is being erected, they put up a scaffolding, which is knocked down when the building is complete. Though he may not be aware of it, Khomeini is being used as a political tool. He should realize that we're now living in a time when the difference is not between nations or between common situations but a basic ideological enmity between people devoted to God and people without God. All the people, whether Buddhists, Jews or Christians, who are believers—who have some common spiritual foundation—should be together on the same side; otherwise when the communists and other anti-religious forces take over there will be neither mosque, synagogue, church nor temple.
>
> Surely the Shah was an enemy of humankind who should have been dealt with in his own country. But even in the case of a person like this, it would not have been an honorable act for another country to have returned him after they had once granted him refuge. Even if a whole empire were at stake, a country would still want to honor their sovereign word. At the

time of the Ottoman sultan, Beyazid, the Mongolian people, who were also Muslims, came and took refuge with the Ottomans. The enemy asked for the return of the Mongols but the Ottomans refused and, as a result, most of the Ottoman Empire was destroyed. But that was that kind of honor that kept the Ottoman Empire alive for five hundred years.

Also, in Mecca during the time of the Prophet, some of the early Muslims took refuge from pagan persecutions with the Christian Negus of Abyssinia. When the enemies of the Muslims came from Mecca and asked the Negus to turn the Muslims over to them, he was insulted and turned the pagans out instead. But what we've seen recently in Iran is what happens when one indulges one's own private, subjective feelings. These acts are totally divorced from the spirit of the holy Qur'an.

On April 23, 1981, Muzaffer Efendi again appeared on the air with Nur Lex Hixon at WBAI, speaking about Sufism and the path of love. This time, Efendi took questions by telephone from the audience. A few callers thanked Efendi for what he was doing and asked general questions about Sufism. One woman asked for a definition of Sufism, and received this concise reply: "In essence, *tasawwuf* (Sufism) is purifying the heart and finding

Allah in one's own heart. Allah's might, power and glory is everywhere, but a specific manifestation takes place in the human heart. That's the barest definition of Sufism."

A Christian man called in asking if people should worship Jesus, "as ordered in" the New Testament. Muzaffer Efendi answered: "We worship Allah Most High. Before Jesus was born, people worshiped Allah; so it is Allah that we should worship. However, I congratulate you. You should go on worshiping Jesus and may you be resurrected with him. At least you have something to worship, because if the non-believers come and take over these lands, there will be left neither Jesus nor Moses nor the Prophet Muhammad, nor mosque nor church. It is a good thing you at least believe in something—that you have spiritual belief."

After this, several callers in a row used the opportunity to criticize Islam and bring up various atrocities throughout history which occurred in predominantly Muslim countries. Muzaffer Efendi dealt with a few specific allegations and answered in general that the existence of a minority of cruel, misguided individuals in Muslim countries who have harmed others does not in itself constitute an across-the-board indictment of the religion. He also pointed out that it does not invalidate the whole beneficial thrust of Islam and the prophets who brought the message of love and unity. Apparently unsatisfied with such answers, other callers called in to argue the point and further vilify Islamic civilization.

Finally Nur stepped in and told a caller, "Let's not get off the level of our original discussion here, which is essentially the reality of Allah, the reality of the Divine Beauty and the dervishes who are living up to that ideal. Certainly, secular states have committed just as many atrocities, if not more, than states who have acted in an insane manner under a misinterpretation of religious doctrine. So let's admit this human frailty and go on to speak to Sheikh Muzaffer about human possibility." Efendi broke in passionately: "I'm here talking about love and trying to get people united—to love each other, feel affection toward each other and respect one another. I'm not here to sow the seeds of discord in the hearts of men. We want to put an end to this fight—blind men fighting other blind men!" At this point, Nur decided to stop taking phone calls and asked Efendi to make a prayer for everyone. The sheikh exclaimed: "We're praying all the time! Allah may or may not accept our prayers for unification, but we're constantly praying for this. Till the end of my life, I will try to unite people, to unite their hearts. Maybe I'll succeed in this mission; maybe not. An ant was walking along and they asked him where he was going. The insect answered: 'I'm going to Mecca, the holy city of Islam, on pilgrimage.' They laughed and said, 'With those feet and those legs?' The ant replied, 'Well, even if I can't make it, I'll die on the way to Mecca.' So I'm working like this to unite people."[27]

Pressed by Nur to pray and address his words to Allah instead of the people, Efendi opened his palms and prayed:

> O Lord, may you make those who serve humanity holy and unite our hearts. May you cause the hatred, coldness and discord that is between us to disappear. The heart that is half-full of hatred and half-full of religion is a sick heart. Transform the hatred into sincere spirituality. Teach us the secret of what it truly means to be human. Make us taste and know the pleasure of serving humanity. You are the Lord of everything, of all humanity, and Your will is done. If this is so, all human beings are brothers and sisters. May You take the enmity that is between two brothers and transform it into love! Grant understanding among human beings and unite us. Adorn us with the love of Truth. Do not allow us to go astray, to harm or think ill of other people. May we become the Truth and enter into Reality. May You grant this for the sake of those who would not put themselves to sleep until dawn, who shed tears for Your love and cry out, "Allah! Allah!" For their sakes, protect us from the disaster of war. If there is another major war, it won't be like former wars. There will be neither men, women, nor children, nor churches, nor mosques left. Surely

You don't desire the extinction of everyone on the face of this earth who would remember You and recite Your name. We love You; may You love us. Unify our hearts with Your love. These are the things which we request and insist upon from you! You have given us endless gifts; do not refuse us this gift. *Amin.*

Universal Islam

Efendi continued to use the *In the Spirit* radio show as a forum until it went off the air in 1984, often using Çinar Kologlu as his translator. Here, in one of the final shows, Efendi was more fully able to elaborate on the theme of Universal Islam.

> Nur: Efendi, who are the true Muslims?
>
> Muzaffer Efendi: The true Muslims are those who have Allah as their Lord and keep their direction. This question requires a variety of answers and, in fact, many books could be written on the subject. Any answers that could be given are like drops of water from the ocean, a ray of light from the sun, or an atom taken at random from the universe. Other possible descriptions of a Muslim are: someone who wishes for others the good that one wishes for oneself. Also: someone from whose hand and tongue others are safe. Further, a true Muslim is a person who obeys the injunctions of Allah, lovingly, without feeling compulsion, who seeks to avoid doing wrong, and who gives to the poor from the sustenance they have received from Allah. Again, true Muslims are those who believe in Allah without seeing Allah and believe in the books which have descended from Allah, including those that were revealed before the Qur'an, such as the Torah, the Psalms and the Gospels.
>
> Nur: So among Jews and among Christians there are true Muslims?
>
> Efendi: Yes. Surely they can be considered as Muslims and good Muslims at that. But it is important for them to recognize the legitimate prophethood of Muhammad, may peace and blessing be upon him. Belief in the prophethood of Jesus and belief in the purity and holiness of the Virgin Mary is also important (peace be upon them both). You see, when that is the case, a Muslim is actually a Jew and a Christian at the same time, with the added confirmation of Muhammad as a prophet. So there's actually no difference between a Christian, a Jew and a Muslim; then we are united. Being humans, we share a

form—the human appearance—and at the same time, we can be united as well by sharing a belief. I don't know if my answers are satisfactory from your point of view.

Nur: Its remarkable the universality that Islam has, because you've said that not only are there true Muslims among Jews and Christians, but you've made a more radical statement that there is really no essential difference between these three great religions and that a Muslim is *per se* a Jew and a Christian.

Efendi: Yes, in fact, without actually being a follower of Moses and Jesus as well as Muhammad, a follower of the Prophet Muhammad cannot be considered a Muslim. A Muslim has to have faith in the Qur'an as well as the Torah, the Gospel and Jesus. Actually, these are not my words. This is what Allah reveals in His holy book, the Qur'an, in *Surat al-Baqara*, the second chapter, which I was attempting to summarize in a concise form.

Nur: So this is not the product of a liberal, modern point of view, but is a universality which comes directly from the original Qur'an.

Efendi: No doubt, this is so. Islam has always been universal. This is not some heretical point of view; it was universal from the Source. And so far, we have only mentioned what we call "the People of the Book" (*Ahl al-Kitab*), namely the Jews and Christians. What we've been saying holds true for others as well. Take for example a Buddhist. With a belief in the Divine Source, the Day of Judgment and the authenticity of the holy messengers, the Buddhist is welcome in the Muslim community as well. Even a fire-worshiper—anyone who follows any religion can be a Muslim if he or she believes in the One Source of Being—God, His prophets and the Day of Judgment, and if such a one performs good deeds, they are bound to enter paradise. There are no other requirements. This has been so from the beginning and will be until the end of time.

Now there are those who speak against Islam without really understanding what it is. I've come across certain people, quite by accident, like Christians, who imagine that Muslims are hostile toward Jesus and Mary, or that Muslims simply don't believe in them nor have any interest in the Bible. This is a totally distorted viewpoint. You see, a Muslim believes in all the prophets—beginning with Adam, the first prophet—and in all the holy books.

The Muslim sees humanity as one family from Adam and from Abraham on. But people have forgotten that they are brothers and sisters because of different understandings of their religion. The reason for the descent of the Qur'an and the mission of the holy Prophet is to unify all people, all creeds, and to erase all major differences in the interpretation of the religion. Humanity is all one family descended from Adam and Eve, but they have divided into tribes, clans, and nations. Islam teaches us all that there are no basic differences between any people or groups of people. They're all equal. The only superiority that can exist is in the form of being close to Allah and obeying Him. In any other sense, there is no distinction, no superiority, so to speak.

The conflict that appears to exist between the People of the Book is like, for example, a number of people from various nations—an Englishman, a Turk, an Arab, a Persian and a German—who are all gathered together. The Arab said, "Let's buy *zibibb.*" The Turk said, "No, let's not buy *zibibb*; let's get some *üzüm* instead." The Englishman said, "Let's buy *grapes*;" the German said, "No. Let's get some *weintraube*;" while the Persian wanted to buy *aungur.* They all fell into dispute and began fighting with one another. Afterward, some grapes were brought in. "That's what we wanted in the first place," they all said, and realized that they had been arguing and fighting over nothing the whole time. The quarrel was over mere semantics, while they were unknowingly united in the object of their desire. This is a simile. . . . In the eyes of Allah, there is only one religion. All the others are sects. This one religion contains Judaism, Christianity and the Muhammadan faith.[28]

Nur concluded the show, issuing an invitation for the public to join Muzaffer Efendi in a celebration of dhikr that week at the Cathedral of St. John the Divine. He added, "There, Efendi will actually have the grapes."

Efendi enjoyed the ethnic, religious and racial mixture of those who attended his public dhikrs, whether in churches, public auditoriums, or at his tekkes. He would say, "Let the priests and rabbis come join us." During the standing portion of the dhikr ceremony, Efendi would raise both arms and gesture to everyone in attendance, calling all hearts without exception to join the circle of dervishes. Often the numbers in the dhikr circle would swell into the hundreds, with three or four concentric circles of pulsing humanity chanting the divine name *hayy*, the Living One, over powerful Turkish hymns and bendir percussion. The taste of ecstasy and exhilaration generated at the height of these dhikr ceremonies can only be compared to the energy of the vast throng of pilgrims circling the Ka'ba during hajj, or a foretaste of what it might be like after the *Mahdi*, or Messiah, had come and joyfully united all the people of the world.

One of the rabbis who came was Reb Zalman Schachter-Shalomi. Born into a devout Jewish family in Eastern Europe before the Holocaust, Zalman trained in the Hassidic Lubavitcher sect. After moving to America, he became an ordained rabbi, university professor, master of Kabbala, and a founding father of the Jewish Renewal Movement. Over the years, Reb Zalman had befriended mystics of other traditions such as Thomas Merton and Alan Watts, gradually developing a broad universalist perspective while still remaining strongly anchored in the roots of his own Jewish mystical tradition. Recognizing Reb Zalman's spiritual stature and aptitude in Sufism, Pir Vilayat Khan made him an honorary sheikh in the Sufi Order International.

Once, while staying in Israel, Reb Zalman desired to find some Sufis and participate in a dhikr with them. After a few inquiries, he located some dervishes in Hebron and spoke to their sheikh. "Are you Muslim?" Zalman was asked. "I'm a Jew," he replied, "but I believe as you do in the Divine Unity and can affirm with you whole-heartedly: *La ilaha illallah, Muhammad ar-Rasulullah.*"

"Then you're a Muslim!" he was told. Zalman qualified their statement, explaining: "I believe in the One God—the God of Ibrahim (Abraham)—just as you do; and I accept that Muhammad was a true messenger of God, who brought the children of Ismail back to the *tawhid* from the worship of idols; but I follow the *shari'a* of the religion of my own people, which was revealed to the Prophet Musa (Moses), *'aleihi salaam.*" Still slightly surprised that a Jew wanted to join their dhikr, the Sufis accepted his explanation with an "*Alhamdulillah,*" and warmly invited him in.

Rabbi Zalman Schachter-Shalomi (photo by the author)

No such explanations were needed when Reb Zalman met Muzaffer Efendi. It was love at first sight, as when any true lovers of God meet and deeply recognize in one another their common spiritual bond. The first night that Reb Zalman came and joined the audience for public dhikr, Muzaffer Efendi noticed him, asked Salik who he was, and then asked to see him. According to Salik, when Zalman met with Efendi, he asked to take hand. Efendi answered, "No, you and I are both teachers with a path. You don't need to be initiated by me. But I will offer you something even more wonderful." Then, in a small ceremony, Muzaffer Efendi placed the white hat of the Order on Reb Zalman's head and accepted him as a *muhib*, a spiritual friend of the Order. After that, whenever circumstances permitted Reb Zalman to come up from Philadelphia, he would joyfully join the circle of dervishes, as did a number of other religious leaders and lay persons of various faiths. Once when Reb Zalman arrived, Efendi greeted him saying, "My blood has been boiling to see you!" This is the way of passionate love.

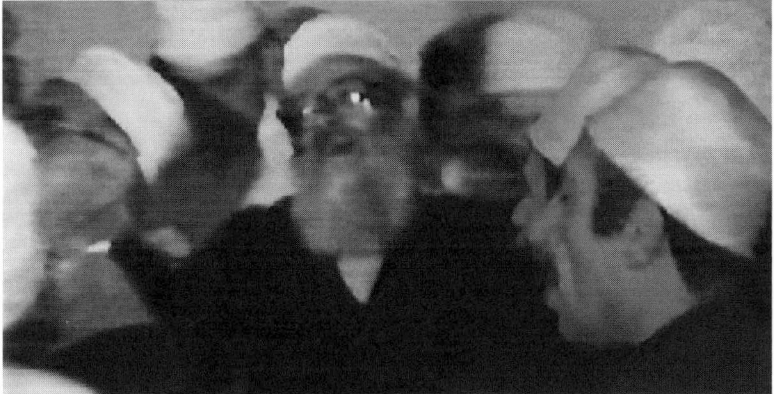

Reb Zalman (center) in the Jerrahi dhikr circle

In the introduction to one of Muzaffer Efendi's American-published books, *Blessed Virgin Mary*, Efendi is quoted as saying of the lovers of Truth in other religious traditions (including even those who might misunderstand Islam and reject her Prophet):

> The genuine love that any Christian feels for the Messiah Jesus will [on the Day of Judgment] be counted as love for the Prophet Muhammad, may the peace and blessings of Allah be upon them both. The sincere love that any Jew feels for the noble Abraham and the noble Moses will likewise be counted as love for Muhammad, the Seal of Prophecy. Why? Because Allah Most High teaches clearly in His glorious Qur'an that all the Divine Messengers share a single essence.[29]

For the person who wished to go beyond the stage of the initial invitation, opportunities existed for them to formally study Sufism with Muzaffer Efendi, and to take *shahada*, confiming oneself as a Muslim. Efendi did accept students who were involved with other faiths, though his general approach was that it was up to Allah and to the Pir to accept the students and to lead them closer to Islam and the observances of Islam. He referred most Western students with other religious affiliations to Sheikh Nur and tended to send more traditional Muslims to Tosun Baba, drawing on the strengths of each. However, as Efendi pointed out, finding one's true sheikh is a matter of destiny, and never happenstance.

Efendi offers a gentle critique

In the Spring of 1981, Muzaffer Efendi and his followers toured the West Coast, meeting with various spiritual groups, both traditional and "new age." In San Francisco, Efendi visited with the disciples of the late Murshid Samuel Lewis, dined with them, saw some of their Islamic Dances of Universal Peace, and invited the American Sufis to join the Jerrahis in a traditional dhikr ceremony. After the dhikr, Efendi took questions and, in response to one inquiry, offered a rare public critique of some of the trends among American spiritual groups which disturbed him. One questioner asked: "Americans tend to be restless and impatient. They want things right away. Is there a fast path?" Efendi responded:

> Yes! Dhikrullah. The path of remembrance of Allah is the shortest way. If you can, while your attention is directed toward worldly tasks, remember God—which is remembering oneself—and say *La ilaha illallah* and let that understanding penetrate, it will jump over seas and flow like rivers and carry you very fast to your desired destination. Indeed, Americans are right. We are given a very short time on this earth. It was just yesterday that I was playing baseball in the streets. Now I can hardly get up out of my chair. You should have seen me when I was young!

Then Efendi was asked: "We see new spiritual communities appearing and growing in America. What is the experience in the Sufi community and among Sufi schools that could be helpful to these American schools and communities?" The sheikh answered:

> Everything has a beginning. A fire starts from a spark. A dragon starts out as a tiny snake and a ram starts out as a cute

little lamb. So as everything has a beginning, let the beginning be as it is and it will find its natural growth.

However, there are certain things that I see that I don't like so much. Please forgive me for telling you that. Perhaps it is something subjective, so please forgive me.

In size and shape, a whip is similar to a poisonous snake. If one is blind, one could get hold of a snake, thinking it is a whip to make one's horse go faster. So, beware. If someone tries to prevent a nation which is hardworking, which is creative—if someone pushes you toward laxness and towards not working, toward just staying in a corner without occupying yourself with what is going on around you, or if someone tells you to divorce your wife and leave your home, and leads you away from your responsibilities in that regard—that is grabbing the poisonous snake instead of the whip. The duty of a teacher is not to make a healthy person sick, but to make a sick person healthy, not to break-up a family but to build one. If there is discord between a husband and wife, the teacher's duty is to repair that, to make them understand and live in harmony with each other, not to destroy a family which is living in harmony and send husband and wife on their separate ways.

Dhikrullah—the remembrance of Allah—is not like some ruminant animal regurgitating what it eats. It is not a game or a dance either. There are so many dancers who can do the samba and the rhumba much better. (general laughter) So what is dhikrullah? It is the aspiration of achieving Truth, of receiving the real remembrance, and it is the manifestation of the joy of that hope, but not the joy of dancing. You can get that better with the samba.

I have no one with me who is without a job, and who is not only working at a profession but striving to do it the best they possibly can. The dervish works by day and prays by night. These two have to work together. It is perhaps a little tiring and heavy to work for this world as if you are never going to die and to pray for the hereafter as though you may die within the next moment. It is difficult and requires a great deal of power. If we did not have the divine power aiding us, we couldn't do it. The difficulty, uncertainty and pain of this world are with us during the day while we are working in the world, but with dhikr and prayers at night we abolish these troubles and gain renewed strength to face the next day. It is like a huge telephone pole resting on a fulcrum—you could possibly lift one end or the other, but you couldn't lift it from the center.

The dervish path is not one of laziness. You have to love the Source and everyone around you. Have you achieved or created something? Have you helped someone in trouble or fed someone who is hungry? Have you wiped the tears of someone who is troubled or helped someone who is lost back to the right path? If not, you not a dervish but an idler. An egg is one of the most nourishing foods, but when it spoils it smells awful. Yes, to be a dervish is not just to chew gum; its more like chewing on an iron ball! Well, perhaps I'm a little bit cross-eyed and not seeing things as they are, but it appears that it is sometimes this way in some American communities. I pray it is not this way.

Last year when I visited America, there was an incident involving the Three Mile Island atomic reactor in Pennsylvania which had a dangerous leak. Without naming names, certain dervishes in New York simply fled the scene and moved out of town! The real dervish is supposed to go and throw his or her body over it to cover it and protect the others, not to run from it. I know of a dervish who, when there was a great fire which burned every shop in the marketplace except his, exclaimed, "Thank God!" when he heard the news. Then for the next forty years, he cried for divine forgiveness because his first reaction had been to say "Thank God," that everyone else's shop was destroyed except his. He understood his mistake.

It is not the dervish way to say, "Uh oh, there's a war, so I had better escape and may God protect me, regardless of what happens to everyone else." One must understand the morality of being a dervish. We are called Halveti. The letter *H* in Halveti means to clear your heart from everything except Truth. The letter *L* means the one who takes his wealth and distributes everything he has to others. The letter *V* is for *vefa*, for loyalty, and the letter *T* is for *tek*, to abandon the worldly, and those who love the things of this world. The whole world can belong to you, but you should belong to Allah. If you pray all of your life, perhaps you may merit a palace in paradise, but if you help a blind person who is trying to cross the road, for this one action you will be granted a far greater palace than what you would receive for a lifetime of devotions. *Hismet*—service, service, service! It is only for later to receive gifts as your reward.

Sacred law and the mystic path

A common question for Muzaffer Efendi was the relation between Sufism and mainstream Islam. Efendi once gave a simple analogy, comparing the shariat to the first floor of a house and the tarikat to the second story. According to the *adab* of Islam, Efendi observed, one always enters through the main door of a home, and wouldn't, for instance, mount a ladder to climb directly into the second story window. If you tried to surreptitiously climb up the back way, Efendi joked, it might be just the moment when the man of the house woke up and decided to urinate out the top-floor window. So it is best, he concludes, to go to the front door, seek permission to enter and then wait to be invited upstairs by the host to their more intimate quarters. The deeper point of Efendi's analogy is that the host symbolically represents Allah, who reveals the mysteries as gifts to those who approach and wait with humility and sincerely. The mystic path of love can then open the way to complete submission to the Divine Will.

Muzaffer Efendi recognized that Western newcomers to Sufism and Islam often needed to adopt a measured rate of learning to assimilate the practices and traditions of Islam, somewhat like Muslim children who start out with a reduced regimen of prayers and fasting, then gradually add more as they mature. If Efendi sensed that a newcomer to Islam was likely to feel initially overwhelmed by requirements such as prayers five times a day, he might suggest that they do one or two prayers a day for a time. Efendi said that the performance of the prayer "lies only between the seeker and his Lord." This is consistent with the broad, non-compulsory spirit of Islam.

Efendi placed great importance on dhikr in the tarikat. Based on various Qur'anic injunctions, dhikr is considered the key to divine union, with the words, *La ilaha illallah*, forming the central basis of Islam, the first of the so-called five "pillars of Islam." In addition to the concentration on divine unity, the shariat of Islam also encourages four other aspects of religious practice, each of which constitutes an unique and important way for the body, heart and soul to progress on the spiritual path. The five times a day prayer allows one to continually renew one's deep connection to the Divine Source throughout the day, consciously standing, bowing and prostrating—losing and finding oneself in the Divine Presence. The practice of alms-giving softens the self-serving ego and allows the heart to open to others in generosity and service to Allah. The pilgrimage to Mecca allows the soul to journey both physically and symbolically to the shrine of the divine heart, the Ka'ba, in communion with millions of other devout souls, all dressed in the humble white shroud of the pilgrim. The fasting from sunup to sundown during the month of Ramadan lightens the cravings of the ego and intensifies the inner life during an annual 30 day collective retreat. Together, these five pillars of Islam provide a balanced context for the practices of the tarikat and offer the spiritual seeker a well-rounded spiritual regimen for daily life.

Muzaffer Efendi's successor, Safer Efendi, observed that the situation of the seeker encountering Islamic Sufism in the West, where Judeo-Christian values prevail, is inevitably different than in Islamic countries, where a person born into a Muslim family might study the deeper teachings with a sheikh after years of familiarity with Islamic culture and basic Muslim practices. The Western seeker is faced with a situation in some ways analogous to that of the earliest Muslims who were seeking to initially establish Islam in Arabia and practice the faith in the face of persecution from their own relatives and countrymen. Western seekers with little knowledge of Islam, often find themselves initially more attracted to the mystical aspects of Islam than to the shariat, the main body of Islamic religious observance. In part, this can be attributed to the influence of negative conditioning about Islam in the West, absorbed through both the media and the pulpit, as well as a more general Western trend toward disenchantment with mainstream religion.

During a visit to America in the early 1990's, Safer Efendi reminisced: "One day my sheikh, Muzaffer Efendi, mentioned to me that verse of Hazrati Yunus, in which the poet says: '*Şeriât, tarikât yoldur varana,*' which means shariat is the path to tarikat." Then Muzaffer observed, 'But these days, it is reversed, at least in America. The tarikat has become the path that leads people to the shariat of Islam.'" Safer Efendi explained, "That is because most of the Jerrahis in America were first interested in the mystical path and it was precisely this interest which drew them to Islam."

Safer Efendi was asked about what seemed to be a real difference of approach to worship by Sufis, who stress dhikr and unity, and non-mystical Muslims, who mostly stress salat and keeping the rules of the shariat. He answered that, in his understanding, authentic Islam unites both of these two approaches, and that Sufis and non-Sufi Muslims can certainly fast together, go on pilgrimage, and make prayers together in the mosque without any distinctions. When this answer did not seem to totally satisfy, Safer offered an example of how these two approaches can be united, pointing to Muzaffer Efendi's great love of prayer, which he had observed close-up during the 28 years he knew Muzaffer:

> I knew him (as an imam) even before he came to Fahreddin Efendi. I passed a whole life with him, night and day; we didn't just talk about religion, but laughed together and had a good time. . . . He was a great man—a great man of knowledge, then a great dervish, then a great sheikh—in that order. He was the imam for 22 years at the Süleymaniye mosque.
>
> One day, as we left after he led the prayers at the Süleymaniye

mosque, Efendi said, "Come, let's eat." So we went over to his house—this was while he was married to his first wife. After dinner he said, "Have you ever made *salat al-khayr*?" I said, "I don't know—what is it?" So he said, "Why don't we do it together?" I agreed, not knowing what we were going to do. Then we made 100 rakats of salat! By the time we finished, the carpet had became like thorns!

Muzaffer Efendi was a man who intensely loved prayers—one could almost say a major *sofu*[30] in his own right. He loved them so much that, during Ramadan, he used to lead the lengthy *tarawwih* prayers at the Süleymaniye mosque, then rush across town to lead them all over again for his own disciples.

I know very few people who loved the prayers of Islam as deeply as he did. And because of our love for him, we have tried to follow him in this.

Sheikh Tosun, Safer Efendi and Sheikh Nur in 1991

Safer Efendi explained that the Jerrahis follow the Hanafi school:

The Shafi'i school believes that if someone purposely abandons the ritual prayers of Islam they can no longer be considered Muslims. But fortunately for us, Hazrati Hanifa didn't say that—he's much more permissive. According to our imam (Abu Hanifa), according to our pir, and according to our sheikh, whoever even once sincerely says *La ilaha illallah, Muhammad ar-Rasulullah* will be safe from the fire in the hereafter. The wording of the hadith doesn't actually say one will go straight to paradise, but of course, that's the implication. One will be safe in the hereafter because whoever can say that sincerely has received the greatest gift of Allah, which is faith—and faith leads to action and to observing the wise counsels of Allah's holy messengers.

Safer Efendi added that people often misunderstand what the shariat is: "The entire religion or *din* is encompassed by the shariat; there is nothing in the spiritual path outside of it. Tarikat, hakikat and marifat are all contained within the shariat (which includes all the qualities such as kindness, compassion, etc.). Our teachers tell us that shariat is a healthy tree; the branches are the tarikat, the leaves are the marifat and the fruit is the hakikat. If the trunk of the tree is not living, neither the leaves nor fruit will have life."

Safer Efendi related a story concerning an encounter between Muzaffer Efendi and a man in Turkey who was demonstrating a rude and distorted idea of the shariat:

Hazrati Eyüp (Ayyub) Sultan was an *ansar*, a companion of the Prophet from Medina, who was present at the time when Rasulullah migrated from Mecca to Medina. Everyone wanted the Prophet to stay at their house when he made his initial entry into the city, so the Prophet told them, "I will loosen the reigns of my camel and lodge at the house where my camel stops." The camel stopped at the house of Eyüp Sultan. Eyüp Sultan lived a long time after the Prophet's passing and was eventually martyred during the Muslim army's attempt to conquer Istanbul (then known as Constantinople). His tomb lies in Istanbul and is held in great esteem by the Turkish people. Incidentally, Hazrati Shemsuddin, who belonged to the Bayrami tarikat, was the sheikh of Fatih Sultan Mehmet, the Conqueror. It was he who discovered the tomb of Hazrati Eyüp. The mosque that stands there now, the *Eyüp Ensari Türbe*, used to be a Bayrami tekke.

The Mosque and tomb of Eyüp Sultan (photo by the author)

We went with Muzaffer Efendi to the mosque at Eyüp Sultan on the Night of Power. It was extremely crowded and there were hundreds of women jammed in front of the saint's tomb making supplications to Allah for their various needs. We sat with Efendi in the little room of the muezzins. Our attention was soon drawn to a man with a huge beard who, like a wild dog, was practically barking at these poor women who were trying to pray in front of the tomb. When Efendi saw how abusively this man was screaming at the women, he became incensed and said to some of his disciples, "Go get that man and bring him over here!" So we grabbed the man and brought him to Efendi.

Efendi demanded of him: "Are you the imam of this place?" The man said, "No." Efendi asked, "Are you the muezzin or in some other way in the service of this mosque?" The man still answered in the negative. "Then what right do you have to so rudely chase these women away?" Suddenly the man who was so brutal to the women looked very sheepish and began offering lame excuses: "Well, some of them had hair showing from under their veils, and others had their socks showing," and so on.

Efendi told him, "It doesn't matter. Even if there is some little infraction, you can't just scream at the women and drive them from the mosque! Proper etiquette for correcting someone is to *gently* inform them of the proper behavior." Then, addressing the man with a strong epithet, Efendi concluded, "Look, you have no business here! There are beaches not far from here filled with women in bikinis. If you call yourself a man why don't you go and try to say something to them, instead of tormenting these women who came here to pray. Now get out of here!" Of course, the man left; he couldn't say anything back, because Efendi was built like a wrestler and was surrounded by a whole group of us, who were like lions at the moment.

You see, this man does not represent the shariat. He was an arrogant, ignorant man, acting like an animal—like a wild dog. The reason I have told you this story is that we have absolutely no right to chase anybody from a mosque or tekke. At the time of the Prophet, uneducated Arabs came to the mosque and did all kinds of questionable, even disgusting things, which sometimes angered the companions.[31] But Rasulullah always calmed them down and told them not to bother these Bedouin who didn't know any better. All these people who did such things at the beginning, by the kindness and gentleness of Rasulullah, left their errant ways and each became a sun, giving light to

> the others to find their way. . . .
>
> To behave like a wild dog in anger is something most unbecoming to a Muslim. May we follow the example of Muhammad, peace and blessings be upon him, in his kindness and gentleness. May Allah Most High grant us the beautiful manners of our master. Amin.

Muzaffer Efendi's earlier Turkish books, taken primarily from *sohbets* as a spiritual teacher and imam in Istanbul, are much more likely to consider issues connected to the shariat than his major American work, *The Unveiling of Love*, which focuses primarily on the tarikat and the mystic way of love. Also noteworthy are the stories Muzaffer Efendi occasionally told emphasizing that it is not absolutely necessary for every seeker of Truth to adopt the shariat of Islam. During one *sohbet*, for instance, he recounted an episode which he said "might surprise some of you." He related how a devout Christian woman, who saw in him a kindred soul, approached him for spiritual advice. He gave her a few words of guidance and then asked if she knew a good Christian priest whom she trusted. When she affirmed that she did, Efendi advised her to go to him and to remain with the Christian faith.

Years later, Sheikh Nur recounted how Muzaffer Efendi came to visit and have dinner at the home of Nur's parents during one of the extended dervish tours of California. Nur also invited a friend who was an American Hindu monk, then living in a monastery in Hollywood. Everyone there enjoyed Muzaffer Efendi's presence as he charmed them with his affable sense of humor and sensible perspective, telling stories and many a Turkish joke, but never once giving any direct teachings about Islam or Sufism.

The next day Nur's friend called and said that he had a powerful dream that night after being with the sheikh. After receiving permission from his own abbot, the friend conveyed the dream to Muzaffer Efendi. Upon hearing the elaborate dream translated, Efendi simply laughed and said, "Just by sitting next to me for one evening your spiritual station—your *makam*—has gone up two levels." The friend confided to Nur that, indeed, he felt as though a breakthrough in understanding had occurred, one that carried over to his own path—and not through anything in particular that Efendi said, but through something spiritually uplifting in his *being*. This episode represents just one of the many times that an influx of divine understanding spontaneously occurred in those who entered the sheikh's presence. Often, as in this case, such breakthroughs happened without any overt discussion of spiritual subjects, much less a formal commitment to Islam. Even those who met Efendi in an elevator or waiting his table at a restaurant were often touched by the love and joy that permeated his being.

When Efendi heard how Bawa Muhaiyaddeen, the one-hundred year old Sufi master from Sri Lanka, had taught his followers in America the basic tawhid, *La ilaha illallah*, for ten years before gradually introducing the shariat of Islam, he raised his eyebrows and said half in jest, "Ahh. That's how we should have done it!"

Efendi once referred to the famous gathering of representatives of the major religious traditions that took place in Kiev during the tenth century C.E. at the invitation of Prince Vladimir, the great grandson of Prince Rurik, the Viking ("Rus") conqueror of Russia. The prince wanted to replace the array of old Slavic and Scandinavian deities with one of the world's great religions as a national faith. After ruling out Judaism and Roman Catholicism, Vladimir was faced with a choice between Islam and Byzantine Christianity, both of which he found attractive. But when the Muslim ambassadors were unyielding on the prohibition against alcohol in Islam, Vladimir told them, "Drinking is the joy of the Rus and we cannot live without this pleasure." On the strength of this one point, Vladimir ruled out Islam and instituted Russian Orthodox Christianity as the national religion for his people.

Efendi reflected, "If I had been the sheikh al-Islam of that time, I would have received all those people into Islam and prayed to Allah to stop their drinking. Over a few generations, with Allah's help, this could have gradually been rooted out."

He continued, "Islam is like clear water poured into different vessels. It takes the color and shape of each vessel." By extension, the water of Islam cannot be limited to any single cultural shape either from the past or from one particular geographical locale.[32]

Muzaffer Efendi advised his senior disciples with the words of the hadith: "Make things easy for people, not difficult. Don't curse the people but unite them in love. Teach people only to the level that they can understand." He advised, "Don't force the shariat. Give a few instructions and then allow people to do what they are capable of doing. If they can fast, make the prayers and give alms, that's wonderful. If not, they can at least respect them as ideals and, for instance, refrain from eating in front of others who are fasting during Ramadan. The important thing is to teach *La ilaha illallah, Muhammad ar-Rasulullah* and what it means for them to accept it, even if they are not able to follow all the precepts. Get people to love Allah! First Allah desires faith; then worship can follow. We are not advocating going off to the mountains to struggle with one's self in isolation. It's much better to be among the people helping to lift their difficulties."

What most disturbed Efendi in America was the conflicts and competition, especially among the Turkish people. "Why not come together instead of fighting?" he would say. "One problem is that many young Turks were raised in Turkey after the closing of the tekkes and never saw a *dhikrullah*; so they come and complain, saying, 'What are you doing? I've never heard of this in Islam.' I don't react with anger toward them but respond, 'Come, come, let's discuss this.' There is a hadith which says: 'I will not abandon the one who abandons me. I will not criticize the one who criticizes me. I will not cut from my heart the one who cuts me off.' That's what dervishhood is all about; that no one should be hurt by the dervish's tongue."

Efendi recommended using one's discernment in the study and reading of hadith among the dervishes. "If you are reading ahadith to people and come to one that's going to upset them, it is better to skip over it." Both for hadith study and Qur'an intrepretation, Efendi emphasized that one should know the conditions under which it was uttered and to whom it was spoken. For instance, was it said under the duress of war, or in peaceful conditions; to a uneducated Bedouin visiting from the desert, to a professed enemy, a hypocrite, to one of his own family, or to an advanced, lifelong follower? "If you take the word that was uttered during the time of war and apply it during the time of peace," Efendi stressed, "you will get confused."[33]

The same holds true for Muzaffer Efendi's own words and stories when reported in print, because the reader in many cases no longer knows exactly to whom Efendi was speaking and on what level he was answering when he made a given statement. For example, Efendi once related how two dervishes went to their sheikh, 'Abdur-Rahman al-Jerrahi, reporting almost exactly the same dream. While it might be assumed that the meaning of these two dreams would be more or less the same, in fact, the two dreams received drastically different interpretations from the sheikh, one boding positive future tidings for the dreamer and the other evoking a reprimand.[34]

To the one who was caught in a narrow, legalistic view of Islam, Efendi might relate a story such as the one where Allah valued the heartfelt sigh of a person who was late to prayers over the one who made their prayer exactly on time without much feeling. Efendi recalled the story of Caliph 'Umar who saw a Bedouin making his prayer, but employing a number of incorrect prayer movements. The caliph approached the man and corrected him, demonstrating the proper form and movements of *salat*. Afterwards, he asked the man to offer his prayers again, this time using the correct sequence and sacred gestures. When the Bedouin finished the second set of prayers, 'Umar asked him, "Now, wasn't the second one better?" The man hesitated and at last replied, "Well, actually, I think the first one was better, the one you didn't like." Surprised at the Bedouin's response, 'Umar asked him to explain. "I did the first prayer wholeheartedly for Allah," he answered, "while I was doing the second prayer to satisfy you."

Though Efendi would relate such stories which emphasized love over formal technique, he was not likely to oblige someone who seemed to want answers that would reinforce a spiritual complacency in their being. In such a case, he might issue a terse, sobering truth from the Qur'an and then add, "Any other questions? Does anyone else want cold water poured on them?" Someone once asked Efendi about loving another in a relationship. When questioned further, he explained that he looked for complimentary qualities to his own in a partner. "Sounds like you're more in love with yourself than the other person," Efendi interjected. The questioner joined the laughter at this quip and admitted that this might well be true.

Efendi occasionally issued a strong warning to his dervishes during a *sohbet*: "Don't fall asleep! A day is coming soon when you will sleep for a very long time. So make the best of your opportunities here before that time when you will awaken from life's dream in the hereafter and find that it is too late to save yourself." Other times, he would deliver the point by means of a lighter story. For instance, there was the Sufi story in which Allah commanded Jesus (Isa) to resurrect a certain poor villager as a lesson to those around him who would witness this miracle. When Jesus commanded the long-dead corpse to rise from his grave, the man suddenly jumped up and started running around saying, "My donkey! My donkey! Has anyone seen where I left my donkey?" This story illustrates the importance of where we place our concentration, as we will be together with and united with the objects of our love in the hereafter. The dervish concentrates upon the Source of Love and Beauty during this life, and repeats the names of Allah, rather than pursuing only the mundane things of this world. Otherwise one may end up like this villager who, when resurrected, could think only of his donkey.

In the course of gathering stories about Muzaffer Efendi from his students, it became clear that the sheikh's teaching could be very individualized, depending on the needs and temperament of the student, and even which cultural background he was addressing. Years after Efendi's passing, I asked Sheikh Ragip Frager about his experience of studying with Sheikh Muzaffer and the different approaches taken by Efendi's spiritual successors, for instance, in regard to spiritual pluralism. He responded that, among those who took hand with Efendi, there were different ideas of what was expected—his own position being that all the great religions contain truth, certainly including Buddhism and Hinduism. He continued:

> I spent twelve years practicing yoga seriously, lived in a Zen temple and had spiritual guides in both traditions. But, in spite of my past background and still current love of these traditions, when I took hand, I made a commitment to follow Muzaffer Efendi, which meant to me that I was committed to following Islam and Sufism. I even asked Efendi about my commitment to a daily yoga meditation practice, and he told me that from this point on he would take spiritual responsibility for me, so I was absolved of earlier spiritual commitments. I still love both of these other traditions, but I have learned not to argue with those Muslims who do not accept the Buddhist or Hindu traditions as

> coming from genuine prophets. I don't agree with them, and I attribute their position to lack of exposure to Hindu or Buddhist scriptures and teachers. As far as Muzaffer Efendi's approach to the tarikat in the United States, I think he was extremely flexible, and perhaps more than flexible, he was extremely patient. He would say "*eyvallah*":[35] to all kinds of ideas and suggestions, if he possibly could without outright violation of the shariat. My opinion is that Muzaffer Efendi allows everyone a tremendous amount of latitude, hoping that the actual practice of Islam and Sufism would bring us into the fold in time. In a sense, Muzaffer Efendi allowed us to "get our feet wet" by beginning with the partial observance of the shariat and Islamic tradition. However, my sense is that his long term intention was for all his dervishes to fully embrace the practice and the traditions of Islam in addition to the traditions and practices of our Order.

I also asked Hafiz Ismail to relate what he had heard from Efendi in Istanbul regarding his aims in spreading the tarikat to the West. Ismail responded that Muzaffer Efendi placed great importance in the supplications which his own teacher, Fahreddin Efendi, had offered. On one special evening, months before his own passing, Fahreddin had raised his palms and prayed for his beloved successor, "May he become well-known throughout the world." All of the blessings which permitted his many travels to the West, Muzaffer later affirmed, flowed from the power of that prayer and Allah's acceptance of it.

Ismail recalls that Efendi sometimes spoke about these issues in his bookshop in Istanbul. In those discussions, Muzaffer Efendi indicated that he wanted to bring the tarikat to the United States so that Americans could practice it, not simply as an expression of Turkish culture, but in harmony with Western culture, without changing the essential principles of the religion. Efendi said:

> The religion is not a collection of cultural values and forms; it is something universal from which all people may benefit.

> We are all brothers and sisters. If an Arab, Pakistani, or Turkish person can be a dervish, why not people from America, England or Germany? How could the dervish way be restricted just to people from the East? The mystic hymns of the tarikat don't have to be sung only in Turkish or Arabic. There is already plenty of variation in how the tarikat is practiced between Turkey, Bangladesh and Syria. So when the tarikat comes to a country, its culture doesn't need to be discarded; the tarikat just makes some corrections and adaptations in that culture.

Ismail said that Muzaffer Efendi often made the point that he didn't need to take the tarikat to Pakistan, Indonesia or any other Islamic country. Efendi said: "I'm not looking to recruit my dervishes from the mosques or the Islamic schools; I need to find people in the nightclubs and pubs and to work with them (people who haven't embraced religion but still have an open mind). We are all servants of Allah, and the Prophet, peace be upon him, is the messenger for all humanity." A similar quotation was attributed to Efendi on a Turkish television special: "Don't bring me people who already go to the mosque. Bring me the ones who don't go to mosques, the ones who are going astray."

Ismail noted that Muzaffer Efendi also placed importance on the famous hadith by the Prophet, peace be upon him, concerning the signs that would precede the last days. This hadith, which is transmitted with variations in the collections of Bukhari and Muslim, relates that "at a time before the end of days, when the truth has ceased to be highly valued by the people, the sun will rise from the West instead of from the East, and when the people see it they will believe."

"So, what does it mean?" Muzaffer Efendi asked. "Does it mean that the physical sun in the sky is literally going to change directions? No, that's not what the Prophet meant. In the tarikat, the sun refers allegorically to knowledge and wisdom." In light of this, Efendi stated that the knowledge which had for so long shined upon the East had changed its direction and was now shining in the West, and this was a further confirmation for bringing the tarikat to the West. Ismail added that, in discussing this, Efendi never indicated that he interpreted this as minimizing the importance of Mecca, Medina and the other places of pilgrimage in the East or as implying that the Islamic religion no longer continues in the East.

Fariha confirmed to the author that Muzaffer Efendi also mentioned to her this hadith, indicating that Islam has now come to the West, after which he discussed the American constitution and the ideal of respect for the rights of the individual, which he considered an essential principle of Islam. As we shall see later in his recorded conversation with Mark Kreiger, Muzaffer Efendi was adamant that the leaders of the Muslim world in his time were no longer following the religion of Islam in the East.

Although Ismail was never able to get off from his job at Beyazid mosque long enough to accompany Muzaffer Efendi on his trips to America, he says he remembers the beautiful stories Efendi shared upon his return about the lovely people he had met there. Efendi said, "I really love going there; I feel very much at home. I feel very blessed to have met so many good people in America."

"People here in America advance very fast," Muzaffer Efendi observed in a talk in New York. "Some of them, in a very short time, advance as much as if they did forty years of inner work under favorable condition. This is because of the unfavorable conditions under which they are working here."[36]

In New Mexico Efendi received a question from the audience about Sufism coming from the East to the West. This time, he didn't speak in terms of movement but emphasized rather, how the East and the West are becoming one:

> It is a question of demand and of search; perhaps because

the materialistic and scientific world has failed to completely satisfy people, the Western world is showing great interest in seeking something further, something more meaningful. The demand is there and that is why it is coming.

In very recent history, time seems to be passing more quickly—things now come and go more rapidly than in former eras. For example, the Egyptian civilization lasted thousands of years, but now things are changing at a faster rate. There were many things in recent history that the East has taken from the West, but now the West is taking from the East. And let us not forget that with the evolution of modern communications, the world has become really very small—there is almost no East and West anymore. The world is still divided in two—especially since the second World War—but the division is no longer between East and West. The division is between the believers and non-believers, and they aren't geographically separated. It's not divided between East/West or North/South anymore. . . . Now people travel much more than they used to and through this there is much more cultural exchange than formerly.

The science and wisdom which we call Sufism is not something new. It is thousands of years old. It is not Islam, nor Judaism, nor Christianity. It predates them all. The first Sufi is Adam. Now as this contact between people has increased, this knowledge has a possibility of spreading much quicker. It's a tree which gives its fruit quite late—perhaps that seed which was planted many thousands of years ago is just now starting to produce its fruits. Or perhaps we could say: those fruits always existed but we only recently started picking and tasting of them.

All disagreement is in words. Truth is simply one. We are beginning to understand this now as communications get closer and are finding that there is only one Truth. The differences of opinion are semantic (like Melvana's story of the people of different cultures and languages who disagreed over the word for grapes when they all had the same fruit in mind, or the story of the four blind men who touched different parts of the elephant, and each described something very different). The problem is that we all carry a divine treasure within us but are unaware of it. The path of Sufism shows us where it is. It's not outside us, but inside. Whatever exists in the whole universe is in humanity. We think of the human as microcosm and the universe as macrocosm, but it's really the other way around. That's why it is said that whoever finds himself finds his Lord, and whoever doesn't find himself cannot find his Lord. So the whole meaning of Sufism is really humanism, but in the sense of deep human self-knowledge.[37]

Muzaffer Efendi's conversations in New Mexico

Muzaffer Efendi meeting Hopi elder Thomas Banyancya and other Native America elders in America.

In March of 1981, Muzaffer Efendi and his entourage traveled to various cites in the Western United States and spent several days in New Mexico, where they met with various Pueblo and Hopi elders. The well-known Hopi elder, Thomas Banyancya shared some of the Hopi prophecies and Efendi responded with the Muhammadan prophetic view, noting many interesting parallels. Although archival recordings of these exchanges are incomplete, they do include an interesting exchange from the final day of talks in New Mexico.

One of the participants gave a short talk, explaining how, when Cortez first landed in Mexico, the native people there were expecting the completion of the cycle of the reign of Topiltzin Quetzalcoatl and the beginning of the dark cycle that was to follow his return. He noted that when these European explorers came with their horses, armor and cross of the four directions, this had already been described to the people, so they were expecting them. They submitted to a small group of conquistadors because they realized it was futile to resist.

The first explorers became obsessed with the idea of seven cities of gold, and they explored the whole continent with the idea of finding these cities, claiming them for Spain and becoming wealthy themselves. When the Spanish explorers would approach a village, the natives would simply point them in the direction of the next village in pursuit of gold. During the time of Coronada, the explorers traveled from Florida through Louisiana all the way to the area just south of where the Hopis lived to the abode of a large tribe known as the Zunis. Finally, a small party came upon seven separate Zuni villages. From a far hilltop, the adobe buildings in the setting sun appeared to glitter like gold. Without actually going down and trying to conquer or further investigate these villages, they sent messengers back to Mexico to report that they had found the gold-filled seven cities of Cibola. In turn, those they informed sent to Spain for more soldiers and priests. When they arrived and saw the error, the friars and priests adopted conversion to their religion as the main justification for conquering.

Efendi responded: "When a person loves something or someone, they see what they love wherever they look. If someone is obsessed with the love of worldly wealth, they will even see a teepee appearing as a golden palace. But when someone loves with great compassion and honesty, even if they see people who don't have these qualities, their loving, compassionate outlook eventually turns these people into expressions of love and compassion." Then he added:

> I want everyone here to understand that those sages who knew in advance of the coming of the invaders were not mere

soothsayers. I say this because, although the four holy books (the Torah, Psalms, Gospel and Qur'an) only mention a limited number of prophets, in the Sufi tradition we believe in the 224,000 prophets which Allah sent upon earth—and some of these must have included our brothers here in America. The (Hopi) beliefs and prophecies related earlier by our brother, which he received from his ancestors and elders, could only be brought by prophets of the One God, the same One Who sent the prophets that we know by name. For if a prophet or divine messenger had not come, man left to himself would have created a god fashioned from his own imagination, who would lead him and others to destruction.

There is a treasure in every created human being, and it is the function of every human to find that treasure; but one may have to search and to dig many holes around oneself unless a prophet comes and shows one where the treasure is located. As the story we heard demonstrates, those who forget God or don't know God, often take gold as their deity. . . .

There is something in the strange history of America that perhaps could have caused an entirely different turn in the unfolding of world history. After Christopher Columbus was turned down for funding by the Portugese king, he came to Sultan Bayezid II in Istanbul and asked the Ottoman sultan for ships and soldiers to go conquer this new land which he believed to exist, but thought was part of India. However, the narrow orthodox Islamic theologians around the sultan advised him that the end of the world was quite near and argued that it wasn't worth going to the ends of the earth, when there were many closer lands to be conquered. The sultan was interested in the voyage for scientific purposes, and was familiar with a number of ancient Islamic maps which indicated the existence of America; however, against his better judgment, he acceded to their counsel. Columbus was sent away without the money, ships or people and had to get them from the Queen of Spain, who was also interested on the basis of scientific knowledge.

That Efendi was aware of Columbus' appeal to Sultan Bayezid, known only to a few scholars in the West (such as Leo Bagrow in his 1964 *History of Cartography*), is indicative of his great love of historical scholarship. His comments also suggest his awareness of the existence of the ancient world maps to which Columbus had access, such as the 1513 map of Turkish navigator Piri Reis, housed in Topkapi Palace, said by the cartographer to be based on older maps going back to the time of Alexander the Great. Piri Reis' amazing map includes the coasts of North and South America as well as the land mass of Antartica, which was only plotted beneath the icecap by Western scientists in the 1950's, using soundwave technology.

During his excursions to the West Coast of America, Efendi found that he was very drawn to the land. In Pasadena, where Efendi stayed at the home of Sheikh Nur's parents, Alexander and Adelaide Hixon, he actually made an *istikhara* prayer to determine whether he had divine permission to stay and settle in California, but did not receive any sign to encourage such a move.

Sheikha Fariha recalled that while in California, Efendi had a conversation with a Chrisitan priest. Efendi asked him, "What do the bells say when they ring?" The priest in turned asked what Efendi thought they said. He replied, "The bells say: Ya Daim," the Eternal One. Likewise, back in New York, when he heard someone complain about the noise of the garbage trucks, Efendi commented that they too were making dhikr. When asked what were they saying in their dhikr, he replied: "*Hayyul-Qayyum*," the Living, the Self-subsisting.

On the levels of meaning in Qur'an

In his teachings, Efendi would sometimes touch upon the deeper aspects of the mystical path alluded to in the Qur'an. Here he shares some of these teachings:

> There were six major races before Adam: the race of *jinn*—created from fire (just as humans are created from earth and water); before that the race of *ten*, created of water. Previous to that was the race of *ben*, created from water vapor, and before that the race of *sen*, created from air. It was not 10,000 years ago that humans appeared on the face of this planet; our planet is 3,313,000,000 years old. No wonder our scientists are objecting to any religious assertions that Adam appeared 10,000 years ago—of course not. From the race of *jinn* only the devil is left now.
>
> Hazrat Allah has created us from nothing and has honored us as a people to whom He has bestowed a vast lineage of prophets from Adam to the Seal of Prophets, Muhammad Mustafa, peace and blessings be upon him. He has given humanity the holy books, with the essence of this teaching contained in the noble Qur'an; and Allah has gathered all that is holy in the Qur'an in the opening chapter, Sura Fatiha. One of that sura's many names is "The Mother of all Books." Allah has concentrated everything essential in the holy books, Qur'an and Sura Fatiha, into the holy phrase, *Bismillah, ar-Rahman, ar-Rahim* [which begins the Fatiha]; and the essence of all this is found in the first letter *ba* [the *b* in bismillah]. The cause and effect, the beginning and the end of it all, is quintessentialized in the dot beneath the *ba*.
>
> Each of the twenty-eight letters of the Arabic alphabet used in the Qur'an have their own special significance. The Qur'an has one clear, open meaning and seven hidden meanings. There are actually infinite hidden meanings, but humanity does not have sufficient intelligence to understand more than these seven hidden meanings; the mind simply cannot weigh everything.

There are some secrets that will cause you to lose your balance, if you try to weigh them with the balance of your mind. You may reach a certain level with your mind alone, but you will not be able to penetrate beyond that. The mind can be fooled. If you put a stick in a pool of water it appears as if it is broken where it enters the water. So the Qur'an contains all of these mysteries.

Alif Lam Mim

Efendi was asked about the letters *Alif, Lam, Mim* and other Arabic letters which are found at the beginning of certain suras of the Qur'an. These cryptic letters are called *mutashabiha*, while the rest of the Qur'an—that which gives us clear guidance for living—is called the *muhkamat*. There are many interpretations about the *mutashabiha*; for instance, Yusuf 'Ali says that A is for Allah, L for Gabriel and M for Muhammad. 'Abdul Mannan Omar maintains in his *Dictionary of the Holy Qur'an* that the letters *Alif, Lam, Mim* are an Arabic abbreviation for "Ana Allah 'Alam," meaning: "I am Allah, the All-Knowing." In answer to the question, Efendi related a story in which he had actually witnessed the unfolding of one of these secret meanings in Qur'an.

One day Hazrati Hudayfa Yamani and Hazrat Ibn 'Abbas were sitting together. As you may know, Hazrat Ibn 'Abbas was the cousin of the Prophet and Hazrat Hudayfa Yemani was the secret knowledge keeper of the Prophet.[38] A person approached and asked the meaning of *Alif, Lam, Mim, Sad*.[39] Hazrat Ibn 'Abbas responded: "It is of no use to you, O Arab. You don't need to know the meaning."

But Hazrati Hudayfa Yemani said, "Do you really want to know the meaning of these four letters?" The man said, "Yes indeed." So he told him, "Come, I will tell you. Sometime, closer than now to the last day, there will be a city which is divided in half by a river; and in that city there will be a prince by the name of Abdullah, descended from the Prophet, peace be upon him. One night, he will be assassinated and the next morning his assassin will be caught and burned."

That city is the city of Baghdad, which had not yet built. That predicted event occurred in 1958 when the son of the then-king of Iraq, Abdullah, whose dynasty was descended from the Prophet, was assassinated and the assassin, Kasim, was found toward morning and burned.

Now—what use was it to that man to know that at that time? I remember very well the day that assassination happened. It was the beginning of a revolt and someone came running to tell me, but I told him, "I know. Someone announced it 1300 years ago." The man said, "Come on, how's that possible?" I went over to a bookshelf, located the book and opened it to that page and said, "Here, see for yourself."

I have given this as an example, but it is only one of the many meanings of these letters. There are countless other secrets contained in the Qur'an.[40]

The story of the sheikh who bought halva

One evening, as everyone gathered for sohbet, Sheikh Nur introduced a new student to Efendi and told him that this person had a sincere wish. Efendi responded, "If something is destined to come to you, it will come to you." After a brief silence, he explained: "There is a hadith that says, 'Whatever is coming to you, no force can prevent it from coming. And whatever is not meant for you, no force can make it come to you.' So if it is your destiny, it will come to you; if not, it won't come to you."

Sheikh Nur queried, "Then what is the use of praying for it?" Efendi agreed that this was a valid question, but added, "If it is not your destiny, then Allah will make you forget to pray for it. Conversely, if it is my destiny, I will remember and pray for it." Then, to underscore the point, Efendi recounted the following story:

> There was once a sheikh who was a very generous person, but he had no income and none of his dervishes donated money to him. Yet, because of his generous nature, he was moved to go beg or borrow money and distribute it to the poor. Naturally, he ran up a lot of debts this way. Finally, he became critically ill and all his debtors showed up around his sick bed, desiring to collect what the sheikh owed them before he passed away. The sheikh told them that he had no money, and whatever he had borrowed had been given away as charity, so the only course was to wait for Allah to bequeath him some money so that he could repay his debts. The sheikh's creditors asked him why he had borrowed money if he couldn't repay it. He explained that he hadn't spent a single cent of the borrowed money to feed himself, but had given to those who really needed it. At this, his creditors only became more upset with him, demanding that he find a way to pay them. So he said, "Ok. Have a seat here around my bed and we'll wait. Maybe Allah will send me something."

At this they became even more exasperated, shouting that they needed to get back to tend their shops, not sit around here where they were neither being repaid nor earning any further money. “Please calm down and have a little patience,” the sheikh advised them. “I’m sure Allah will soon provide something with which I can repay you.” Then, in the street below, they heard the sound of a young boy crying that he had halva for sale, a sweet Turkish dessert. The sheikh got up and went to the window and called out, “My son. How much are you charging for your halva?” The boy replied that it was one cent per piece. Now, there were some other poor children playing in the street—kids who rarely got to taste dessert—so the sheikh told the boy to go distribute all his halva to them and then come up and see him. The creditors spoke up, saying, “Look, you obviously have money to buy all this boy’s halva. Why don’t you pay us?” The sheikh replied, “I don’t have any money. I’m just using the child as a medium to get some money.”

After the boy gave away all his halva, he ascended the steps up to the sheikh’s apartment and held out his hand for payment. The sheikh told him, “Look. I don’t have any money.” The boy looked shocked and said, “What do you mean, you don’t have any money? You just had me give all my halva away and now you’re telling me you don’t have any money? What am I supposed to tell my boss if I come back without any halva or money? I’ll be in big trouble! I need that money, now please pay up!” The sheikh only repeated that he didn’t have any money.

Now the little boy started crying, and wailing and begging for his money, in a most pitiful voice. At this, the other creditors became infuriated with the sheikh, saying, “Isn’t it bad enough that you did this to us? Now you’ve done the same thing again, cheating this little boy out of his money right in front of us! What a terrible person you are!” They were just on the verge of attacking the sheikh in his bed, when a loud knock came on the door. It was an emissary from the palace of the sultan, who entered the room and handed a huge bag of gold to the sheikh. The sheikh opened the bag and paid off all of his creditors and the child as well. Then the sheikh addressed the merchants,

> saying; "You see, if this child had not cried so long, so longingly, and so bitterly, that money would not have come to us."

Then Efendi concluded, "I don't know if I have been able to convey this adequately to you. If one cries like a child, losing oneself totally, lamenting and crying for what one wished, then Allah will certainly reward you with what you wish. Whatever the reason, whether it was a matter of money or something else, that boy in the story lost himself and—perhaps out of fear of his boss—he forgot all about the rest of the world, and even the afterlife. This one thing became his center, and with this center he lamented and cried. If you could just pray like that, there is no doubt that you will receive your wish." Referring back to the original person that came with their wish, Efendi added with good humor, "To be able to afford you your wish, I have to cry in the presence of the tomb of Hazrati Pir like that little boy." Efendi concluded with a chuckle, which was joined by the others, "Either I have to cry like that or you have to."[41]

The Language of the Animals

Often, Muzaffer Efendi would relate one long story with commentary, which would run through an entire evening's sohbet. Here, continuing to expound the deep mysteries of destiny, he recounts an entertaining, yet profound, barnyard fable from Fariduddin Attar's classic collection, *The Conference of the Birds*:

> There was a farmer in the time of Moses who came to the prophet and said, "O Moses, Would you pray to your Lord on my behalf, that I might learn the language of the animals?" Moses, who is called *Kalimullah*, the word of God, answered him: "O man, instead of trying to learn the language of the animals, why don't you try to learn the depth of your own language? Do you think you already know that?" (If humans knew their own language and how to read the book of their own life and see the treasure within, that would be a great accomplishment indeed.) At this, the man went away, but before long Allah spoke to Moses and said, "That servant of mine looked upon you as his messenger and inquired about learning the language of the animals. Why didn't you bring his request before me? As a lesson to him, I will teach him the language of the animals—but he must exercise great caution, patience and restraint in reacting to what he hears from them." Moses answered, "O Allah, if it is Your will, so be it;" and he went and found the farmer and advised him as to what God had said, repeating the divine warning that he should be most careful about acting upon anything he might hear from the animals.
>
> A few days later, the farmer was passing by his stables when he heard the donkey conversing with the cow. (Everything that exists has a language—some through words, some through actions.) The cow was complaining to the donkey, saying, "Woe is me. I've had enough of these human beings. They barely feed us and they make us work so hard. I have to pull the plow and carry so many burdens. Whether I am tired or sick, I still have to work all day; and finally, when I'm too old and worn

out to work they will cut my throat and eat me. They will even make clothes from my skin and make use of my horns after I am gone."

The man listened intently as the donkey answered the cow, saying, "You idiot! You have such a big head but such a tiny brain. You're so dumb—even when you are sick, you don't look sick. You need to play dead, play tired, play sick. Lie down on your side and act like you can't get up. Haven't you noticed how sometimes I won't get up. Believe me, if you do this, you'll be left in the stable where you can eat and drink all day, without having to work."

. . . Now, the cow, like a student, listened very carefully to its professor, the donkey. She was very grateful and expressed her thankfulness to her instructor.

Muzaffer Efendi storytelling

The next morning, the cow was laying on her side when the farmer entered the stable. The man kicked the cow but she wouldn't budge. The cow peered up through one eye toward her master to see what was going to happen next. The farmer kicked her again and pulled her tail and her ear, but the big animal wouldn't budge. The man said loudly, "Woe is me. I was going to harness the cow to run my carriage; but the cow is sick and it looks like I'm going to have to harness the donkey instead. With this, he grabbed the donkey and harnessed him to the cow cart and set out for town. The poor donkey was not used to such a heavy load and only proceeded under duress from the master's blows. When someone along the way saw the donkey straining to pull the large cow cart and being whipped, he asked indignantly, "What are you doing?" The master answered, "Never mind! This donkey has a great punishment coming to him!"

Later, the poor donkey returned to the stable, hardly able to hold himself up. There he found the cow sitting comfortably, munching her food. "Get up! Get up!" the donkey said in a frantic voice. "Why?" said the cow. "You gave me such wonderful advice that I was most comfortable today and will do the same thing tomorrow." The donkey answered, "Listen! While I was pulling your carriage today, someone asked our master why the cow wasn't pulling the carriage. He answered, 'Well she's sick today, but if she's still sick tomorrow I'm going to slit her throat and sell the meat.'" Meanwhile, the farmer was again eavesdropping outside the stable; he smiled to himself as the donkey continued, "You'd better recover quickly or you're going to lose your life!"

Bright and early the next morning, when the master came to the stable, the cow was standing up, looking strong and digging the ground with her hoof, pretending she was a bull—because she saw death coming. The man mused to himself, "How strange that Moses should tell me it isn't necessary to know the language of the animals. If I hadn't known this language, how would I have seen through this intrigue that these two animals were plotting?"

He heard the rooster and the dog communicating with one another. The rooster asked the dog, "Why did you take away my bread?" The dog answered, "They didn't give me enough meat today, so I became hungry and grabbed your piece of bread." The cock replied, "But this is my due! Why did you steal it? If you could have been a little bit patient, our master was going to butcher the cow tomorrow and you would have had plenty to eat left over from the meat." The farmer, who was still listening, decided the rooster must know something he didn't about the cow's imminent death; so he took the animal at once to the market and sold her. The man was pleased with himself and felt that he knew better than Moses. After all, had he not outsmarted the animals and saved himself from the lost revenue of a dead cow?

Later, he went back to the barn and eavesdropped again on the dog and the rooster. The dog was complaining to the cock, "You told me the cow was going to die and we would have plenty of meat, but now the master has sold the cow!" The rooster answered, "Look, I'm not lying. If a cock crows before sunrise they take it and cut its head off. Believe me, I knew what I was talking about! Now, just wait until tomorrow and you'll see—the master's servant is going to die. Then there will follow a funeral feast and plenty of leftover food for us."

Hearing this, the master rushed off to the market with his servant and sold him. As he counted his money, the man was pleased that he hadn't listened to Moses and that he had been able to sell the cow and the servant without any loss of money. He didn't realize that sometimes it is preferable—it can even be a great gift—for a person not to know certain things. If one knew one was going to die tomorrow, one would never work or build anything. As it is, people work and gather things as though they will never die.

The next day, the farmer went back to listen, but what he heard did not please him at all. The dog was reproaching the rooster over all his failed predictions. The cock defended himself, "Look! Everything I said was true; we just didn't see it happen. Tomorrow, you'll see for yourself an even bigger feast—because the master is going to die." The man became pale when he heard this. What could he do? He couldn't sell himself off at the market. It was his own death coming. He didn't know the secret that if his cow had died, his servant would not have died; or had his servant died, the master's own end would not have come due.

Here is a great secret. Sometimes, when apparently bad things happen to us, these in turn prevent a greater misfortune from befalling us. What was the farmer to do? People imagine that they are self-sufficient and only as their last breath approaches do they turn to their Lord. Until then, they only work for their ego. The intelligent person remembers Allah always, whether in favorable or adverse conditions. In every situation, Allah is with you.

The man rushed to Moses and told him everything. Then he pleaded, "O Moses, my death is coming! Please save me." Moses answered, "O man, didn't I warn you plainly that you should learn the language of your own being, instead of the language of the animals?"

If a person was able to answer all questions and to penetrate all secrets, he would not have a single moment of comfort in this world. Sometimes heedlessness is necessary. If we lived in continuous fear, there would be no way of supporting that. . . . The last words Moses spoke to the man were: "The lot of one who seeks his happiness in the misery of others is death."

We have heard and received many lessons from Hazrat Attar's *Conference of the Birds* tonight. All that I have shared and more is given for the ones who are able to see and to hear. If we view the whole universe as a theater, we ourselves are the actors and actresses—sometimes we laugh, sometimes we cry, sometimes we cause others to laugh and cry. May Allah give us eyes that know how to take lessons from what we see. May we take lessons from what we observe instead of becoming lessons for others. May our hearts be filled with Divine Light and may our faces reflect the light of faith. Amin.[42]

Democracy, Leadership, and Islam

Efendi seldom commented on socio-political issues during his sohbets. However, when he did, his insights were thought-proking. One evening at Spring Valley, Efendi engaged in a lengthy dialogue with questioner Mark Kreiger. The sheikh was asked what could be done to address the lack of spiritual development apparent in politics and business today, when the leaders in these fields are being trained to emphasize worldly gain and self-interest above considerations of the greater good and the Divine Will. Efendi replied:

> We have the same problem in Islam. We also have narrow-minded imams who invite people, not to God, but to their own self interest. They propagate what their limited minds understand and invite people to that. Worse still, they reject whatever doesn't fit into this narrow framework. They reject people and they become a barrier between people and God. So this situation is not just a question for the Western world. One has to get beyond that.
>
> Of course we all want success in this world! Success is necessary; if you are not successful you become a slave to this world. We have two enemies, and they are both in human form. These enemy forces are continually attacking us, from within and from without, with the goal of enslaving us. Of the two, the strongest enemy is the one within—our ego.
>
> All these people in America are talking about freedom and some of them claim that they are free. They may not realize it, but they are in a worse kind of slavery; they are the slaves of their egos—of their *nafs* We have to save ourselves from that. In this world it is necessary. In Islam, the world is added to the hereafter; or, we could say, the hereafter is added to the world—they are not separated. We pray daily, "O my Lord! Grant me what is best in this world and in the hereafter." First, we want to plant in this world because this world is the field of

> the hereafter. Your question, if I have understood it, is: in this worldly environment, how are we to keep from forgetting the Truth of our Creator, our Lord?

Mark responded: "It's a bit more than that. The milieu of this country is such that the ego is not seen as an enemy. So the question is how, if at all, can one help others if they don't see this—if they value the ego rather than seeing it as an enemy?"

Efendi answered that people must follow the laws of scripture rather than the impulses of their own egos. Then he continued:

> There are so many cases in history of people doing exactly what this civilization is doing. A prime example is Rome. They had a huge and powerful empire with an immense administration spread over a vast area—and you see what happened to them. . . . The eyes which don't draw lessons from what they see are like two enemies on one's head. Those leaders who don't take lessons from what they see and what has happened in the past will themselves become examples for future generations who will see what befell them.
>
> Democracy, as I understand it, is like two neighbors with a fence between them whose rectitude is such that, even if the fence were not there, they would behave lawfully and respect each other's property as though it were there. That's my understanding of democracy—that which is lawful. This sort of democracy is destined for mature souls who deeply understand this and are able to act on that knowledge. Even if the fence weren't there, one would not invade another's territory—whether in land, in spiritual life, or in thought. But humans under the sway of their animal nature become obnoxious and charge in like rams as soon as the fence is removed. When you see people under the sway of their animal nature working within a system of democracy, that is what happens.
>
> A democracy is for humans who have reached a certain level of consciousness and of understanding. At that level, if you went on a journey and entrusted your wife to my care, I should be able to preserve her honor and sustain her even

better than you would, since she has been given to my care. But if, as soon as you turn your back, I throw her in my room and take advantage of her, that is the kind of "democracy" we often see today. Somehow with the animal nature, instincts take the place of education. In essence, what characterizes the mature human understanding is the realization that there is only one Divine Source, Who is all that exists. Everything should be centered around that.

Question: "If this does not exist within the minds and hearts of those men and women who are being trained to lead in business, how are they to lead? "

A society is composed of individuals. You cannot put the blame on the leaders alone. If the society contains individuals who are faithful, then the future will bring forth leaders who are also faithful. But indeed, there is a battle to be fought—an intellectual battle, a spiritual battle; it could even involve a physical battle or ordeal. Haven't you heard how the faithful who believed in Christ were fed to the lions in the arenas by the Roman government; then afterwards, the Roman leaders themselves became Christians?

Question: "Is there anything that could be done to avert this? "

Let us be clear: I am not saying there has to be bloodshed! Today we are living in a civilization where, if a battle exists, it must be fought on the intellectual and spiritual level. The possibility of progress through raw force, with bodily clashes, is extremely limited. You see, the Qur'an says, "O Muhammad! Invite them! Invite them to your Lord with wisdom and with sweet words"—not beating them up and insulting them. It says: "They are not going to accept you—they are going to torture you—but in spite of that, continue in this way, debating with them and trying to convince them with sweet words and kindness." Now it is possible in this battle, that you would receive physical blows from your adversaries; and, according to Islam, if someone uses brutal force to suppress you, you may defend yourself. But it is best if we can be patient.

In the beginning, the Muslims conducted themselves like Jesus, who ordered that if someone slaps you on one cheek, you should turn the other. But finally—after turning the other cheek—they kicked! It was either that or perish. The reason that permission was given for *jihad*, for defensive fighting in Islam, is that—although the Prophet showed a great deal of patience in the beginning as they threw stones at him, tortured his followers and finally tried to exterminate them—they ultimately had no option left but to fight to defend their lives. In the end, if Allah had not permitted fighting in defense of the faith, Islam would not have survived—and Christianity would not have either if their followers had not finally fought back.

But never mind that! We are going to make our battle with our intellect. For instance, you write a spiritual book and a materialist writes another book to refute it; then you write your own refutation of his book. That is how the battle is waged. From this dialogue, the ones who are destined to understand and see the truth are going to see the truth, and the ones who are not so destined will not see it. Some will take your side and some will side against you.

Question: "Efendi, what would you change in the present world of large corporations where individuals are secondary?"

First, people have to be taught that no society can live without submission to God, without faith. They may, but only for a short period of time. . . .

You ask a technical question. Perhaps one important answer is this: One should not expend one's forces to change the existing situation; that is, to try to convert an unfaithful one to see Truth. It is important to concentrate one's forces in terms of future generations—working with children. . . . People change generation by generation. Our actual generation is what it is. To change it is almost an impossible task. So in the terms you are talking about, if you wish the Truth for other people, then the best thing is to try to work within the educational system, and to work on one's own children. Of course, you cannot fight on behalf of future generations without doing battle with the existing generation. You don't have to change the life of people in this generation who are already set in their ways. Instead of asking a smoker to quit, if you ask them to help keep their child from ever starting to smoke, they might well go along with that. People are often more receptive to that kind of approach.

The conversation continued with Efendi being questioned further about the problem of corrupt corporate leadership, and what answers might be provided by Islam. Efendi responded:

What Islam does is to introduce Allah to people's hearts. Then Allah places in their hearts the love of Allah, then the compassion and love of His creations, as well as the fear of Allah, so that they are not left Godless. Since you ask me, I will tell you: that is how Islam works. But why don't you also include the leaders in the world who call themselves Muslims? They're not exempt from this question either. They haven't followed the religion of Islam; and this is why their people are so miserable today. You have complained about your leaders and I'm going to complain about ours. I have witnessed many beautiful acts of kindness and consideration in Muslim countries, but I must say these things occur in spite of the leaders. Our leaders are as bad as yours!

When some of the Turkish students began to question Efendi further in this direction, he responded:

Look! I don't like to be the bearer of bad news, but the world is pregnant, and before long we are going to see all these corruptions and sins giving birth. That's as much as I want to say about it. I count on Allah's compassion on those who love Him and who abide with His laws to save us from this coming holocaust. . . . I really hate to give this kind of news, but you've forced me to.

The Prophet, peace and blessings be upon him, has said: "Even if the last day of the world has begun, with the earth shaking and the mountains falling—if you have a little date seed in your hand which you were about to plant, then plant it." As a believer, you have a duty to try, because the ones who came before us planted seeds and we ate from them. The Prophet has also said that if you see something ugly and corrupt, you should knock it down, if not with your hand, then with your pen or your mouth. If circumstances constrain you from even writing or speaking against it, then at least shield your heart from embracing it. That's the bottom line of faith. So plant the seed—if you don't, nothing can happen. Then perhaps after the holocaust that date tree will grow, and others who come later will find some dates to nourish themselves.

It seems to me that there is some sadness in these questions; but don't fall into sadness! Not only here, but throughout the universe, it is as I have described. It is like a jar of jam with some flies inside trying to get out, while on the outside of the jar some other flies are trying to get in. That's the state of the world.

Look, I've seen all over Europe and the Middle East. I've surveyed the whole situation, and—regardless of religion, industry and level of civilization—it's the same everywhere. Humanity is wounded. May Allah send us medicine in the form of faith to heal this wound. In Iraq, in Kuwait, wherever you go in the Muslim world it's the same. But, indeed, I am still very much impressed with what's going on now in America. There is an on-going search for the Truth; and people value other people here. How do I know? Because you are a part of this society and you are here asking these questions. You could easily stay at home in comfort and watch TV or enjoy other entertainment—that's my point.

"But there are so few!" came the lament. Efendi rejoined: "That doesn't matter. What is valuable is what is scarce. Jewels are valuable because they are rare. If they were as abundant as rocks what value would they have? Allah says in His Holy Qur'an:

'My faithful servants are very few.' My ideas could be wrong, but still you've rushed out to hear the sheikh speak. You are like the seeds. The seed gives one hundred to one." Then Efendi added with a chuckle:" It is said that you should even seek the counsel of a fool—but do the opposite of what he says!"

> Why do we come here? This is the third time I've come. I've got lots of things to do and people back at home. But obviously, I feel that there is a need here—that's why I'm here. Even if it were one single person it would be worth it. Ten million people going in different directions is not a society. If you have even three people who understand one another, who see and feel alike—that would be a society. With patience and a single direction, small forces have been made victorious over large ones. Why do you think that that which is little is unimportant? Doesn't a great fire start from a tiny spark? Indeed, no matter how few, there are people in this society who are seeking truth; and without doubt, these few will be victorious over the many, because when they find truth they will have the power of the Divine behind them—a force which no numbers can withstand.[43]

Later Efendi would add: "Wherever there is justice, compassion and help between people, Allah blesses that land and abundance reigns there. How do we know if a nation has the curse or blessing of God? Look at their leaders. If they are kind, compassionate and just, then know that the divine blessings are upon that nation. When you see that their heads of state are tyrants, know that the divine displeasure has come upon that country."[44]

Mysteries of the afterlife

Muzaffer Efendi often discoursed on the afterlife, emphasizing not only the importance of the eternal realm in relation to our relatively short temporal existence on earth, but the value of our earthly deeds and intentions in relation to our experience of the next world. His teaching stories involving the afterlife often carried unexpected, intriguing implications.

One such story involved a holy fool who approached a wealthy miser in a cafe, demanding that the man buy him some yogurt. The rich man was irritated and refused the beggar, as he always refused such requests. But when the beggar became loudly insistent, refusing the offers of other patrons to buy him food, saying that this particular man should give for the sake of Allah, the miser finally handed over one coin for a yogurt, thinking it was worth it just to get rid of him. The beggar bought the yogurt but was not satisfied; he returned and asked the man for some bread to go with it. This time, he was driven off by the infuriated miser, who, by now, was too upset to enjoy his own food.

That night, the miser fell asleep and dreamed he had died and entered paradise. He enjoyed the beautiful scenery for a while, but soon became hungry, and sought out a heavenly denizen to ask for something to eat. Upon receiving a simple bowl of yogurt, he inquired if he could also get some bread or something else more substantial to go with it, but was informed that there was nothing else available for him to eat. "But this is paradise! Surely there's more to eat here than just one bowl of yogurt," he insisted. "I'm sorry," he was told, "but that's all you sent over from the other side." When the man woke up, he was relieved to find that it had been a dream and he was still on earth. He quickly dressed, ran out to the street and began to distribute alms to every beggar he could find.

Efendi also related a similar story involving Behlul Dona,

the wise fool who was the court advisor of the famous 'Abbasid Caliph Harun ar-Rashid, associated with the tales of *A Thousand and One Nights*. One day, Behlul needed some fire to light the wood in the fireplace, so he decided to make a quick visit to hell in order to borrow some fire from that realm. When he arrived, he was surprised to see only green meadows and no fire. When he asked someone where the fires of hell were, he was told, "O, we don't keep any here. Everyone has to furnish their own—that which they bring with them." Efendi added, "You see, hell is in degrees and levels just as your misdeeds are. There are seven levels of paradise and seven levels of hell. In hell, one burns with the fire of one's own misdeeds, no more, no less. . . .[45] Actually, everyone burns in some way. Every soul will at least taste the fire; but the righteous souls when they die become intoxicated with the beauty of the divine and because of this, do not experience it as pain... The best way of burning is to burn with the fire of love. Whoever burns with the fire of love disappears. When the self has disappeared in the fire of love, then there exists nothing left to burn."[46]

Aware of the modern tendency toward dismissing hell or the existence of any negative states in the afterlife, Efendi insisted:

> Wherever one lives, one must abide by the laws of that country or risk ending up in prison. There also exists a Divine Government and laws of Our Creator; those who don't abide by the Creator's laws will end up in the prison-house of the Divine Government.
>
> I was brought somewhere in America and was speaking about the fear of God and the love of God, when someone got up and said, "How could anyone fear God? What is important is to love God." But it must be understood that when I speak about the fear of God, it is not fear of punishment that I mean, but rather, caution about taking God's love and favor for granted. We should be sensitive to the possibility that one could lose the

divine favor, to the point that Allah would in effect say, "You are no longer my servant." That's the real "fear of Allah", which is simply another aspect of the "love of Allah."

Everything has two sides, a positive and a negative side. Everything has a *jamal* (beautiful, gentle) side and a *jalal* (powerful, intense) side. Take water for example: you experience its beautiful side when you are thirsty and you can drink and be cooled and satisfied by the water, or when you water a plant and it grows. But the strength of water can be something terrifying, creating floods and typhoons. It is the same with the air: a beautiful breeze cools you but a tornado destroys. Fire also warms us and allows us to cook our food—that is the *jamal* side—but there is also the *jalal* side which can burn down a whole city.

Allah has these *jamal* and *jalal* qualities as well. When Allah's attributes of beauty show forth, even the devil begins to dance about and say, "O, Allah is going to overlook everything I've done and have mercy on me." But when Allah's might is manifested, even Gabriel trembles like a piece of cloth in a great wind. If there existed only the beautiful side of things—if Allah had only His *jamal* and not His *jalal*—it would mean Allah was lacking and incomplete. *Estaghfirullah.*

Yes, I know we all want beauty in everything, including Allah. But how about each of you? How much beauty, kindness and mercy are you manifesting? How many orphans have you fed? And how many tearful eyes have you wiped? Or do you sit around worrying about your money and calculating your checkbook? Your wealth will not last forever. The keys to both paradise and hell are available here in this life."[47]

A questioner said to Efendi: "I hear lovely descriptions of paradise, but somehow this doesn't seem like it could be the end of the soul's journey." Efendi responded:

Of course, there is something beyond paradise. The believers may go to paradise, but the seekers of Truth directly receive the Face of God, the Divine Truth Itself. Entering paradise is like entering a garden; there is a garden, but also an Owner of the Garden.

The question one must ask oneself is: "How do I go to paradise? And why?" To find this out you must ask yourself: "Why was I created? And why as a human being and not as a rat?" Everything in our universe was created for our benefit as human beings, and we ourselves were created for Allah. If you want to enter paradise during this life, affirm, "*La ilaha illallah. Muhammad ar-Rasulullah.*" You will either go to paradise or to the Owner of Paradise. . . . When unity, *tawhid*, has become your truth, then Allah is actually closer to you than you are to yourself. . . . .[48] There are one hundred gates to paradise and unity. *Tawhid*, provides a key to enter them. There are also three basic levels of paradise: the level of your actions, the level of Divine Attributes, and the level of Pure Essence. Those who enter this last level are in the very Presence of the Divine Face.[49]

One of the dervishes asked Efendi to elaborate on how one goes about practicing the remembrance of one's own mortality, *dhikr al-mawt*. The sheikh replied:

Visit the graves; attend funerals and don't objectify your own mortality or remain mentally aloof. You yourself must feel what it would be like to be buried all alone in that tomb in the cold ground, and consider what it is like to have everything you ever loved or possessed gone. This is not a great stretch of the imagination because soon that's exactly what is going to happen to you. The soil you are walking upon today might have once been the flesh of an important king or a beautiful woman. Within one hundred years, most of the people alive on the planet today will have passed. What does the Sufi do about this? The Sufi feels his own nothingness, which all souls have in common, and realizes that all souls have come forth from Allah. We have all come from the realm of Allah and will all return to Him. It is Allah Who grants life and rescinds life.

Another dervish spoke up, inquiring: "Efendi, if one was really this aware of death all the time, how could they have any joy in life?" Efendi answered:

Ahh . . . The ones who remember death have such joy that they laugh at us who think we are having fun while we ignore death. The prophets and saints are trying to make us taste the joy which they have—but we don't seem to be receiving that message. In fact, the same question was asked by the companions of the Prophet. They said: "You talk to us about death, but really, we are still afraid of it." The Prophet guaranteed them that when the moment of death would come, they would rush to it with joy. The ones who should really fear death are the ones who inflict injustice on others and cause them suffering.

Death is achieving union with the Beloved. How could one fear or have anxiety about meeting the Beloved? It is like going into exile from the country of one's origin and then returning home. There are two types of homecoming: one is returning home unsuccessful with a blackened face from having failed to achieve anything, while the other is like returning with fame and honor to one's home.

Someone dreamed about one of the devout who had passed

away and they asked him in the dream: "What is it like at that terrible moment of death?" The deceased man answered, "All I can tell you is that as I was dying, a person of great beauty appeared and gave me a lovely rose. When I smelled its sweet perfume, I suddenly became aware of looking down and seeing my corpse laying on that stone slab, being washed and wrapped in a shroud."

Is the one who is dead afraid of death? The lovers pass away before death. How could a lover fear death when he's already in that state? That is why the Prophet, peace and blessings be upon him, says, "Die before you die." What does this phrase mean? It means you submit your will in such a manner—just like a corpse in the hands of its washers—when they lift your hand or turn you, you don't resist. So in this manner you give up your separate will and submit to Allah in such a way that your will proceeds from His One Will. When one dies before death in this way, there is no death any more. It is nothing—just smelling a rose. The ones who love Allah cannot fear death. When you go knock on the door of the Beloved—are you going to be clobbered over the head? No! You will be received with open arms and kisses. "I love You but I'm still afraid of You," means that you don't fully love Him.

There was a very upright aristocratic person who had never in his life been cursed. One day, someone came and hollered at him, calling him a donkey. The aristocrat was so shocked by the insult that he fainted. The people surrounding him told the man who had done the cursing that the man who fainted had been very sheltered and had never been called a donkey. So the man bent over the prone aristocrat and began to repeat, "Donkey! Donkey! Donkey!" The others screamed, "What are you doing? The poor man already fainted when you first called him a donkey!" The man replied, "Oh, I'm just trying to get him used to it." So, as your sheikh, that's what I'm trying to do—to get you used to death. The holy Qur'an promises, "Be consoled, O beloved and lovers of God, for there is neither fear awaiting you nor sadness."[50]

In 1983, Lou Rogers was hosting a series of television

interviews with spiritual teachers, called *Turning Inward*. He invited Muzaffer Efendi on the show with Çinar Kologlu as translator. On one of these broadcasts Lou inquired as to how the Sufi faces "the dark specter of death". Efendi answered:

> There is no such thing as death. There are only births. There is no such thing as ceasing to be. Nothing perishes or is lost and no one dies. But every creature who is ornamented with a soul *tastes* death, just as I am now tasting the water in this glass. *(Efendi takes a drink of water.)* From the realm of the spirit to this world, there are various stages of births. A drop of semen entering a woman produces one stage of birth. The embryo that forms in the mother's womb regards that womb as its entire universe and doesn't want to leave it. When the baby comes into this world, it cries, imagining it is losing the comfort of the womb and coming to a worse place. But they are actually coming to a much wider place that offers many more opportunities. In the same way, we imagine that when we leave this world we will be losing something. Babies are born crying, their fists tight, meaning that we are very demanding toward the world and eager for what it can offer. On the other hand, when we leave the world, our hands are wide open. The significance of this is that no one takes anything with them from this world. A poet wrote: "When you came into this world, you cried while everyone else laughed. Lead such a life that when you die, everyone will weep while you will laugh."
>
> For those who lead righteous lives of service and goodness, there is nothing to fear in death—only union with the Beloved. Souls are not visible, but bodies are. It is as if the soul rides on the body in the way they are joined. For those who are attached to this world—like two lovers who do not want to part—separation of the soul from the body at death will be painful. Though a lover may have some attachment to this world, if Allah loves this soul and so wishes, Allah shows to the eyes of this lover's heart during the moment of death such a vision that the lover totally forgets the separation from this world and

experiences no pain. It is similar to the Qur'anic story of the Prophet Joseph, where Zuleika invites some women friends to visit her house to see the beauty of Joseph. When he enters the room, the ladies are cutting up fruit with sharp knives. They are so enthralled with Joseph's beauty that they cut their hands instead of the fruit, without realizing it. They don't feel the pain of it because of the beauty they are beholding. In the same way, at the moment of death, we see a vision of either Allah's beauty, or a vision of paradise, or of a greatly beloved person, perhaps a saint. In this way, one is lost in love and beauty and feels no pain. Everyone should accustom themselves to death. As long as they remember death, they won't commit evil. . . .

There are two ways of departing to the hereafter. As the person is making their transition at the moment of death, the angels come to soothe him and assure him that everything is all right—or the person might be met by a loved one who has passed before him, such as his mother. But for those who have led lives of extreme negativity and who have not asked nor understood why they were here, no one comes to meet or comfort them. They feel the pangs of the separation vividly . . . because there is no beauty—no Joseph—to contemplate.

In the hereafter, there are seven heavens, and the souls go to one of these seven celestial spheres. But the souls of those who have led lives of injustice and spiritual denial stay imprisoned within the earthly sphere with their soul still attached to this world, and the heavens do not become apparent to them. The first celestial sphere is the level of the ascetics. Worshipers are found in the second level. Righteous people inhabit the third realm and martyrs, the fourth. On the fifth are saints; on the sixth, prophets; and on the seventh, the greatest prophets.

Although the television interview ended at this point in Efendi's explanation, at a later date the subject resurfaced during a discussion with the dervishes.

As we have enumerated before, there are seven levels of the soul, from the lowest mineral and animal soul to the highest soul, the *ruhu sirr*. This highest level of the soul is the mysterious, secret soul, the divine part of a person's makeup which is located neither inside nor outside the body—it is beyond creation. For the unbeliever at death, this highest soul is drawn back to the Creator, but unless the other lower aspects of the soul have been improved, they are drawn to remain with that person, imprisoned within the sphere of the earth.

The highest soul is where the divine name *al-Hayy* manifests. It is that which gives life to the soul. As Allah mentions in the Qur'an: "We all come from Allah and all return unto Him." (2:156) So every person's highest soul, or *ruhu sirr*, returns back to Allah. As for the destination of the lower aspects of the soul, that depends on a person's qualities. If a person has learned that they have a calling, a destiny to fulfill in this world, and has striven for it, that person will find their station in the hereafter according to their own affinity and rank within the spiritual stations. Paradise has different levels, some for the lovers, some for martyrs, prophets, and so on; each person is drawn to the heavenly station appropriate to their spiritual level. As for those who never made the effort to discover their purpose in this world, the lower aspects of their soul are attracted to remain in the earthly sphere, while their highest soul returns to the Source.

At this point Efendi was asked: Can we aspire to attain knowledge of and become one with the *ruhu sirr* ? Efendi replied:

This is what we're all trying to do, to find and be one with the *ruhu sirr*, the secret soul. That soul is very close to us but we are far away and distant from it. This is the root of the matter—to deepen our relationship with the soul. When, in answer to the question about the soul which was directed to the Prophet, Allah revealed: "Say that the soul is of the command of Your Lord (*ar-ruhu min 'amri Rabbi*), of which you have been given only a little knowledge," (17:85b), it was this soul to which He referred. When Allah continued: "We have given you only a little knowledge concerning the soul," it was

> the other lower categories of soul that were being addressed. Also, when we speak of "the realm of the souls," this implies creation and creatures, so it is the other souls which have been created. Conversely, the *ruhu sirr*, which is the receptacle of the manifestation of the name, *al-Hayy*, is something totally different from the other souls. *Hayyul-Qayyum*—Allah, the Ever-living, the Self-subsisting—is the greatest name.
>
> Also in the verse where the primordial souls were asked, "Am I not Your Lord?" (*Alastu bi-Rabbikum*; 7:172), it was the *ruhu sirr* who was asking the other souls, and it was the human and sultan souls which replied.[51] It is the same with the hadith, "Allah was alone and there was none else beside Him," or, "He who knows himself knows his Lord." We're always talking about the same thing, but sometimes we change the terminology by which it is expressed.

On still another occasion, the sheikh was asked about the justice of this arrangement, in which some souls find Truth and ascend to higher planes than other less capable souls. The questioner felt that for one's place in the hereafter to be truly just, everyone should be created equally capable of reaching the Truth. Efendi answered: "Indeed, it is everyone's right to reach the Truth, but how close they can come to Truth is according to each one's ability."

The questioner responded: "But that's what I don't understand. That doesn't seem like justice." Efendi answered: "One person comes forth from the Divine blind, another crippled, another retarded. Where is the divine justice in this? One dog lays in front of the butcher store hoping to be thrown a bone while another dog is pampered, traveling in a Cadillac, eating *filet mignon*. Is this justice?"

"No," was the reply. "In that case," continued Efendi, "according to your understanding, God is not just, but a tyrant. If God were to be just according to your view, everyone would have to be the same sex, look the same, and have all the same qualities;

everyone equally wealthy or poor—no difference." Efendi added with a chuckle that if one wanted the last mentioned justice, it was available in communist Russia.

> Now, let's say I have one thousand dollars, and I line up ten people to whom I can distribute this money. If, out of my own money, I desire to give one $900 and the rest $10 each, have I been just in the distribution of my money? If you start asking, 'Why did the other person get more, and I got less?' it will soon come to the point that the animals will be asking, 'Why did I become a rat?' and so forth. If everything was equal in this world, it would be no fun at all. As it is, you see the sick one and can be thankful for your health, or see the poor one and be grateful for your wealth.
>
> There was a Russian czar who called an Islamic scholar into his presence and asked him why everything was not created equal. He wanted to know why there are different religions instead of just one. The scholar answered, "That's easy to explain. Call your orchestra together and I'll show you." So all the musicians in the orchestra assembled and the scholar said, "Let only the bassoon player play, and no one else." So the bassoonist honked away for a while until the czar became very bored with his song. Then the scholar explained to the czar, "If everything was equal and the same, that's how this whole universe would sound." Then he had the whole orchestra play together and told the czar, "Now, experience the full harmony in the orchestra and in the world."

Efendi concluded, "It is the harmony in the orchestra, like the harmony in the universe, with all its rich diversity, that brings real justice into place." Then he added, jokingly, "If everyone reached the truth equally, who would I be speaking to now? No one would need to learn anything or be interested in listening to anybody else. But God, in His Divine Wisdom has created the diversities of this world; and, as such, very seldom does a human reach to Divine Perfection."[52]

The Training of the Nafs and Breaking of the Inner Idols

One evening Muzaffer Efendi was asked about the way of transformation offered in the tarikat. He responded:

> The tarikat is the path. By divine decree, the heavenly soul has been sent to earth and has united with the physical body. The human is formed through a marriage of body and soul, of heaven and earth. But the soul's inclination is to fly to freedom, to the realm of its heavenly origin. It feels somewhat out of its element in the physical realm...When the soul, by Divine Will, comes into the body, it becomes intoxicated by the realm of the senses and forgets its spiritual origin; but when the body dies, the soul awakens to its original state. A few souls remember their origin while in the body, but most do not.
>
> The tarikat, then, is the path that awakens the soul to its true nature and shows it how to return to its true home, by cleansing the heart and receiving spiritual guidance. The word *tarik* in the dictionary is said to be the "path" or "road", but *tarikat—tariqa* in Arabic—is "the path to Allah." In the *Qur'an al-Karim,*[53] Allah says: "We have created humanity most exalted and beautiful." There is nothing on earth equal to the greatness of the human soul. "And," it continues, "We have sent humanity down to earth"—into the realm of density. Therefore, if the soul finds the path to its original place while in this world, it reaches the heavenly state; but if not, one remains attached to the earth in an abased condition. You see, it is the soul that animates and shines in the body. No one is too keen to hang around a lifeless corpse. Only when the soul comes into the body is it possible to have loving relationships among human beings.
>
> When the soul enters the body, there are seven earthly attributes which it takes upon itself. These are: arrogance, jealousy, hatred, love of possessions, love of wealth, and love of rank and power. The prophets are sent to teach us how to overcome these abased qualities and transmute them into positive qualities: arrogance into humility, love of possessions into the love of

God, and so on. The prophets show us how to transmute these earthly qualities, how to reach God and how to become fully human. After the prophets, their students and successors are the sheikhs and murshids, coming down to our time.

According to the prescriptions of the tarikat, each of the seven characteristics of the earthly body is purified by the seven divine attributes: *La ilaha illallah, Allah, Hu, Haqq, Hayy, Qayyum and Qahhar*. There are 10,000 veils associated with each of the earthly qualities, making a total of seventy thousand veils, which separate us from our Divine Source. Each of the seven Divine names is a remedy for 10,000 of these veils. In the nativity poem of the Prophet, the *Mevlud*, Süleyman Chelebi mentions these 70,000 veils, which were lifted for Muhammad.[54]

You see, the Truth is very close to us, but through spiritual blindness we separate ourselves far from the Truth. In the Qur'an,[55] Allah states: "I am closer to you than the jugular vein of your neck." So the Truth is closer to us than we are to ourselves. But from the human perspective, the Truth is seen as separated by 70,000 veils. In the struggle with one's limited self, with one's arrogance and so forth, the dervish makes use of the prescribed medicine, the seven divine attributes, and in this way removes the 70,000 spiritual veils, 10,000 at a time.

There is also a kind of hypocrisy that needs to be avoided, called *ujub*, in which one is proud of all one's good works and long prayers in a judgmental way. This self-righteous attitude can cause one to see oneself as superior to everyone else; it is a quality worse than arrogance. If you depend on religious worship and prayers self-righteously, the 70,000 veils of suffering can turn into 70,000 veils of light which still will separate you from the Truth. That is why Shams-i Tabriz, the teacher of love—as Mevlana's sheikh—threw all Rumi's books into the well. Mevlana protested that these were priceless books of knowledge, especially the one by his father, to which he was especially attached. But in reality, these books were a veil between him and Allah. Shams retrieved the book by Mevlana's father from the well, still dry, and shook the dust off it—meaning he removed the dust of earthly attachment. In this case, the knowledge had become a veil, a veil of light, which is slightly different than the veils of suffering caused by negative attributes.

You cannot see yourself clearly enough to prescribe your own spiritual medicine. For that, a doctor or sheikh is necessary. If you wish to travel to another city, it is most expedient to find a guide who already knows the way—unless you want to wander a lot. The sheikh trains the dervish and helps him overcome the unbecoming qualities such as arrogance. In some cases, the dervish might have to clean bathrooms for a while, which is a difficult task for a haughty person. Or if someone comes to a sheikh and has an inordinate love of money and possessions, the sheikh may say, "Bring all your money." The sheikh would not accept it himself, but would ask the dervish to throw it in the river or spend it on the poor. That's how the training of the ego, or *nafs*, proceeds.[56]

During the West Coast tour of 1981, Efendi had also spoken about the process of removing the 70,000 veils. He listed the seven divine qualities that are prescribed for the initiate, from *La ilaha illallah*, to *Qahhar*, and then added:

Theoretically, if you chanted these seven esmas 10,000 times each, it would remove all these veils, but often you have to persist beyond this. If there is someone in a house that you really need to get to, you keep knocking and knocking and knocking. If you keep knocking, eventually someone will answer.

Also, in our work, it is not absolutely necessary to go into seclusion and do various preparations before reciting your practice. What is more important is continuity. You can be working and doing two things—actually three things at once is even better. You could be driving or working at the same time you are reciting and remembering. You can do all these things at the same time. In fact, this will enhance your work or activity, if done properly: your hand at work, your tongue reciting the names of Allah, and the love of Allah in your heart—all three at the same time. If you can keep that up, I will take my hat off to you!

Now, I don't mean to say that you shouldn't ever do your practices in the more traditional way—making exterior and interior ablutions, preparing oneself, turning toward the kibla, and achieving a state of purity and inner peace before you begin. But the times being as they are, with people's busy schedules and responsibilities, we have to adapt. Therefore, your hand is at work, your tongue beautified by His name, your heart beautified by His love, and your eyes seeing only Him—because Allah is in His creation, the artist is in his art; so the eyes also participate, which gives us another concentration.

> Your image is in my eye,
> Your love in my heart,
> Your name on my tongue.

Efendi also spoke about the efficacy of making prayers, even at the more advanced levels of the path:

It is only through being a servant of the divine that one becomes aware that *Haqq*, or Divine Truth, is in one. Prayer helps you come to this realization. You might further say, "Fine, I understand that prayer helps me understand and become conscious that the Truth is within me. So why continue with prayers and meditations after you've realized that God is within, that God is nearer than one's jugular vein? Once you've attained this realization, then to Whom will you pray? Whom will you glorify and serve when, beyond time and place, the servant and the served have become one?

Then what you will do is pray from the Divine Attributes to the Divine Essence. Because your exterior being is coarse, but your interior reality is divine, or belongs to Truth. The Divine Essence is one, but the attributes are many; for instance, Allah has 99 attributes. When you reach that state of *fana*, of oneness, of attainment, you still need to connect the attribute to the Essence, so you still continue your prayers. This is not easy to understand. Some teachers may teach that they have

> attained and no longer need to make prayers, but even the prophets—who have attained—continued to worship and offer their prayers. In the act of prostration during the *salat*, you come closest to the servant merging with one's Lord. In fact, there is an *ayat* in the Holy Qur'an which says, "Make prostration and come close to Allah."[57]

Efendi added that he would not recite the verse in Arabic just then because everyone is supposed to prostrate upon hearing it recited, according to the sunnah. Then Efendi was asked about the struggle with the *nafs* as the "greater *jihad*". The term was coined by the Prophet, when he and his companions were returning from a fierce battle with their enemies in which many were killed. The outward struggle for righteousness is called the *jihad*—or lesser *jihad*. On this occasion, the Prophet announced, "Now the greater *jihad* can begin." When some of them asked whether they were about to meet an even greater army of enemies, the Prophet explained that the fighting to improve outward conditions was only the first step, but the struggle with the *shaitan* or *nafs* within oneself was the real spiritual battle, the greater *jihad*. Muzaffer Efendi responded to the question by saying:

> You see, the greater *jihad* is having pity on yourself—having so much pity on yourself that you really long to turn into a true human being. You treat your body well. The great battle has nothing to do with torturing yourself, with depriving yourself of sleep for days on end and hurting yourself. It is a spiritual and psychological struggle to change your attributes—to transmute them. One doesn't want to slay, annihilate or cripple the self. No, there is great pity, great compassion involved in this work; you are gradually turning into a human being, something of much higher, greater value. "Slaying the self," "torturing the self"—these are completely out. Someone may speak in terms of killing the *nafs*, or annihilating the ego or lower self, but it is not really appropriate. The goal is not to kill, but to improve.

We have the choice of either turning ourselves over to a guide who will gradually educate us, train, drill and improve us or simply turning ourselves over to an executioner who will lop our head off. The second is not a desirable outcome. . . .

The struggle is between our *nafs al-ammara*, the commanding self—which has some of the qualities we described such as arrogance, greed, anger, and lust—and the higher attributes intrinsic to the soul, which have been inherited from the Divine Throne itself. In the top echelon of creation, we see three main realms: the realm of human beings, the realm of angels and the realm of animals. If we take animals, for instance, we can say in a general sense that they have lust, but little intellect. Angels have intellect—a kind of transcendental intellect which deals with the beyond—but no lust. But in the case of humans, both lust and intellect coexist.

In the continuous battle for domination between these two qualities, humanity is capable of rising higher than the angels or sinking lower than the animals. It all depends on which qualities are dominant. If the intellect dominates lust, the human spirit is higher than the angels (who were made to prostrate before Adam in paradise), but if lust dominates, the human operates beneath his or her potential and becomes lower than the animals. The point is that we want to transform the undesirable attributes of the self into more beneficent, useful ones. This takes great undoing and doing at the same time. It can be a very difficult struggle.

We came to this world as human beings and it is important to leave as human beings. One might become a vezir, a sultan, king or president, but it is very difficult to turn oneself into a human being. To change our animal-like qualities into human qualities is what is needed; a battle with machine-guns is nothing compared to this.

Take the example of a person who makes fun of people. Externally that person might appear as a human being, but inwardly he or she is a monkey. A person who hurts their fellow human beings with their tongue, by insulting them, lying about them or slandering them, is inwardly a snake or scorpion. A

> person who earns his living through theft is inwardly a rat, feeding upon unlawful food, like what is obtained from the sewers. It is easy to attain a high rank with the qualities of a rat, but infinitely more difficult to turn someone who is inwardly a rat into a true human being.
>
> When Moses was ordered to throw his staff to the ground before Pharaoh, it turned into a snake. Why a snake and not some other animal, like a tiger or an elephant? Because the Pharaoh's cruel deeds were like those of a snake, and the staff of Moses was like a mirror upon which Pharaoh's qualities were reflected. When Pharaoh died, his inner being went into the afterlife as a snake, rather than as a human being.[58]

Efendi explained that another aspect of the path of ego-purification was to rid oneself of all forms of *shirk*, meaning associating partners with Allah, which, in effect, denies the All-Powerful Sovereignty and Oneness of the Creator. Efendi pointed out that to believe that the limited self exists at all, as an entity separate from Allah, is a subtle form of *shirk*. The dervish ardently strives to avoid this, as Allah has revealed that "*shirk* is the one sin which cannot be forgiven" [*shirk* being essentially the dualistic perspective which denies that there is ultimately only One Reality]. Sheikh Nur questioned how it could be possible that *shirk* was unforgivable, since it would follow that almost everyone except extremely advanced souls would be judged on this. Efendi responded: "You are correct. The reason is that there is an opposite to every imaginable sin and forgiveness possible for each one, but there is no opposite to the Divine Truth. It is One and beyond opposites and consequently out of the realm of what can be forgiven."[59]

A few weeks later, during a discussion which again turned upon the ramifications of *shirk*, Sheikh Nur asked Efendi: "If the souls of humans came forth from Allah and Adam received in his very nature the gift of faith from Allah, how then could humans ever really, in their heart of hearts, believe in associating partners with Allah?"

Efendi responded: "Indeed those who have faith, or *iman*, cannot commit *shirk*. But in the universe of souls, Allah offered faith to everyone, but not everyone accepted it. Allah asked the souls, 'Who wants this faith?' He also asked, 'Who wants to be the assassin of Imam Husayn?' and somebody voluntarily agreed to do it. Everything was decreed in this way, but transmitted in subtle form through the Qur'anic question, '*Alastu bi-Rabbikum?*' ('Am I not your Lord?') and the response of every soul, '*Bala*' ('Yes'). Every soul was there in the *'alam-i arwah*, and all said yes to the Truth. But they did so in a pure environment. When they came to earth and were mixed with impurity and experienced their own will, they changed and didn't keep their word. Keeping one's word is an attribute of a real human being."

Efendi then used Shaitan as an example, referring to the Qur'anic version[60] of his divine rebellion:

> When Shaitan revolted against Allah, his absence of *adab* affected all those who committed *shirk*. He said to Allah, "It is You who fooled me." He didn't comprehend the mystery of humanity and thus wouldn't prostrate before Adam. Allah foresaw all of this in advance, because He had already declared before the creation of Adam: "I am going to choose one amongst you as my opposite, my enemy."
>
> At this time Shaitan was known as Harith, the most enthusiastic worshiper of Allah alone. When the angels heard Allah's declaration, they went to Harith and begged him, "Please pray for us that none of us will be chosen as God's opponent. So he opened his palms and prayed for them, but did not pray for himself—because he was made to forget. You see, in a reverse way, there was already *shirk* in his attitude. He went to Allah and said, "I will prostrate before You, but not before Adam." So there was *shirk* in his very act of separating Allah and Adam into two. Prostrating before Allah and Adam is the same thing, but the devil wasn't intelligent enough to realize this. Prostrating

> to Adam was prostrating to Adam's heart, where Allah was. It's the same as prostrating toward the Ka'ba. It is not toward the bricks themselves that we prostrate. If we prostrated to the Ka'ba itself, we would be pagans. Rather, we direct ourselves toward the Ka'ba, while prostrating to Allah alone. The angels prostrated toward Adam, but they knew they were prostrating toward Allah.[61]

"There are levels in *shirk*," Efendi continued. "Worshiping a stone idol would be one level of *shirk*. In the case of a dervish who reached the level of *fana fi'llah*, where nothing exists except Allah—if, in that state, the dervish thinks that he exists, that would be associating partners with Allah, making an idol, a separate deity of the self. Another example of *shirk* would be a person who worships Allah because he wants to avoid hell or attain paradise. If this is the intention of his prayers, he is actually praying to his own ego and associating partners with Allah. One must worship Allah for His Own sake, not for any ulterior motives. Nothing exists apart from Allah. During the dark age of spiritual ignorance known as the *jahiliyyat*, the Arabs used to worship stone idols. Therefore it is said that the nonbelievers have one kind of idol; but the Muslims believers have a thousand kinds of idols which they must break."

"What are they?" he was asked. Efendi answered: "Whatever is other than Allah is an idol; there are more than thousands or even millions of idols." Then Efendi related a story:

> There was a great sheikh who had many khalifas, scholars and followers. When he was about to pass from this world, he gathered all his followers and told them that a certain person from another village, a man who happened to be a Christian priest, would be their sheikh after him. On his last meeting with the priest, the sheikh gave him some specific instructions. When the sheikh died, some of his disciples doubted his

selection of a successor and thought maybe he wasn't thinking clearly when he chose the priest so near to the time of his death. Others insisted that they should certainly respect their sheikh's choice and try to follow his appointed successor.

After the sheikh's funeral, the priest came and sat on the sheikh's post. Then he arose and said to the dervishes: "Your sheikh has instructed me to come here after his passing and destroy my idol, which I shall now do in your presence." Then he took from around his neck the cross that hung over his chest, cut it in half and cast it away. "But as for you," he informed them, "your sheikh has instructed me that you must cut your unmanifested idols, the idols you carry in your hearts. He asked me to cut my external idol that I carried, and to help you cut the idols you carry in your hearts."

"Therefore," Muzaffer Efendi continued, "when one reaches the seventh level of the self, *an-nafs-i safiya*,—if in that state one says, 'God exists and I also exist,' then one is engaging in *shirk*. At the highest level, only Truth exists and nothing else. Some of their idols were women, some were money, some prestige. That's what they meant by 'cut the idols in your hearts.' Anything other than God is an internal idol. Any external totem is an external idol. It is easy to clean your hands when they get dirty, but very difficult to cleanse the heart when it gets dirty. Only Truth can cleanse the heart and give repentance. That's why, when the dervish submits himself to the sheikh, the first thing he asks him to do is to repent. The first step on the path is repentance, *tawba*—repentance from sins, then repentance from repentance. It depends on the degree and the level."

Sheikh Nur asked, "What if the idol is oneself?" Efendi answered, "Then one experiences hell—even if one ultimately goes to heaven—because one is separated from the DivineTruth, *Haqq*, and is still suffering in isolation. You see, the reality of heaven is that one is united with Truth. Whenever you are separated from Truth, you suffer; your own limited self is the veil that hides the Truth. When you say with absolute sincerity, *La ilaha illallah*, or 'There is no truth other than the Divine Truth', then the "you" disappears in the realization of that Absolute Truth. The dervish must have a name but not a self. There is something in Turkish literature called an *anka-bird*. No such animal exists in reality, but there is a name for it. The dervish should be like that bird. That's the goal—to be destroyed in the Truth."

On hearing this, Nur commented, "It is easier to be destroyed by love." Efendi answered, "Yes, its much better. But to be destroyed by love is not really destruction; rather, it is coming into Being. From true non-existence—from the complete negation—emerges the positive. Therefore the ones who lose themselves in Truth become one with the Truth, and eternal."[62]

During another evening discourse, Efendi elaborated further on the subject of *fana*, saying:

> One meaning of Sufism is to be contented with one's fate. The one who has not achieved that state, if he tries to imitate it, is going to receive a very big slap. At that level, you cannot—even if you wanted—petition Allah in prayer, since that would mean you are disagreeing with what Allah has given you. We are speaking of the level of union with the Divine. Then you come so close to God that the eye with which you see will be the eye of God; and the ear with which you hear will be God's ear; and the tongue with which you speak will be God's tongue. Allah sees through your eyes and hears through your ears and speaks through your tongue. That means there is no separation between you and Allah.
>
> You ask me, "How does this happen?" When you place an iron sword in the fire, what happens to the iron? It becomes fire. You must become like that as well. But when you pull the iron sword back out of the flames, it becomes iron again—you return to your servanthood. This fire is the fire of love, which comes from Allah. The sword has two edges: it cuts both ways. This [unitive state] is the final gift, of God's will, which we

hope to receive.

I don't know the degree of love for God in your hearts, so I have initially given you the *shariat*, the lawful religious teaching for the ordinary person's state vis-a-vis prayer. But I could not withhold telling you something of the higher levels. The *tawhid*, *La illaha illallah*, is the prayer for beginners. At the next level, *La maksudi illallah*, "there is no goal or destination except Allah." The level above that is *La mahbudi illallah*—"there is nothing to be loved except Allah." The fourth is: "there is no action except Allah." Finally, "Nothing exists except Allah." That is the highest level.[63]

Another aspect of this theme arose during a television interview with Lou Rogers. There, Efendi further elaborated on the paradox of becoming nothing in order to become Reality, when asked about the famous hadith of the Prophet, "He who knows himself knows his Lord." Efendi offered the following explanation:

The first level of interpretation is that whoever knows their own self, knows the weakness of that self. One realizes the nakedness of the self and its mortality, and recognizes their dependence upon someone to clothe them and sustain them. One knows one's smallness, one's nothingness, and seeks for something greater, something immortal. After that comes another type of knowledge.

There is an "I' inside this "I"; there is another personality, an essence within the human soul which is connected with the Divine. Knowing the second stage is difficult and cannot be realized except by one who has gone through the first stage. The "I" within the "I" means that there is a manifestation of the Divine within the human being. By analogy, if we gather a cup of water from the ocean—it *is* the ocean. In another sense, it is not the ocean; yet it is certainly not other than the ocean. In the same way, the human body is like foaming bubbles on the ocean waves. These are only inexact metaphors; but beyond making such metaphors, the only thing that the one who knows and tastes Reality can do is to remain quiet.

During one of Efendi's last sohbets in America, he was again asked about the "I" disappearing in the One (*fana*) and the non-dual state of *baka* that follows. He was asked if, at this point, one still has an individual will or one's servanthood. He responded:

> As there is no duality, one's service is from the attribute to the Essence. There is a meeting of flesh and soul (life). There is a meeting of soul within soul—the two are one. So it is with the attribute which is united with the Essence. They are neither separate nor wholly apart. There are two different ways of understanding unity: *wahdat as-shuhud*—the unity of witnessing, meaning the universe exists only as a reflection on the mirror of Truth—and *wahdat al-wujud*, the unity of all existence. But *wahdat al-wujud* is the better way of expressing it, because unless there is an existence, there is no reflection of a Being—there would be no image on the mirror, nor any mirror. So there is no witnessing or contemplating unless there is a Being reflected by an existence. Moment by moment, this mirror, which is the universe, receives grace from either your might (*jalal*) or your beauty (*jamil*), and from this reflection is derived either sorrow or pleasure.

Another person asked: "Does the Creator know the creation by means of the creation?" Efendi replied:

> Allah is above and beyond such limited means of knowledge. Allah had full knowledge of His creation prior to creating it. With a superficial reading of some verses of the Qur'an, one might get the impression that Allah knew His creation through the creation. There is such a passage in *Surat al-Mulk* (67:2) where it says "Allah has created life and death in order to see who will be successful in good deeds." But it is really meant to be read in the sense that Allah, Who already knows your nature, is testing your soul so that *you* will know. It is not that Allah needs to observe in order to find out what you are going

to do—the tests are not for the edification of Allah but for us, so that we might learn about ourselves. Allah reveals our level of servanthood through these tests, or we see and learn from the tests of others what their levels are, high or low. So the gnostic knows about the states of others by observing what they are going through, and they in turn also understand something about the gnostic by observing his tests, deeds and sufferings.

There is also a verse in Genesis (1:3-4) in the Old Testament where it says: "God created the light. . . and saw that it was good." If we thought that God was like a chemist in His lab who had to create something experimentally to find out whether or not it would work, and then decided it was good enough to remain, this would be a distorted understanding of the meaning of the text. Allah has all the perfect qualities and neither lacks anything nor needs tests to discover our stations. Anything that implies a lack of knowledge on God's part is attributing ignorance and imperfection to Allah and is an unacceptable interpretation, far beneath His majesty. Those who envision Allah as lacking in qualities are projecting their own shortcomings onto the divine. . . . Rather, these passages are always about the hidden treasure, the hidden qualities of humans which are waiting to be discovered, and not about Allah needing to know or discover. Allah's existence is known through the servant because if He hadn't created the creation there would be no one to search, find and know Allah. Otherwise Allah would know only Himself. . . . As the *waliyullah* says of God, "Neither are You known without me, nor do I exist without You." So existence comes from Allah, but the knowledge of Him, apart from His self-knowledge, comes from the servants of Allah.

Changing Hats: Reincarnation and Tawhid

During one of his sohbets, Efendi was asked: "Do the souls in the *Alam-i-Arwah*[64] ever appear more than once?" He replied:

> No, they only come once, according to our belief. There are certain mysteries on this subject of destiny which cannot be revealed. This much however can be said: Each time a body and soul leaves this planet, someone else, so to speak, dons the hat which has been left behind. Imagine a walnut tree whose walnuts fall to the ground and from them another walnut tree arises. When that walnut tree dies, another has been left to take its place, yet it is not the same walnut tree. It is not reincarnation. To give another example, I am a sheikh and have a sheikh's turban-crown. When I'm gone, someone else will come and pick up the crown and wear it, and continue my function and duties. All messengers, all sheikhs and teachers, who have somewhat of the same nature, same methods and teachings—their places are filled. A Moses goes and a Moses comes back; a Pharaoh goes and a Pharaoh comes back. The attributes are carried over and the function is filled; but it is not the same person. The attributes could appear in my son or my grandson, or my neighbor's son—it's a different matter; it's the filling of the space. Even the Prophet Muhammad, who was the last prophet, has his attributes inherited and his place filled by someone else, even though that person is not a prophet.
>
> There is no returning as a donkey or a snake. If beings had to be recycled that way, it would mean God is limited to a certain number of souls going and coming back repeatedly. One of the divine attributes of Allah is the Limitless One, *al-Wasi*. As *Wasi*, God never recreates anything He has already created. Even identical twins have different fingerprints and are not the same being. This filling of the place applies to everyone, but should not be understood as limited in respect to space and time. They may appear in Egypt, in America, or in China, but the attributes are acquired by another being.[56]

One evening after the dhikr ceremony, Muzaffer Efendi posed a question to those who had stayed for tea and sohbet: "If someone put a little poison in your food, and you ate it but had the belief that it would not kill you, would that belief save your life?" Most of the people answered, "No." Efendi then proposed: "How about if someone said *La illaha illallah*, but they refused to believe in it or accept its blessing, would the blessing contained in *La illaha illallah* still save them?" Most answered affirmatively. Efendi continued:

> Even if someone said it in imitation or without any faith in it, *La illaha illallah* would still save them from the fire of perdition. *Tawhid*, the phrase of unity, is a seed, and as you say it you are planting it in the ground. It will grow, even without your knowledge, and its sustenance will save you. For each *tawhid* you repeat, even in imitation, 5,000 past sins will be lifted from you.
>
> When the Prophet David was presented before Allah Most High in the Day of Judgment, he was shown an enormous scale where the balance of good deeds and sins were weighed. David asked: "What must be placed on the scale to even the balance?" Allah answered: "If on one side of the scale you balanced the entire universe, and on the other side the words *La illaha illallah,* the latter would tip the scale."
>
> Beyond what I said about 5,000 sins for each *tawhid*, here is Allah saying: "One *La illaha illallah* will outweigh the whole universe." There is only one single sin Allah will not forgive, which is *shirk* or duality. *Tawhid*, the phrase of unity, goes beyond any possibility of dualistically associating partners with Allah, because it says, "Nothing exists except the One, *Allah*." In our tradition, regardless of which prophet you believe in, you must first say *La illaha illallah* before you mention: *Muhammad ar-Rasulullah, Isa Ruh-Allah, Musa Kalimullah,*[66] or any of the other prophets. First, you must clearly see that nothing exists except Allah. Then after that, you can tie yourself to whatever religion you belong to.

The beginning of this endeavor is to recite the phrase of unity and, once said with heartfelt sincerity, Allah will lift all your sins. Not only will He forgive your sins, but, for the sake of *La ilaha illallah*, He will inform the angels: "On behalf of this servant of mine who sincerely proclaimed my unity, I have not only forgiven all his sins, but have transformed them all into good deeds." This is promised in the Qur'an. There Allah says, "If We so wish, We will transform all the bad deeds of our servants into good deeds."

On the Day of Divine Evaluation, the Prophet will be allowed to intercede for all souls who have even a grain of faith in their hearts. Then he will ask again for the sake of those left who have a grain faith in their hearts even as tiny as a mustard seed and they will be forgiven. Again the Prophet will prostrate before Allah and intercede for those who have even an atom of faith in their hearts. A fourth time he will intercede for those who simply once in their lives said, *La ilaha illallah*—even if they had no faith in their hearts. These last will be accepted, not for the Prophet's sake but for Allah's sake, because they proclaimed His unity.

Whether you believe this or not, know that it will be so. You may think that we are made of earth and that it will be dust to dust when we die, but it is not so. It is spring now, and nature is showing us how everything resurrects from the ground after it has died in winter. The spring for humanity is the great Day of Evaluation when we will be raised like plants from the ground. Those who say *La ilaha illallah* will win eternal salvation. Allah knows best. How thankful I am—and we should all be thankful—that Allah has gathered us here to say *tawhid* and that Allah has seen and heard our remembrance.

Asked about chanting dhikr internally (*qalbi*), Muzaffer Efendi replied:

Everyone has an exterior and an interior. The first attribute or name of Allah that we chanted in the standing dhikr was the name *Ya Hayy*, the Everliving, Deathless One, the Giver of Life. First we say it aloud with our mouths and our breath, outwardly, but finally it sinks into the heart so that you can't tell whether the sound is generated in your mouth, nose or ears, or in every pore and cell of the body. It is coming from your heart. The hearts of those who chant the name *Hayy*, the Everliving One, will not perish when all other hearts die. Their hearts will be joined with Allah. Others who haven't repeated God's Everliving name will indeed become ashes to ashes and dust to dust, but the heart which has said *Hayy* will endure forever.

"O Allah, Who has created this universe without template, I ask of You: establish my heart with the light of the knowledge of God." The highest level of the knowledge of God—*marifat*—is to know God, to see God and to Be God. There are four levels in one's development: *shariat, tarikat, hakikat* and *marifat*, the last being the knowledge of God—becoming one with God at the highest level. So we should pray that our hearts would be built with the light of the knowledge of union with the Divine, so that when other hearts die, our hearts will survive in tact. Pray this in whatever language you know.[67]

Muzaffer Efendi's Final Visits to America

Muzaffer Efendi giving sohbet in Yonkers, N.Y. (1984)

Muzaffer Efendi and his core group of Turkish disciples continued their semiannual visits to the United States until the end of 1984. During the fall visit in 1982, Efendi had resided downtown in Masjid al-Farah in an area separated off with curtains. One night during that stay, Efendi had become very ill, almost to the point of death. Given this unpleasant experience and the lack of privacy in the sleeping area at the mosque, Haydar made a search for more suitable and comfortable quarters before Efendi returned to America.

In the spring of 1983 a large stone house in Yonkers, New York, near Manhattan, was purchased by Haydar and Fariha to provide a permanent guest residence for Efendi and his senior Turkish followers during their subsequent visits to America. The estate provided spacious grounds and dozens of guest rooms on several floors, and a particularly expansive Tudor-style great room on the second floor, where everyone could gather with the sheikh. By the fall of 1983 it was ready for use. Efendi was delighted with the house and began to give sohbets there, often seated on a favorite burnt-orange divan under the windows on the south side of the central meeting room.

Fariha recalls how, after Efendi moved to Yonkers and began to invite people to his adopted home for spiritual discourse, the feeling of closeness with his spiritual family in the West grew more and more palpable, as though he was moving beyond formalities into a deeper state of spiritual intimacy.

It was also here, on the third floor of the Yonkers house that Safer Efendi and several other Turkish musicians stayed and, over a period of many weeks, produced music manuscript copies of almost all the well-known Turkish ilahis of that time, transcriptions which are still used by the Jerrahis to this day. The massive effort was aided by office copy equipment provided by Salik Schwartz, who, since Efendi's initial trip to America, had handled the sound equipment and taped all of Efendi's sohbets, dhikrs and musical concerts. According to the eminent Turkish singer, Sami Özer, Safer Efendi, during his lifetime, accumulated the largest collection of Sufi music in the world. In the early days, Safer Efendi lugged primitive recording equipment through villages all over Turkey, collecting on tape hundreds of old ilahis that had never been written down or recorded and would otherwise have been lost to posterity.

Amina Teslima, named after the mother of Hazrati Pir, is a vibrant Puerto-Rican-born sheikha in the Order who today resides in Mexico City. Around 1983, she joined the Jerrahi Order and was initially assigned to manage the Yonkers household. A television journalist who headed the News Bureau of the Spanish International Network in New York City, Amina was given permission to film a few of the public dhikrs at St. John the Divine (only short out-takes of the footage have survived).

After Efendi's passing, she transferred to Mexico City, where she organized a substantial community of Jerrahi dervishes who are still very active today. She also translated many of the Turkish ilahis into Spanish and produced several quality recordings of the Spanish ilahis in conjunction with various musicians in the Mexico City Jerrahi community.

Amina recalls that during the final years of Efendi's visits to America, particularly in 1983, the schedule of events in New York usually featured: Monday night *meshk*, an evening of singing ilahis, usually accompanied by musicians; Tuesday night public dhikr at the Cathedral of St. John the Divine; and a Wednesday concert with the Turkish musicians. Thursday night was the traditionally designated night for dhikr, held at Masjid al-Farah, followed by Friday noon prayers and *khutba*. Friday night generally featured teachings by Muzaffer Efendi; and on Saturday night the community would gather once again for dhikr at the Spring Valley tekke. Sundays were rest time.

During the times of question and answer after sohbet, dervishes occasionally told their dreams to the sheikh. If they were of a personal nature, they were told to Efendi privately. Sometimes he would offer brief interpretations, occasionally informing someone if their dream revealed that their spiritual level, or *makam*, had been raised. In such a case he might also change or add to their practice. Often, he would simply hear a dream without comment; and on occasion, if the dream was not propitious, he was even known to "erase" the dream or to open his palms and pray to Allah that the destiny of the dreamer would be changed from what was being shown in their dream.

Efendi recounted an interesting dream from Ottoman times in which a women dreamed that her son had been executed after having performed various unpleasant deeds. The mother went to the sheikh and told him the dream, but because she found the content so embarrassing, she attributed the dream to her neighbor's son. The sheikh asked her directly if this was actually her own son's dream rather than her neighbor's son, but she continued to insist that it was the dream of her neighbor's son. "In that case," the sheikh answered, "go and tell your neighbor that her son is going to be the prime minister of the Ottoman Empire." When the mother heard that, she objected, saying, "No, no! It really was my son's dream." The sheikh said, "I'm sorry but you insisted it was your neighbor's son's dream and now the interpretation has been given. Now it is he that is going to become the prime minister." Indeed, it came to pass that the neighbor's son became the prime minister.

In this same vein, Muzaffer Efendi pointed out that "sometimes, if you want to do something in life, but have no means, Allah brings it to pass for you in a dream. For instance, if you sincerely wished to build a hospital but don't have the money to do this, you may dream you did it and will be rewarded for your intention just as if you had done it. Sometimes, if there is in your destiny an accident or something undesirable, Allah may have you dream it instead, in order to protect you from it."

Speaking further on the mysteries of intention, Efendi added: "The rule is, one is not responsible for the impulses which cross one's heart. Even if you were to intend to do something evil and then decided against it and refrained, instead of deserving punishment for it, you will be rewarded." This is based in part on the Muslim and al-Buhkari hadith transmitted from the Prophet by Ibn 'Abbas:

> Whosoever intends to do a good deed but does not do it, Allah records it with Himself as a complete good deed; but if he intends it and does it, Allah records it with Himself as ten good deeds, up to seven hundred times, or more than that. But if he intends to do an evil deed and does not do it, Allah records it with Himself as a complete good deed; but if he intends it and

does it, Allah records it down as one single evil deed.

Efendi also quoted a similar saying from the Qur'an (6:160): "Whoever performs a good deed will be credited with the equivalent of ten good deeds, and whoever performs a bad deed will only have one bad deed counted against them."

Efendi added that while one's good deeds normally stop accruing at death, if one has started an orphanage or built a hospital, a school, a library or some other service that continues to help humanity after one's passing, one continues to receive the merit of these good deeds posthumously. He mentioned that if one couldn't afford to build a hospital or clinic, one could pray for its manifestation or make some effort to try to bring it into being, which also has merit according to one's intentions. Returning to the subject of dreams, Efendi explained:

> The value of true dreams are 1/46th of the value of prophetic revelation. The revelations to the prophets first started in the form of dreams. For instance, the command to Abraham, peace be upon him, to sacrifice his son came in a dream. Joseph dreamed of eleven stars, the sun and moon prostrating to him, and he reported the dream to his father, Jacob. Many important people throughout history have received powerful dreams which have come true and are now part of our historical legacy.
>
> Since there is actually nothing in front of your eyes to be viewed while you sleep and dream, what are the images that appear and who is seeing the dream? There are four main souls in the body: the vegetable soul, the animal soul, the human soul and sultan soul. We should also mention the secret soul, *ruhu sirr*, which is located neither inside nor outside the body. These different souls in the body dream different types of dreams. For instance, from the level of the vegetable and animal soul one has dreams stimulated by indigestion, hunger, thirst or sexual desire. Therefore, you dream of food, water, going to the bathroom or a sexual encounter and these satisfy the physical part of the body. In your sleep, the lower souls extend out of

> the body like a lightbeam from a flashlight, attempting to fulfill their needs—searching for the bathroom, the refrigerator, or whatever. Of course, they can't actually open the door of the refrigerator and eat real food.
>
> As for the higher souls, the human soul dreams are usually interpreted non-literally, as something other than what appears in the dream. For instance, if in a human soul dream, one dreams of excretion, it might be interpreted as wealth; or if you see a fish it might symbolize fertility. If you dream of a snake, it might mean money is coming to you, but with envious people observing it. Now, these are more ordinary dreams interpretations. If you were a dervish and dreamed these things, it might have a different meaning in the interpretation of the sheikh in the context of the tarikat. If the sultan soul dreams, its dream is straight-forward and clear. These are angelic-level dreams. The sultan soul radiates light from the body which falls upon angels, and thus receives information from the angelic realms. In the highest, secret soul, the dreams appear with the attribute of peace, of *salaam*. If a king and a shepherd dream the same dream, their dream will have a very different interpretation.[68]

Efendi also mentioned that in dreams, each of the seven levels is associated with a particular color: blue for the mineral soul, red for the vegetable soul, green for the animal soul, white for the human soul, yellow for the kingly soul and black for the sacred soul.

Sheikh Nur noted that Muzaffer Efendi would not normally apprise a dervish about the spiritual level of his or her dream, as the interest in finding out one's level tends to be an egoic concern. He related how one dervish sister related a powerful dream to Muzaffer Efendi and was told that she had moved up a level. She was happy to hear this but wanted to know what her level was now. Efendi explained that he usually didn't tell but, when she was very insistent, he finally told her. She was crestfallen when her level turned out to be lower than she had hoped, and even quit coming to the Sufi gatherings for a brief time, confirming

Efendi's conviction that it is better not to tell.

Muzaffer also used to joke about vaguely remembered dreams. He recounted how one person went to his sheikh and recounted a dream in which he thought he remembered a light, but he wasn't sure what color or where it was, and then he thought maybe someone else came but he couldn't remember whether they were male or female. The sheikh stopped him and said, "I must tell you that your dream forebodes a great punishment coming to you!" Smiling, Efendi continued: "But because of the vagueness of the dream, I cannot tell you how severe it will be or whether this punishment is going to come sooner or later, or even in this life or in the hereafter."

In the same vein, Muzaffer Efendi recounted how the great 'Abbasid caliph, Harun ar-Rashid was visited by Azra'il, the angel of death, and informed that his death was coming. The angel held up five fingers and then departed. Harun wasn't sure what to make of this. Did it mean in five minutes, five days, five years or what? The caliph did not die anytime soon, but all of this uncertainty about when it would happen greatly tormented him. Efendi concluded with a chuckle, "It is better not to know."

Those who attended Efendi's talks would often bring Efendi gifts of fruits, flowers, and cartons of cigarettes which he would distribute to the dervishes as a kind of blessing. An American dervish named 'Alia relates how, one day, Efendi was distributing ten dollar bills. 'Alia had a background in Buddhist studies and had a great appreciation for simplicity and emptiness. She had great love for Efendi and had received much spiritual blessing from him; as such, she didn't really desire a material gift from him. When she saw Efendi coming her way, she inwardly hoped he would not give her any money. He passed by her and handed the rest of the money to some other people. Then he began distributing cigarettes to the smokers, tossing and handing them out until they were all gone and he was left holding an empty carton. He looked over at 'Alia and handed the empty carton to her. She happily received it and felt it was the perfect gift.

Fariha once asked Efendi if he would prescribe a *salawat* for her to repeat, as he had for a few others. Later, he came back with a drawing of the Sandals of the Prophet, inscribed in Arabic with one of the most noble *salawats* or blessings on the Prophet, a supplication which also appears in the Jerrahi morning litany. Muzaffer Efendi explained that the Ottoman sultans used to wear this salawat, folded up in their turbans, for protection. Fariha feels that the salawat goes beyond something for her personally, and is really a gift to the American lovers.

Haydar and Fariha Friedrich with Muzaffer Efendi in Yonkers (1984)

The *salawat* surrounding the sandals is translated into English as follows:

> *O Allah Most High, please bless our Master and Prophet Muhammad among the first, and bless our Master and Prophet*

among the last, and bless our Master and Prophet at every moment and at all times, and bless our Master and Prophet in the highest assembly until the Day of Judgment. And bless all of the prophets and messengers and the servants of Allah and the righteous ones and those who follow them among the people of the heavens and the earths with spiritual perfection until the Day of Judgment, and resurrect us and have mercy on us together with them, O Most Merciful of the Merciful.

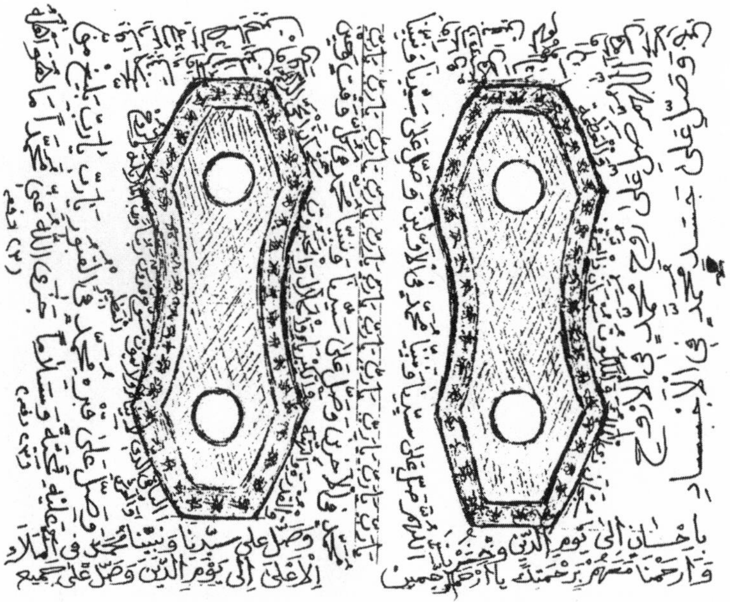

Salawat with sandals of the Prophet drawn by Muzaffer Efendi

During Efendi's last three visits to America, the house in Yonkers was filled with people almost on a daily basis. According to Fariha, who still resides on the estate, around 50 to 75 people a day would come daily, often with as many as 100 for dinner, made possible with a whole staff of cooks. She says it was like a constantly functioning tekke for Efendi where he could receive visitors and dervishes. The musicians would sit opposite Efendi on red couches where they would sing or compose. Efendi loved the intimacy of the place and wanted people to come there, scaling back his visits to the masjid in downtown Manhattan to about twice a week.

Not only were there frequent concerts by the Turkish musicians, but once Efendi and everyone present were treated to a dance performance by the Concheros from Mexico. One of Efendi's students, Merhaban, was a Conchero dancer and arranged for the whole group to dance in full Native American costumes, with their short shirts with conches and shells on their ankles. Efendi was so delighted by the performance that he asked for an encore.

The direcction of prayer in the main hall at the residence in Yonkers where Efendi stayed (photo by the author)

In one of his last talks at Yonkers, Muzaffer Efendi was asked about music and the effects of various music scales or makams on the psyche. For those readers who may not be familiar with the system of Turkish and Arabic musical makams, these modes are somewhat like the major and minor scales of Western music, only in Middle Eastern music there are far more musical scales in common use. There are as many as twelve main makams (*makamat*) in Turkish music, some, such as the Hijaz makam, dating back to the time of the Prophet. The mystic hymns are sung with melodies in various makams and even the five times a day prayers are begun with a melodious call to prayer, each time of the day having its own recommended makam. Makam is also the word used to refer to one's spiritual level or station. Here Efendi mentions some of these considerations in relation to music:

> Musical modes or makams have a very close relation to the time, place, audience, season and time of day. For instance, mountain people like the Hüseyni makam while people from the plains are very much impressed by either Hijaz or Uşşak. The Rast makam is very good for ailments of the digestive system. Music in Segah, Saba or Dugah is very effective before sunrise. At noon, Rast, Hüseyni or Suzinak are best. In the afternoon, Nihavent, Hüseyni or Uşşak is most effective. In the early evening, Segah or Hüzzam is favored and for the time of the night prayers, Hijaz, Segah, Nihavent, or Hüzzam is best. When we travel to Europe and the West, we often perform in the Nihavent makam because their modes are similar to this and they enjoy it very much. Albanians prefer Nikriz. Kurds prefer a certain version of the Hüseyni mode. Every nation naturally has a preferred makam.
>
> Music and dance can be of either a carnal or spiritual nature. Music and dance that addresses the carnal body leads one to carnal, sexually provocative dancing, but spiritual dance and music that addresses the soul leads one to Truth. Disco music addresses itself to the animal part of the soul that is made of clay, but *dhikrullah* evokes the higher aspects of the soul; so

> one performing the ceremony of dhikr is approaching Allah and is not meant to experience lust as a result of this kind of spiritual dance. The way one responds all depends on one's inner states and maturity. You see, if a spiritually immature man and woman are dancing together, this will bring out their lustful inclinations, but if they are spiritually mature and on the way to perfection, neither of them will have lustful inclinations and their tendencies will be toward Truth and finding union with Truth. Sexual attraction between a man and a woman is a necessary part of life, and when rightfully applied, it is a desirable quality. However, when a feeling of lust arises within one while performing a religious ceremony or ritual, then this creates a veil between oneself and Truth.
>
> This is the reason why in mosques, when Muslims are doing their ritual prayers, the men line up in rows separate from the women's lines. The separation is not because of anything inherently wrong with the men or women, but because if there are any lustful feelings or inclinations toward the opposite sex during worship, this becomes a veil between the servant and Truth. Sex can be sacred too, but if it comes into one's heart during ritual worship, it becomes a veil.[69]

As his visits to America continued over a span of six years, many different types of people were drawn to Muzaffer Efendi, including Islamic scholars and writers. Imam Feisal Abdul Rauf was a talented individual of this type who encountered Muzaffer Efendi and was profoundly affected by him. Born in Kuwait in 1948 into an Egyptian family steeped in religious scholarship, Feisal was educated in England, Malaysia and America, with a degree in physics from Columbia University in New York. In April of 1983, after the opening of Masjid al-Farah, Imam Feisal came and met Muzaffer Efendi and was invited to attend the Thursday dhikrs. Efendi was quite taken by him. Thus, when Efendi returned to America in October of 1983, he sent one of his interpreters to ask Imam Feisal to meet privately with him. When they met, Muzaffer told him,"I'd like you to become the imam of this mosque." Imam Feisal accepted immediately, saying later that the offer was "not something you can reject." In the introduction of his book *Islam: A Search for Meaning*,[70] Imam Feisal mentions one of his early encounters with Muzaffer Efendi:

> In April of that year, when I first met him, I visited the mosque one Friday evening. I had brought some fresh dates as a gift to him. His talk over, he changed from his outer robe into his traveling clothes, proceeded to walk towards the exit with a crowd of dervishes following him, and stopped a couple of feet in front of me. He glanced at me with a wry smile and began fishing in his trouser pockets. I knew he was looking for something to give me, and I remember telepathically saying, "That's very kind of you, but you really don't have to." He telepathically insisted, and with a glimmer in his eyes indicating that he found something worth giving, he fished out a roll of Rolaids and graciously presented it to me. In our Eastern culture, to refuse a gift is bad manners, and I therefore accepted it with gratitude, chuckling at the Rolaids; as a teenager I had suffered from gastritis, a condition which stayed with me till I was nearly thirty.

From 1983 to 2007, Imam Feisal served as the imam of Masjid al-Farah. Although there was usually one other imam assigned to the mosque, it was Imam Feisal who preached the sermons at the Juma prayers on most Fridays for the next 13 years, always inspiring the congregation with his eloquence and scholarly erudition. He has transmitted two important sayings of Efendi: "A river passes through many countries and each claims it for its own. But there is only one river." And: "Sufism without Islam is like a candle burning in the open without a lantern."

Continuing in the spirit of Muzaffer Efendi, Imam Feisal has dedicated his life to building bridges between Muslim perspectives and Western sensibilities, and has become a leader in the effort to build religious pluralism and integrate Islam into modern society. In 1997, he founded the American Society for Muslim Advancement (ASMA Society), and also became the architect of the Cordoba Initiative, an inter-religious blueprint for improving relations between the Muslim World and the West. Particularly, since the 2001 attacks on the World Trade Center, Imam Feisal has emerged as an important public speaker in America and a tireless advocate for ecumenical solutions in the ideological struggles between Palestine and Israel, as well as between traditional Muslim countries and the West, appearing as a moderate Islamic spokesman on CNN, BBC, PBS, NBC and the other major American networks.

Imam Feisal Abdul Rauf

His fame soared for a time during the 2010 election season, when his plans to build Park51, a 13-story Islamic community center containing a mosque two blocks from the site of the World Trade Center, became the controversial subject of an American media frenzy, revealing a great ongoing reservoir of post-9/11 fear and resentment in the collective American psyche—even for peaceful, moderate expressions of Islam. (The Park51 building plans eventually fell through.) In recent years, Imam Feisal has authored a number of successful books, such as *What's Right with Islam is What's Right with America* (HarperCollins, 2004) and collaborated on collected works such as *The Universal Spirit of Islam: From the Koran and Hadith* (World Wisdom, 2006)

Another person who was deeply inspired by Muzaffer Efendi during his final visits to the United States was Imam Wali Nureddin, a young African American brother from Harlem who began to attend Efendi's sohbets and dhikrs around 1983 or 1984. Wali had a background in the teachings of the Nation of Islam but in time felt himself being drawn closer to Islamic Sufism, the path of mystic love. Because of the crowds and the demands on Efendis' time, Wali was not immediately able to converse with the sheikh. In the meantime, his long-held plans to make hajj to Mecca came together and he was able to travel there in 1984. The journey, however, would evoke an unexpected state of bewilderment for the pilgrim.

Wali relates that when at last he laid eyes on the ka'ba and made the seven ritual circles around it, he experienced a strong, unsettling feeling that somehow *this was not the true ka'ba*. Wali says that only after he returned to America and took *bayat* with Muzaffer Efendi, did the full implications of his insight about the ka'ba become clear: for him the true ka'ba—that for which he had been spiritually seeking—was in the West, in his sheikh and in the sacred shrine of the human heart—of all humanity.

On Dec. 24, 1984, during a gathering of the dervishes at Masjid al-Farah, Efendi's powerful voice broke the silence with an urgent question: "Did I teach you *La ilaha illallah*?" After some of those present answered "yes," Efendi repeated the question in a more urgent tone. The answer "yes" filled the room more strongly. Then a third time, Efendi asked, "Did I teach you *La ilaha illallah*?"

Hearing a strong, unanimous "Yes!" from everyone present, Efendi sat back and relaxed. He knew that the time of his own transition was not far off and that he had accomplished his mission in America. His passing, he realized would be difficult for those with whom he was joined so deeply in love. He told them in advance, "Do not look for me in my tomb, but in the hearts of my dervishes."

Ragip Bey stands behind Muzaffer Effendi and his wife, Baji Sultan. (photo: James Wentzy)

During his last visit to America in 1984, Efendi was suffering from rapidly deteriorating health problems. He had given up cigarette smoking at the advice of his physician and was letting his beard grow out. One night, he became so ill that he feared that he might expire in his bed right then and there. Still maintaining his sense of humor, he joked with the doctor the next day and quipped to his wife that perhaps they should return to Istanbul before the Americans ended up having to send him back in a box. But with medical treatment he began to feel better.

Efendi's devoted personal attendant, Ragip Bey, was also ill and didn't make the fall trip; he passed away in Istanbul in early November 1984. Ragib was the son of Efendi's former music teacher, Ismail Hakkı, and they had been close friends since their early days. After losing contact for many years they were re-united in the late nineteen-sixties and at that point Ragib became not only Efendi's disciple, but volunteered to serve from then on as his personal valet. Efendi mentioned his passing and told how Ragip Bey had for years said to him, "May Allah extend your life by giving you a share of my life." Efendi revealed that he began to feel much stronger—almost like a young man—as soon as Ragip Bey passed. "Maybe his prayers were accepted," Efendi said. "I stayed and he passed away. I didn't ask him to make this supplication, but if his wife finds out about this she may come and bang me on the head with her shoe. Words are like seeds planted in a spiritual field. Once they are uttered they cannot be retracted. Sometimes these things do happen."

Then Efendi mentioned how the venerable saint, also named Ismail Hakkı, was asked by his dervishes to write a spiritual commentary on Rumi's *Masnavi.* He wrote one of seven proposed volumes, only to have it revealed to him that his time on earth was soon to end. He explained the situation to his dervishes, and one of them volunteered to offer his life to Allah so that the sheikh would have time enough to complete the commentary. They said a *Fatiha* for the dervish and he passed away within minutes, while the sheikh lived just long enough to finish his seven-volume book.[71]

Muzaffer Efendi's health remained relatively good throughout the rest of the trip. He stayed until Christmas of 1984, and then returned to Turkey, while his daughter stayed on in the Yonkers house for the winter. What follows is an excerpt from one of Ashki Muzaffer's final sohbets at the Masjid al-Farah on the subject of Divine love:

> By nature, human beings have been given both arrogance and humility—the knowledge that we are in ourselves nothing and are totally dependent on Allah. Humanity has also been given anger and, in opposition to that, softness and gentleness. Some of these qualities are human qualities, some are animal qualities, but all are necessary when used in the right proportion at the right time. When this is the case, a person exists in a truly human state. Neither devils nor angels know what love is—only Adam was worthy of being granted love—because love is the mount on which humans rise to reach and find Truth.
>
> The path that leads you closest to Allah is worship and devotions to Allah, offered freely with love and affection. Even the Angel Gabriel does not have love. I realize that some people equate the word love primarily with lust and sexual intercourse, but this is not the love of which we speak. If it were, then donkeys would rank first in the field of love. Divine love is beyond description—it has to be tasted for oneself. It is the most notable and desirable attribute which can be found in a human being. This love and affection is the point of union between servanthood and Lordship. When one finds true love for the Divine, then neither the eight paradises nor the spiritual pleasures they contain will be desired; nor will the world and what is in it have any attraction for one.
>
> Allah has crowned the universe with humanity. We always find joy and companionship with other human beings. Why? Because people are mirrors of Truth—mirrors in which Allah's manifestation is reflected. Allah has created humans as mirrors for Himself, mirrors which are the jewels of the universe....[72]

Muzaffer Efendi's Last Days

Muzaffer Efendi in 1984

In late December, Muzaffer Efendi said his farewells and returned to Istanbul. He spent time with his family, met with his followers, and worked at the bookstore, apparently in good health. Safer Efendi recalls how, years previously, he had made a supplication after the manner of Fahreddin Efendi, saying, "O Lord, let us come to you in faith, and may you take us to You without much pain." Muzaffer Efendi said, "What are you talking about? Ask Allah not to give us *any* pain!" And indeed, he left this world without any extended illness. According to Hafiz Ismail, Efendi had added on this same occasion: "You'll see. I am going to pass away without any pain and I will even dance before I die."

On February 8, 1985, the Friday before Muzaffer Efendi's passing, Ismail reports that he had a strong feeling that he should take off from his work at the Beyazid mosque and go hear Efendi preach and lead Juma prayers in the small Jemili Han mosque. He attended Efendi's Friday sermon and midway through the talk, heard him say, "I know that you are not paying too much attention to what I am saying, but you should listen because this is the last Friday you are going to hear me speak. I won't be here after this; but don't worry! My place will not be left empty. Someone will come and take care of things after me." He continued, alluding to a local cemetery, "I have been invited to go to Edirnekapi and I will be going there soon." Then Efendi added in Arabic, "Did I make my meaning clear?"

Efendi went on to tell part of the story of Mansur Al- Hallaj's passing, explaining why Mansur had said, "*Ana'l haqq*"—"I am the absolute Truth." However, Efendi didn't complete the story of Mansur during his sermon, but elaborated on it more in the bookstore that afternoon. Then Efendi tarried a while, saying goodbye to everyone and seeming very happy, as Ismail recalls.

On Monday evening, Efendi attended the meshk as usual, sang the liahis and was very lively, making everyone laugh. The next morning at breakfast, as his wife, Baji Sultan recalls, Efendi told her and their son Junayd—then 15 years old—that he would pass that evening. He advised Junayd that he wanted him to graduate from school. He also recounted the dream that had come to him during the night. In the dream, Efendi found himself among his dervishes sitting at a banquet table full of food, but he had no more desire for food and, acting quite out of character, none of his beloved followers offered him anything to eat.

Baji Sultan relates that Muzaffer had been hinting for months at his own passing, telling her, "Your Army time is over," or "Your job in the army is finished," but at the time she didn't fully grasp his meaning. He was also commenting to others how the sun was getting very close to the horizon. Junayd also recalls that during Ramadan, the previous summer, Efendi had stated that it would be his last. He had also made a rare Fatiha prayer for himself at dhikr the previous Thursday, explaining that he sent it ahead so that it would meet him in the next world. Recently, he had shown Junayd his hands saying, "These hands have washed thousands of corpses." He added that Junayd would in turn wash his body, but first Efendi would "wash himself."

Efendi in airport returning to Turkey

On the morning of Tuesday, February 12, 1985, Efendi went into the bookstore at the covered bazaar as usual and was there most of the day. His secretary, Ibrahim, relates that in the afternoon, around the time for *'asr* prayers, he witnessed a strange visitation by two unusual men who entered the shop, and spoke not a word but just gazed intensely at Efendi, who immediately turned toward the Ka'ba and began to make prayers. Ibrahim understood them to be angels in human form whose presence signaled that Efendi's time had come and quickly began to make his own prayers as well. Muzaffer Efendi left the shop early and asked Ibrahim to take care of closing everything up. He embraced everyone there, glanced one last time around the shop and said, "I leave everything entrusted to Allah."

According to his family, Efendi did not mention any unusual encounter at the bookstore when he came home, but remained as certain as he had been in the morning that he would not survive the night. Yet, he was in good spirits, even dancing with joy that evening, according to one report. Junayd recalls that his father seemed especially jubilant on his final night, prompting him to inquire why. Efendi responded simply, "This is my best day."

At dinner, Efendi asked for his favorite dessert, *suhlach*, a milk and rice dish his wife often made, which he ate with great satisfaction. According to Baji Sultan, she and Efendi stayed up late that night reading together. He also encouraged Junayd to stay up with him—he was very affectionate, hugging and caressing him—but as it got late, Junayd became very sleepy and finally went to bed. Efendi and his wife often read and studied books together, such as Rumi's *Masnavi*, and on this night they sat together and read past midnight.

Sometime around 1 or 2 AM, Efendi put the book down from their reading and offered salat, while Baji Sultan waited across from him in their large living room. She thinks this was probably the *Isha* salat—which he often did very late—but it is possible that it was the extra *tahajjud* night prayers. At the conclusion of his prayers, Efendi was kneeling on his prayer carpet, reciting the *tesbih*, with which he normally ended the prayers, when his wife heard him call out very forcefully, "Allah, Allah, Allah!" Then, still kneeling, he exhaled very deeply and his head slumped forward toward his shoulder and chest. Baji Sultan cried out and ran to his side and held him.

Efendi praying in his Istanbul home

Immediately his mother-in-law, who was living with them, came in from the next room and called Baji Sultan's brother who lived nearby. Safer Efendi, who also lived in the area, was called and quickly came over. At first they thought it was a heart attack, but when they realized the sheikh had quit breathing, they laid him out on the floor. They didn't wake Junayd and it was very hard on him when he woke in the morning to find his father had already passed during the night. Efendi had told Baji Sultan for years that he would die in her arms and indeed this came to pass. This occurred during the early hours of Wednesday morning, January 13, 1985. Officially, Efendi passed at age 69, though he may well have been a few years older, according to his family.

His secretary, Ibrahim, says he received a phone call asking him to come over to Efendi's house around 2:30 AM. Though it had been warm the previous day, by this time it was 16 degrees outside and a snowstorm had just begun to fall on the city. Also, around the time Efendi passed, a great tree in his yard fell over. A doctor and other disciples were called as well, but by the time they arrived Efendi's spirit had already passed into the Realm of Beauty. His body was taken to the lodge at Karagümrük to be washed and prepared for burial.

When the ablutions were complete, his body was placed in a box. Then they waited for Efendi's daughter, Ayşe, and various followers and friends to arrive from America for the burial. Years before his passing, Muzaffer Efendi had been brought two small stones from the soil of Karbala, the site of Imam Husayn's martyrdom. Efendi had said, "When I die, place these stones on my eyes. If tears of blood come forth, you will know I am a true lover of the *Ahl-i-bayt*—the Prophet and his immediate family: 'Ali, Fatima, and his grandsons, Hasan and Husayn.

Presently, one of Efendi's long-time followers arrived carrying the sheikh's last will and testament, as well as these two stones from Karbala. He placed them on Efendi's cheeks just below the tear ducts of his eyes as the sheikh's corpse lay in state in the wooden coffin. To the astonishment of all who witnessed it, Efendi's cheeks began to blush as warm tears flowed out of his eyes toward the stones. Amazingly, the tears did not flow with the force of gravity out of the corner of his eyes, as one might expect, but flowed copiously down his blessed cheeks toward his mouth. It was an emotional moment for those who witnessed it, and they soon veiled Efendi's face because they could not bear to continue to watch him weep.[73] Later, just before Efendi was put into the grave, his son, Junayd, observed that his father's tears had turned to blood. Nineteen years earlier, Safer Efendi had similarly observed pools of blood in Fahreddin Efendi's casket hours after he himself had gently placed stones from Karbala upon the sheikh's eyes.

The next day, Muzaffer Efendi's funeral services were held at the Fatih Mosque. He was to be buried with the other Jerrahis sheikhs and Pir Nureddin Jerrahi in the lodge at Karagümrük. As the funeral procession returned to the burial site—the casket and turban lifted shoulder high above the people—the funeral crowds began to swell until thousands jammed the streets, including riot police sent to keep order. Snow was falling as the streets were filled with walls of humanity, including dervishes from America and other countries, all there to pay their last respects to a great teacher and friend of Allah, the Emir of Divine Love to modern humanity, Haji Muzaffereddin Ashki al-Halveti al-Jerrahi.

The tomb of Muzaffer Efendi in Karagümrük

AFTERWORD

Much has occurred in the decades since Muzaffer Efendi's passing. The Halveti-Jerrahi Order has continued to flourish, not only in America, but in new centers around the world, its fire of love spreading undiminished. A number of other principals in this account have since passed into the Realm of Beauty, among them Safer Efendi (1926-1999) and Sheikh Nur/Lex Hixon (1940-1995), may their souls be ennobled. We have not attempted to cover developments in the tarikat after the time of Muzaffer Efendi—the process of assimilating Sufism into Western culture will take many years to find its proper balance and its authentic Western mode of expression. Meanwhile, during the course of this book, we have endeavored to convey some sense of the various directions taken by those entrusted by Muzaffer Efendi to carry on the teaching in the West.

I would like to close with an account of a dream, recounted in 1993 by Sheikh Nur, which was the dream of an American dervish who lived in the Ozarks and had never met Muzaffer Efendi. Nur relates that in the dream the dervish found himself with Muzaffer Efendi where Efendi is *now*.

Muzaffer Efendi was sitting at the end of a long table and the dervish came up and made a prostration, in reverence, beside Efendi. Muzaffer Efendi leaned over and touched the dervish's forehead and three places on his back, and the dervish went into a state of ecstacy. Kneeling there, he realized that he should ask something of Efendi, as this was a great opportunity. So he asked: "Efendi, what are you doing now? What is your function?" and Efendi answered: "I'm meeting with a lot of souls that are going down, descending into time and space, and I'm planting a lot of seeds in them. I'm also meeting with a lot of other souls who are coming back and clarifying many things for them." Then he added something that sounds very typical of Efendi: "I'm saying a lot of Fatihas for a lot of people."

May the infinite sweetness of the good pleasure of Allah rest upon all humanity, and may the light of Divine Love illuminate the heart of each one who has endeavored to read this humble account. Amin.

POSTSCRIPT

In the Overflowing Divine Compassion and Love

I am very grateful to the author of this book, Sheikh Muhammad Jamal, for inviting me to participate in his work with my personal account. Please forgive me for any mistakes, oversights or omissions. This account is just one ray of the huge light that was Muzaffer Efendi, may he be embraced in the most beautiful Divine peace.

On a day of heavy spring snow in April, Haydar and I stepped for the first time into the living room of Tosun Baba and Jamila Baci's home in Spring Valley, NY, where the Sheikh was living during his stay in America. And there he was, on the couch surrounded by his dervishes, singing his love to Allah with every cell of his body and soul. I saw the living Jesus with his disciples before me, and without choice I became his, wrapped in his love, his life, and his destiny.

From then on Haydar and I stayed on Efendi's side as much as we could, in America, on travel and in Turkey—from the spring of 1978 when he first set foot on American soil until December 24 when he left for the last time. During this time Haydar was inspired to put in place several of the structures and venues that served Efendi and the community in his latter years, such as the Masjid al Farah in New York City and the Dergah home in Yonkers.

At Efendi's bookstore in Istanbul

In Istanbul we sat in his bookstore every afternoon in the wooden chairs to the right of his desk reserved for visitors. In this hub of humanity we watched as people came and left, some coming from across the world to meet him and some wandering in thinking this was just another bookstore in the book bazaar. And every day his closer dervishes came after work to be with him, to kiss his generous hand and to receive his baraka. We sat for hours. And I gazed at him for hours, internally moving in a deep dance of joy and at the same time feeling intensely the pain of my own imperfections cooking in the cauldron of his love. There was no other place to be on earth than in this mystical cooking pot, sitting in these wooden chairs a few feet from Efendi in his small, crowded bookstore. Nothing on earth was more attractive than his company, nothing more beautiful and divine than his presence. It was through his presence that we traveled the path of the heart, it was in his presence that we were absorbed into Divine life. The science of Sufism unveiled its secrets in his presence. The path to Allah could not be more direct or more beautiful. Wherever Efendi was, God was revealed.

Park Hill, Yonkers, a birth place of the new spiritual community in America.

It is April 1983. Overflowing with exuberance and joy, Muzaffer Efendi has just arrived from Istanbul with his beloved wife Mehlika, his daughter Ayşe, (Muhammad Junayd remained in school on this visit), and more than twenty Turkish dervishes and musicians. For the first time he steps into the house on Park Hill that is to become his home and Dergah in America for the remainder of his life. This dwelling, which seems to have been destined for him, was built by a visionary Quaker at the turn of the 20th Century. It was ample enough to contain the large group traveling twice a year from Istanbul and staying two months at each visit. The Spring Valley home/tekke of Sheikh Tosun Baba and Jamila Baci who had been devotedly hosting Efendi and the dervishes and visitors in the early years, could no longer hold the growing size of the new community forming around this Sufi master of love. By now, approximately fifty to seventy visitors were coming daily to see him and to share a meal and a feast of mystical wisdom.

Efendi traveled only with the divine permission that came through dream. He came to America in the last seven years of his life as a culmination of his life work, for a new spiritual awareness was arising here. In America he imparted Shariat, the luminous outer form of Islam, Tariqat, the mystic path of the heart in a community of love, Haqiqat, direct transmission of the truth, and Marifat, the perfect embodiment of the Divine attributes in human form and in human life. Efendi felt that here in America the sacred lineage of 124,000 Prophets, of which the Prophet Muhammad (pbuh) was the confirming seal, would continue to flourish. It was here that Sufism, the true face of Islam, would spread.

Efendi's temperament was well suited to the people of America who were themselves from all different cultures and nationalities. He was a naturally frank, open and spontaneous being, and he enjoyed the frankness and spontaneity of Americans and the relaxed social atmosphere in the gatherings of those who came to see him. He valued the American sense of justice and the commitment to human rights and the rights of the individual—all of which he saw as signs of the spirit of Islam. This prompted him to say one day in Yonkers that the guiding light of Islam which had flourished so magnificently in the East had come to the West, to America in particular. Efendi admired the level of spiritual intelligence in the American people, and he was enamored of their thirst for God and their quest for spiritual knowledge. For this he became their servant and devoted friend, and so there grew a spirit of friendship, joy and spiritual intimacy within the new community developing around him.

This does not mean that Efendi unreservedly accepted American culture. He was astonished and pained by the great amount of waste in America, both of materials and of food. One year he took with him back to Istanbul a large empty glass bottle because he did not want it to be thrown away. And food was sacred. It was a gift of God and intended to be consumed gratefully and shared generously with others. Efendi had personally experienced periods of hunger in his youth when he was alone supporting his aging mother with whom he lived, and he had witnessed the impoverishment and hunger in his country following the dismemberment of the Ottoman Empire and the World Wars. He never began a meal without *Bismillahirrahmanirrahim*, in the Name of the All Compassionate, and he always concluded with *La ilaha illallah* and prayers of gratitude to his Lord and blessings on the cook and the sources of food. He instructed us to pray, "O Allah may this food bring strength and healing to my body and light to my heart and consciousness." Not even a cup of water was drunk without giving thanks.

We had much to learn. Yet, despite our shortcomings Efendi loved us, and it was his love that conquered every other condition. The love that we had read about in the Gospels and other mystic traditions, but had never tasted, or had tasted but never fully experienced, this love was here unstoppable. Love drew us to him every day, and this love erased the boundaries of religion, culture, age and gender. Love absorbed us into a mystical body, a Sufi community of lovers of God that had a life of its own and was moved, nourished and guided by Love. Efendi was the living Jesus, and we were the disciples. We were the companions of the Bridegroom who did not toil or fast but who kept constant company with the Bridegroom. This was the direct way to God—complete absorption of our hearts in the Divine Presence manifesting through the grace of Efendi.

Every day one could drive up from the city to the house on the hill, enter the open door and climb the wide curving staircase which gave directly onto the large living room with high ceilings where Efendi was sitting. He might be speaking intimately with someone through the help of a translator, or telling a story to the visitors or singing ilahis with the musicians. Whatever burden one had been carrying disappeared instantly in the ocean of love surrounding this magnificent being called Efendi. In the ecstatic atmosphere surrounding him one could openly be a lover of God and humanity without reservation. One could cry out to Allah in the ilahis and dhikr, feel immersed in Allah's embrace sitting with this man of Truth, and deepen one's knowledge every day through the subtle spiritual transmissions coming from his heart. One could hug one's companions, sit shoulder to shoulder on the rich red carpet, and openly express one's holy love to others. It felt that only here, in the presence of this mystic guide could one truly be oneself.

This community under the banner of Love was immensely diverse. Youth, artists, elders, priests, rabbis, imams, scholars of religion, Native Americans, wealthy business people, homeless poor and simple lovers were all gathered together in the orbit of Efendi. No worldly divisions were felt as everyone related to each other through their shared humanity, naturally and joyfully. And within this group the Turkish Babas, some of whom had been loyal dervishes for over 40 years, would hover protectively like spiritual mothers, radiating light, praying with every breath, attending to guests, and always anticipating Efendi's call. Sometimes they would banter with him and humor him if the atmosphere became heavy. They were highly evolved spiritual adepts and they were among his closest allies in transmitting the spiritual path in Turkey and abroad. His life in America would not be possible without them. They were his mystic body and he would know instantly if one of them was missing.

Often, to lighten things up and add a little surprise and humor, Efendi would toss cigarettes into the laps of the dervishes and guests gathered around him. He had a precise aim and he would delight the visitors with this attention. Whether they smoked or not, they could feel that these little flying gifts were gestures of love toward them and transmissions from heart to heart. And sometimes Efendi would just burst into singing. When he sang his whole being sang. He loved the ilahis, and composed many himself. He said that music was natural to the soul and loved by the dervish heart for it carries the vibration of Allah's original call to humanity in pre-eternity, "Am I not your Lord and Lover?" And all the souls without exception fell into ecstasy and replied, "Yes, You are our Lord and Lover for all eternity." This sublime ecstasy of union was always around Efendi. At moments he would sit quietly, deeply absorbed, eyes overwhelmed in Divine presence and his state transmitted wordlessly to all present.

Sometimes the house filled with children who had come with their parents. Efendi loved children and always looked out for their welfare. In Turkey, where he came across poor children every day on the way to his bookstore, he would never fail to give them something and gently stroke them on the head and speak kind words to them. And he always reminded parents of their responsibilities toward their children—caring for them in the womb, naming them beautifully, and providing them with proper food, clothing and education, both spiritual and practical. On the days when more children were present in the Yonkers house, Efendi would have them line up in front of him and one by one he would give each a giant Hershey bar. Once in a while there was a special transmission to a child. This happened to our daughter who was barely one. She stood before Efendi to take her bar, a tiny tot before a mountain, when he spontaneously began repeating *La ilaha illallah* very rapidly, moving his head, and like a mirror image, her head began moving quickly in sync with his. In the open space of love age was no barrier and Efendi gave transmission to all open hearts.

In the East, Efendi was widely recognized among the Sufis as the spiritual inheritor and living representative of the Prophet Muhammad, may he be always embraced in mystic union. Efendi embodied the light of his wisdom and the beauty of his manner. If one desired to meet the Prophet in person one came to meet Efendi, as the one closest to his nature. His love to the Messenger was of a kind that most of us in the West had not known. Yet by witnessing his powerful frame humbled in the passion of his love, the state of a servant of God and a servant of the Messenger of God, we were drawn to love God and the Prophet of God as naturally as a child would love its mother.

In a dream that Efendi recounted from previous years he was in the back of a great crowd of people in the Prophet Muhammad's mosque in Medina. The Prophet (pbuh), was standing in the front of the mosque, and he called to young Muzaffer to come to him. So Efendi advanced through the assembly as carefully as he could, trying not to jostle the people or step on their toes. When he came to the front, the Prophet gave him the order to clean his Mosque. This order became Efendi's life, and he gave his life to fulfill it.

He cleaned the hearts of the community of the Prophet. He spread the path of Sufism and he renewed the spiritual Tradition by helping to free it from false teachings so that it could regain its pristine humanity. He dismantled many of the historical accretions which were strangling the religion and bringing a great burden onto people. One of the distortions he addressed was the belief that the Prophet forbade representation and the making of images. He declared this to be an invention that came after the Prophet, who himself left in place a picture of Mary and the infant Jesus which had been hanging in the inner chamber of the Kaaba. This naturally brought the Tradition closer to Christianity and other religious Traditions which convey teachings and spiritual transmission through sacred imagery. And to strengthen the bonds with the people of other sacred Traditions he would meet with their representatives and engage in spiritual discussions emphasizing their common ground.

Efendi moved widely. He was able to open many closed hearts in his own Tradition through his profound knowledge of the Qur'an, of the Hadiths, and of the science of Sufism. He met with the very people who were propounding narrow teachings. He strove to open their minds and hearts to the greater compassionate reality. And he reasoned with the rationalists in the religion whose faith was limited by materialism, preventing them from opening to the miraculous. Could they accept that the stones in the hand of the Prophet Muhammad (pbuh) declared his prophecy, or that the pillar against which he was accustomed to lean to deliver his Friday sermon moaned when he had to leave it for a higher platform in order to be heard?

Within his own community of dervishes Efendi rarely quoted the Qur'an or Hadith. He simply was the Qur'an, and he was the Hadith. He was the true Sheikh al Islam. He was the Sheikh of sheikhs, and he set the standard for Sufi sheikhs from his generation forward. He gave permissions to his followers that made the practices more accessible. He made the way lighter, just as the Prophet had done. He would declare that one cry of 'Allah!' from the depths of the heart would open the Divine floodgate of Mercy. He himself made the gate so wide that many could pass through. He informed us that he was the 19th Khalif of Pir Nureddin Jerrahi (r.a.), and he emphasized that the number 19 was the number belonging to the Divine Name *Bismillahirrahmanirrahim*, the All Compassionate and Loving God. Efendi was the living *Bismillahirrahmanirrahim*, a mercy to all beings. Whoever met him was blest. Heart to heart he guided souls directly to the Truth. He did it with utter sincerity, with no thought of self-gain. He did it with the passion of his prayers and the transmitting grace of his glance, with the humble kindness of his demeanor, with his generous manner of welcoming people, with his humor, with the gusto with which he told Sufi stories handed down through generations of Sufi sheikhs, and with the power of his magnificent dhikrs which brought prophets and angels into the circle of remembrance.

In this powerful field of love most members of the American community asked for initiation. They took the hand of Efendi and pledged themselves to God and to a holy way of life. They entered the path of Unity. This was the same heart initiation given by the Prophet Muhammad to his companions and followers 1,400 years before. Efendi had come to pass on the torch of the Prophet and the essence of *La ilaha illallah* to America.

Efendi and the Feminine

Efendi developed strong bonds of spiritual friendship with women in the West, addressing them with the same level of seriousness as his male dervishes. He viewed the feminine as a high divine emanation, following the guidance of the Prophet Muhammad (pbuh) who was usually accompanied by the women of his community, particularly his beloved daughters and wives, whom he always consulted on important matters and who became significant transmitters of his way after his passing. His vision of the feminine was adhered to by some of the great mystics such as Ibn al Arabi and Mevlana Jelaluddin Rumi, may they be immersed in divine Mercy.

Efendi stated that we were actually in the age of the woman and that she would help guide humanity out of its present impasse. Some of the women in the community were given close access to his person. They sat with him, served him, discussed with him, laughed with him and loved him. This was not just amusement or pure relaxation as some assumed. The spiritual companionship led to spiritual fruition, and today some of these women are themselves guides in the American Tariqat and inheritors of Muzaffer Efendi's light.

I will mention some of them individually, among others not named, because they stood out so uniquely.

Efendi, Nur and Amina in Yonkers

Amina Edlin Ortiz had been appointed by Nur to head the household in Yonkers during Efendi's visits, which meant managing the service structure that supported the daily life of Efendi, his twenty dervishes and all of the guests who came every day to meet with him. It was her responsibility to see that all was flowing and satisfying, from the smallest needs of the Turkish dervishes, their daily food, the constant tea service, to the large dinners served every night to the 50-75 guests. Amina tells how she would often come into the living room in the mornings after everyone had gone to sleep and find Efendi by himself deeply absorbed in *tasbih*. She would sit quietly with him until he went back to his room. Efendi loved her and informed her, from a dream she recounted to him, that she would be one of his representatives in the West. Today she is heading the large dervish community in Mexico City, with extending centers, and is representing Sufism in international conferences relating to interfaith and women leadership.

Sixtina and Saskia Friedrich

Saskia and Sixtina Friedrich, daughters of Haydar Friedrich, were also part of the very close circle around Efendi. Only in their late teens and twenties at the time, they nevertheless plunged into the life of the dervish community around Efendi, sleeping in the house during his visits and keeping him company throughout the day and night, together with the Turkish Babas. Saskia, now known as Medina, took many of the pictures that we have of the Yonkers gatherings. Efendi loved them both and initiated them into the Order, giving them the names Lale and Gul, Tulip and Rose. He also confirmed them as future spiritual guides who would carry the light of the Order in the West. They both learned Turkish, particularly Gul who translated some of Efendi's books into English, such as *Adornment of Hearts*, a manual of Sufism, and *Garden of Dervishes*. Gul worked on the translations with a young English woman named Louise Temple, who also became part of Efendi's inner American circle. She was given the name Karima by Efendi, and she was hired by Haydar Friedrich to head the distribution of charity from the community and to care for homeless people. This was carried out in collaboration with Mark Greenberg who worked at the Cathedral of St. John the Divine.

Brigitte Minel was a young Frenchwoman who met Efendi in 1979 when he offered dhikr for the second time in the cultural festival of Rennes, France. She was 22 years old at the time. Their relationship was even more unusual than most as she had a strong and independent character that challenged the norms beyond the norm. He loved her dearly and was always overjoyed to see her. In the note he wrote for her in his book, *Unveiling of Love*, he called her the 'Rose of Paris.' Personally he affectionately called her 'Birujuk', meaning 'my only one.' He pointed her out as someone who would contribute to the new face of Islam and its interface with Christianity.

Another very unique individual in Efendi's entourage was Dharma Fatima. She is the one who declared that she could hear Efendi's blood chanting *La ilaha illallah* one evening as she touched his feet. Efendi said of her that she was hidden behind his throne, but that she would soon be distinguished in the world with special divine knowledge.

Elif was still in high school when she became part of the community. Loved by Efendi, she served in the Yonkers house and became very close to some of the Turkish Babas. She went to live in Istanbul during the last months of Efendi's life and was there for his passing and his funeral.

Jamila Baci, the wife of Tosun Baba, was also close to Efendi and loved him very much. She devotedly attended him and the Babas during the years they stayed in the Spring Valley tekke.

Louise Rifkin, given the dervish name Lutfiya, was another beloved of Efendi who continued her discipleship with Nur after Efendi's passing.

Among the Turkish women was Ayten, wife of Necdet, who cooked many delights for Efendi and kept company with Efendi's wife, Walide Sultan, when she came.

"He came to the West to find his beloved friend."

We were Efendi's beloveds, and Nur was his heart. It was evident that a very powerful bond of divine love and spiritual transmission existed between Efendi and Nur. This great love spilled over all of our gatherings in the early years as Nur and Efendi would sit side by side on the couch in Spring Valley, or Nur would sit at the feet of his guide, his preferred place, sometimes with his eyes closed. Efendi would lovingly prod him by saying, "Open your eyes and see the Divine before you." Nur's spiritual mood tended to the more contemplative, the more inward and quiet, trained as he was in Eastern meditation and Western contemplative practice. His spiritual inclination was toward divine clarity and wisdom. It was Efendi, his master, who took him from the state of meditative tranquility to the state of divine love, 'askh'. This was Efendi's great gift, divine love. So each became Shams and Mevlana to the other. They poured the wine of love into each other's cup and their hearts were married in the stormy ocean of love. And the new stream of the lineage was born, 5,000 miles away from its homeland where it had flowered in the extraordinarily rich Sufi culture of the Ottoman Empire.

In August of 1978, four months after Efendi's first visit to America, Nur flew to Istanbul to spend the month of Ramadan with his new sheikh. During this month of fasting from food in the day and feasting on the Qur'anic revelations chanted in the Mosques, they would sit side by side in the great Beyazit Mosque near Efendi's bookstore, listening to the entrancing beauty of Qur'an in the late summer Ramadan afternoons. It is there that Nur had his vision. "…I was granted the vision of a translucent emerald mosque, above even the highest heaven. There were no human figures visible, only a vast Koran whose letters radiated light and whose pages turned gracefully as it spontaneously chanted itself. Later, the Sheikh confirmed to me that this had been an authentic mystical experience…"

At fast break they would join together with dervishes in one of the many restaurants that Efendi liked, or they would go to Efendi's home where Walide Sultan, Efendi's wife, would prepare paradise dinners. On these visits Nur was deeply affected by Efendi's love to his wife and his two children. For him it was a living demonstration that the family and its responsibilities was not separate from the life of the spirit, but rather an expression of the intimacy of divine Love. During the day Efendi would take Nur to visit the precious shrines of saints located throughout the city where they offered Fatihas for the friends of God buried there. Like Mevlana and Shams, they seemed to be inseparable. On the Night of Power, the night when Efendi wanted to crown his beloved friend with the Taj of the Order, the night that commemorates the descent of the Qur'an into the heart of the Prophet Muhammad, Nur was overcome by an intense desire to flee. Maybe it was the accumulation of spiritual power that had gathered during their month long companionship. Maybe it was the heaviness of the religious sermon that was spoken that night in the Dergah by a visiting preacher. Maybe it was the desire to flee from the responsibility that was coming onto him as a successor of Muzaffer Efendi. Maybe it was the divine guidance flowing in Nur to call Efendi away from Turkey into America where the new stream would be born. It could have been any of these, or other reasons we do not know. But in the middle of the evening, just before the crown was to be placed on his head, Nur fled. He ran out of the Dergah, not even stopping at the entrance to take his shoes. He ran back to his hotel and a few hours later he boarded a plane to New York.

The impact on Efendi was huge, unimaginable. He wrote three letters to Nur which give us a glimpse of what he suffered. These letters have not been published, and are still in private keeping. In one of them he confesses that this experience was like a huge rock falling on his heart, but a sentence later he states that this rock came only from his Lord, and therefore he accepted it fully. His family and his close dervish Babas came to his side the best they could. This was when they witnessed the burning of Mevlana for his friend. That winter Efendi became very ill, and many felt that he would not survive. Yet he did, and soon after his recovery he wrote the book dedicated to Nur and the Americans, *Ask Yolu*, the Path of Love, given the English title of *The Unveiling of Love*. When Efendi returned to America in the spring of 1979, eight months later, Nur met him expecting to be rebuked for his sudden departure in the summer. But no mention was made about the flight from his teacher. There was no lover's complaint, no reminding of past impropriety, only the joy of reunion.

Under Efendi's guidance Nur blossomed into a full Sufi sheikh, continuing and spreading Efendi's legacy. He left us a remarkable spiritual portrait of his beloved guide in the chapter called 'Heart and Countenance of the Sheikh' in *Atom from the Sun of Knowledge*.

Haydar and Fariha Friedrich with Efendi

Efendi's Passing

Efendi was the descendent of Imam Husayn, may Allah be pleased with him and envelop him in boundless mercy. At times Efendi would sing hymns dedicated to his great ancestor and weep. His person emanated the 'ashk', the particular fervor and love that is a sign of the spiritual presence of Imam Husayn. He would tell us that when he died, if the earth of Karbala where Imam Husayn was martyred was placed on his eyes, tears of blood would flow. And it happened exactly as he had said. The earth was placed over his eyes as he had requested, and tears of blood flowed forth from under his closed lids.

On the cold and sleet filled February day of his burial, thousands of people, including Haydar, myself, our infant daughter Duha and soon to be born son Aziz in my belly, followed his bier as it made its way, carried by his dervishes, from the Jerrahi Tekke to the Fatih Mosque where the funeral service was given. The Sheikh who was chosen to offer the sermon and prayer cried out at one point that every one at the funeral gathering was a friend of God, a *waliyullah*. This cry was a gift from Allah to Efendi and to all those present. The same statement was made at the funeral of Hazreti Pir Nureddin Jerrahi, may he be embraced in divine mercy. All those who are attached to a beloved of Allah are also beloveds of Allah.

The implications and consequences of Sheikh Muzaffer's thirteen visits to America, where he planted seeds of light in fertile hearts, is vast beyond understanding. We cannot know all the places where these seeds have grown and borne fruit and we can never know the full extent of blessings that a man of Truth like Efendi brings to the earth. What we do know is that since he and other noble spiritual masters have set foot on American soil there has come about a marked change in our larger society from obsession with materialism to a maturing relationship to the realm of the Spirit and the vast potential it holds for human transformation and happiness. Many more people are pursuing spiritual paths and turning to their Source to seek the meaning of life. The great field of love and wisdom where the Prophets and Holy Ones have sown their seeds is flourishing again and a new humanity rooted in compassion and new knowledge is emerging. Efendi came to sow the seeds and announce the harvest.

May the power and beauty of the light that he transmitted to America help to further this new spiritual civilization and may it continue to enlighten hearts and bring forth creative manifestations for centuries to come. May the Source of Love send continuous blessings and radiant peace upon the beloved Muhammad, Jewel of humanity, and upon his blessed family and noble companions, and upon all of the magnificent Messengers, Prophets, Mothers of the faithful and the Divinely guided beings who embody the light of Truth for humanity.

Effendi's Sufi lineage continues in America in two main streams. One is the more traditional form, adhering to the beautiful Turkish expression of the Tariqat, and the other is the more Western form which evolved with Shaykh Nur and is continuing to evolve under my responsibility. The latter is called the Nur Ashki Jerrahi Sufi Order, and it has spread into many centers of the West.

Efendi lives, and he continues to manifest through the living hearts of his community and family.

Fariha Nur Ashki Jerrahi
Yonkers, NY
Ramadan 2015 / 1436

NOTES

Section One

1. Jalaluddin Rumi, inscription from Konya.
2. Recorded *sohbet*, March 30, 1980, Harvard University
3. Recorded *sohbet*, April 14, 1980, Rice University
4. Recorded *sohbet* March 21,1981, New Mexico.
5. Recorded *sohbet* of Muzaffer Efendi: April 15, 1980.
6. *In the Spirit* radio interview with Lex Hixon, WBAI, New York; April 11, 1978.
7. Muzaffer Ozak, *Ashki's Divan*, p.102
8. As recounted by M. Fatih Citlak on a Turkish television documentary
9. Recorded *sohbet*, New York, Oct.23,1982.
10. Recorded *sohbet*, New York: November 9, 1984.
11. Muzaffer Ozak, *The Unveiling of Love*, p.3.
12. *Ibid*, p.5.
13. Recorded *sohbet*, N.Y.,1980.
14. *In the Spirit* radio program, WBAI, New York, Nov. 19,1980.
15. *In the Spirit* radio interview, April 11, 1978; *sohbet*, April 15, 1980; *The Unveiling of Love*, pp.5-7.
16. *In the Spirit* radio interview, April 11, 1978.
17. Recorded *sohbet*; New York, April 13, 1981.
18. *Ibid*, pp.8- 9.
19. *Ibid*, pp.9-10.
20. Stoneman, *A Traveler's History of Turkey*, pp.184-5.
21. As related to the author by Safer Efendi on January

13,1996.

22. Mustafa Özdamar, *Gönül Cerrahi, Nureddin Cerrahi Ve Cerrahiler*, pp.175-7.
23. Ozak, *Ashki's Divan*, p.18.
24. As related to the author by Safer Efendi on January 13,1996 and further elaborated by Muzaffer Efendi in a recorded *sohbet*, April 15, 1980.
25. This is confirmed by Muzaffer Efendi's son, Junayd, and is also documented in the autobiographical introduction to *The Unveiling of Love*
26. Ozak, *Ashki's Divan*, p.83
27. Özdamar, pp.182-9.
28. Recorded *sohbet* by Safer Efendi, Spring Valley, N.Y., Nov.1, 1992.

Section Two

1. This section of his book, as far as we know, has never previously been translated into English
2. Kudsi Ergüner, *Journeys of a Sufi Musician*, p.96
3. New Dimensions Radio interview of Lex Hixon (host: Michael Toms), 1989.
4. *Ibid*
5. Lex Hixon, *Heart of the Koran*, p.8
6. From a Rochester newspaper article dated April 14, 1979.
7. From the Introduction to the Turkish version of Muzaffer Efendi's *The Unveiling of Love*
8. R. Frager, *Love is the Wine*, ix-x.
9. Muzaffer Ozak, *Ashki's Divan*, pp.iii-v, forward by Lou Rogers.

10. Recorded *sohbet*, N.Y., April 5, 1980.
11. Recorded *sohbet*, N.Y., April, 15, 1980.
12. Recorded *sohbet*, Boston, March 30, 1980.
13. *Ibid.*
14. Sheikh Fadhlalla Haeri, *The Elements of Sufism* (web document). Qur'an 9:32 translation based on Muhammad Assad's *The Message of the Qur'an*
15. Recorded *sohbet*, San Francisco, March 14, 1980.
16. As told by M.Fatih Citlak on a Turkish television documentary.
17. Recorded *sohbet*, March 26, 1980.
18. Recorded *sohbet*, October 19, 1980.
19. Recorded *sohbet*, April 21, 1980. The life of Pir Nurredin al-Jerrahi is treated in another book by this author, The Garden of Mystic Love
20. *In the Spirit*, radio interview, March 27, 1980.
21. Recorded *sohbet*, April 10, 1980, N.Y
22. Recorded *sohbet*, April 13, 1981, N.Y
23. Muzaffer Ozak, *Ashki's Divan*, p.85
24. Recorded *sohbet*, March 22, 1981, New Mexico.
25. Lex Hixon, *Atom From the Sun of Knowledge*, pp.115-6
26. Recorded *sohbet*, April 4, 1980, Rice University.
27. The end of the story is that the ant, during his journey, sought out some food on the blanket of a passing caravan. As he was nibbling on some bread crumbs, the blanket was suddenly wrapped up and put away with the ant trapped inside. When the caravan finally arrived at its destination, the blanket was again rolled out and the ant fell to the ground. Looking up, he saw that he had been taken to Mecca.

28. *In the Spirit*, radio interview, October 17, 1982. The story of the grapes is from Rumi's *Masnavi*.
29. Sheikh Muzaffer Ozak al-Jerrahi, *Blessed Virgin Mary*, p.ix.
30. An ardent, even zealous, advocate of religious piety.
31. In one famous incident, an ignorant Bedouin visiting from the desert, decided to relieve himself in the middle of the Prophet's mosque
32. As recounted by Sheikha Fariha Friedrich.
33. From a taped interview in Istanbul, March 1982.
34. They both dreamed of climbing to the top of a minaret to give the call to prayer. The sheikh congratulated the first, saying he would soon make hajj, and told the other dervish that he should repent and give back what he had stolen. We should note that the interpretation of the authentic mystic guide is not based solely on the outward events of the dream; rather, the sheikh looks within his heart and feels the emotions, images and inspiration that come through as the dream is being recounted. It is important for the dervish to receive the sheikh's interpretation of a dream before it is told to others, if repeated at all, since the first interpretation of the dream is preeminent and has a strong effect upon the dreamer. Also, it is best not to share important dreams with those who would criticize it or not appreciate it properly.
35. *Eyvallah* is used in Turkish to signify agreement, acceptance.
36. Recorded *sohbet*, Oct.16, 1982, N.Y.
37. Recorded *sohbet*, March 22, 1981, New Mexico.
38. He was entrusted with highly sensitive strategic

information concerning the loyalties of key parties in the Prophet's community during the time of war.

39. *Alif, Lam, Mim, Sad* is one of the letter configurations placed at the beginning of a Qur'anic sura
40. Recorded *sohbet*, May 1 & 19, 1982, N.Y
41. Recorded *sohbet*, April 07, 1980, Spring Valley, NY
42. Recorded *sohbet*, Oct. 29, 1982, NY
43. Recorded *sohbet*, April 8, 1980, Spring Valley, NY
44. Recorded *sohbet*, Nov. 15, 1980, NY
45. Recorded *sohbet*, May 11, 1982, Masjid al-Farah, NY
46. Recorded *sohbet*, April 22, 1983
47. Recorded *sohbet*, October 22, 1982.
48. Recorded *sohbet*, May 18, 1982, 7 East 82 nd St., N.Y.
49. Recorded *sohbet*, May 21, 1982.
50. Recorded *sohbet*, April 22, 1983.
51. Recorded *sohbet*, Nov, 18, 1984, Yonkers, NY. Note: the seven levels of the soul are: the mineral soul, the vegetable soul, the animal soul, the personal soul, the human soul, the sultan soul (these six come into the realm of creation), and the secret soul or *ruhu sirr* (the highest level, which is our transcendent divine aspect).
52. Recorded *sohbet*, May, 11, 1982, Masjid al-Farah, NY
53. Qur'an: Sura 96 (Tin).
54. Recorded *sohbet*, April 28, 1982.
55. Qur'an 50:16.
56. Recorded *sohbet*, April 11, 1982.
57. Qur'an 96:19
58. Recorded *sohbet*, Oct 26, 1982; Masjid al-Farah, NY
59. Recorded *sohbet*, May 11, 1982.

60. See Qur'an 2:30-39, 7:11-25, 15:26-44, 38:65-88.
61. Recorded *sohbet*, April 28, 1982.
62. Recorded *sohbet*, May 11, 1982.
63. Recorded *sohbet*, April 13, 1981, NY
64. The *'alam-i arwah*. (mentioned in Qur'an 7:166) is the universe of souls, the timeless dimension where souls dwell before coming to earth.
65. Recorded *sohbet*, April, 8, 1980; 82nd St. N.Y.
66. Muhammad, the Messenger of God, Jesus the Spirit of God, Moses the one who speaks with God.
67. Recorded *sohbet*, April 24,1982, Spring Valley, NY
68. Recorded *sohbet*, March 13,1981, California.
69. Recorded *sohbet*, Nov.18, 1984, Yonkers,NY.
70. Feisal Abdul Rauf, *Islam: A Search for Meaning*, pp. xi-xii.
71. Recorded *sohbet*, Nov.16, 1984, Masjid al-Farah, NY
72. Recorded *sohbet*, November 9, 1984.
73. As related by Muzaffer's secretary, Ibrahim Akkökler.

ABOUT THE AUTHOR

Gregory Blann has been an active student of Sufism and the world's religions for over three decades. He received initiation from Pir Vilayat Khan in the Sufi Order International in 1980 and served as a representative in that order for a number of years. In 1990, he received *bayat* (initiation) in the Halveti-Jerrahi Order from Sheikh Nur al-Jerrahi (Lex Hixon), and also studied with Safer Efendi. He was given the name Muhammad Jamal, and became a Jerrahi sheikh in 1994. He worked closely with Sheikh Nur for four years, translating the traditional mystic hymns of the Jerrahis from Turkish into English, to be sung by dervishes in the West.

Sheikh Muhammad Jamal received a degree in music and art from Vanderbilt University in 1974 and continued his studies at Massachusetts College of Art in Boston. He also trained for ten years in Carnatic South Indian music. In more recent years, he has worked in the graphic arts and web design field, published numerous articles on spirituality, led local Sufi groups in Nashville, Tennessee and taught Sufism in various cities throughout the United States. He has also been a frequent participant in ecumenical dialogues and panels, serving on the board of the Interfaith Alliance of Middle Tennessee. Sheikh Muhammad Jamal brings to the present work the experience of over thirty years on the Sufi path, as a member of both a contemporary universalist Western Sufi Order originating in India and a traditional Islamic dervish Order with Ottoman Turkish roots.

ACKNOWLEDGMENTS

I would like to express my sincere thanks to all those who helped and encouraged us in the writing of this book, whether by providing information, translations or help with the editing of the manuscript. These include: Safer Dal, Ömer Tugrul Inançer, Ibrahim Akkökler, Tosun Bayrak, Ragip Robert Frager, Ismail Çimen, Fatih Tatlilioglü, Reb Zalman Schachter-Shalomi, Salik Schwartz, Nur Lex Hixon, Sheila Hixon, Mehlika Ozak, Junayd Ozak, Fatma Ayşe Ozak, Amina Teslima Ortiz Graham, Sixtina Friedrich, Saskia Friedrich, Haydar Friedrich, and Fariha Friedrich.

I wish to extend special thanks to Kaan and Ayşegül Erdal, who translated the Turkish introduction to Muzaffer Efendi's *The Unveiling of Love*, most of which has never before appeared in English. While the author is responsible for the final English form of these translations, these recollections of Muzaffer Efendi would not have been accessible without their kind help. I am also indebted to those at Masjid-al-Farah who generously made available hundreds of hours of recorded talks by Muzaffer Efendi as well as many fine photographs.

Permission has been sought and credit given in all cases where the photographer or artist was known; any omission in this regard is strictly inadvertent and will be corrected as soon as we are notified. We would like to thank Peri Fezier, who kindly made available rare photographs of her relative, Fahreddin Efendi. Our thanks also to Fahrettin Dal for making available a number of older photos collected by Muzaffer Ergür. We would also like to thank Amina Teslima for allowing the use of stills from her videos of dhikr at the Cathedral of St. John the Divine.

Photographer James Wentzy was hired by the DIA Art Foundation in 1980 to photograph Efendi and the dervishes. He has graciously allowed the inclusion of a number of his dynamic photographs—mostly black and white originals—which beautifully reflect the power of the dhikr ceremony. I invited him to contribute something about his experience in shooting these photos, and he agreed. His own statement appears at the end of the acknowledgments along with an interesting pair of self-portraits, one from the early eighties and the other in 2005.

Sheikh Nur (left) with the author (photo: Saskia Friedrich)

A special note is necessary regarding the English ilahi translations of Sheikh Nur (Lex Hixon), who passed from the earthly realm on All Saints' Day, November 1, 1995. From 1991 to 1994, the author collaborated with Sheikh Nur on approximately fifty English settings of Turkish mystic hymns or ilahis. Some of these hymns, which are presently sung in a number of Jerrahi dervish circles throughout America, are quoted in the course of this book with Sheikh Nur's full permission and blessings. In a very few cases, where Sheikh Nur's adaptations freely depart from the original text, I provide fresh renderings from the primary Turkish source.

Finally loving thanks is due my wife, Sylvia, who reviewed the various drafts of the working manuscript, offering suggestions as to editorial and grammatical improvements. Thanks also to Abdul Malik Massie, Abdus Salaam Manakas, Abdul Karim Chisti, Habiba Ashki and Mahmud Kabir for all their help and encouragement.

Sufi Remembrances

I have had a large photograph of the circling Ceremony of Dhikr (Remembrance) hung on my wall since its photography, twenty five years ago. The image was inspired by the Dervishes, realized by synchronized mechanics of the camera, formulations of reflected light on film, finessed time and space within a frame, and printed image on paper. However, for me the image was always more than memorabilia, reflected light from circling Dervishes time-lapsed onto paper; the image becomes a representation of the commonality with everything, of self without identity, and form without volition.

Photographer James Wentzy, 2005

Remembrance is a particularity of perception, with its own transcendence of space and time. Photography has a particular affinity with remembrance, as memorabilia deposited for future recollection. When remembering the experiences of photographing the Dervishes many years ago, the past becomes present. My memory of Muzaffer Efendi is as conductor of a symphony, centered and orchestrating form in the middle of whirling formlessness, an anchorage of stillness like the eye in the middle of a hurricane. My memory of the Dervishes, when I was in their company, was of an openness and inviting camaraderie, like the warmest embrace you'd give to your closest friend. And I remember their almost child-like playfulness and exuberance, when they were crowded around looking over pictures of themselves that I had previously photographed. (I particularly remember their nodding approval with the Dhikr time-lapse pictures of themselves, circling as blurred waves without identity.)

James Wentzy, 1980

I have long-used photography as repository of memories and perceptions. I had actually photographed my reflection, at the conclusion of photographing the Dervishes, finishing the last frame of the last roll of film. In reflecting back on this photography, I look back at myself, this time twenty five years ago, marveling over the span of time and the immediacy of memories; surprised with the unrecognized memory of youth (it only becomes a "memory of youth" after the fact) yet aware enough to have photographed this time, a captured reflection for a future recollection past.

James Wentzy, 2005

BIBLIOGRAPHY

Erguner, Kudsi. *Journies of a Sufi Master*. London: Saqi Books, 2005. (Translated by Annette Mayers)

Frager, Robert. *Love is the Wine*. Threshold Books, 1987.

Friedlander, Ira. *The Whirling Dervishes*. N.Y. Collier/ MacMillan, 1975.

Hixon, Lex (Nur al-Jerrahi). *Atom From the Sun of Knowledge*. Westport, Conn: Pir Publications, 1993.

Ozak al-Jerrahi, Sheikh Muzaffer. *Ashki's Divan*. Westport, Conn: Pir Publications, 1991. (translated by Muhtar Holland and Sixtina Friedrich)

Ozak al-Jerrahi, Sheikh Muzaffer. *Blessed Virgin Mary*. Westport, Conn: Pir Publications, 1991. (translated by Muhtar Holland)

Ozak al-Jerrahi, Sheikh Muzaffer. *The Unveiling of Love* (translated by Muhtar Holland). NY: Inner Traditions International, 1981. Aşk Yolu Vuslat Tariki.

Özdamar, Mustafa. *Gönül Cerrahi, Nureddin Cerrahi Ve Cerrahiler*. Istanbul: Kirkkandil, 1995.

Rauf, Feisal Abdul. *Islam: A Search for Meaning*, Costa Mesa, CA/Mazda Publishers, 1996.

GLOSSARY

Note: All foreign words in the glossary are of Arabic origin, except where otherwise noted.

A

'Abbasid. The second Islamic dynasty, descended from the Prophet's uncle, al-'Abbas; they succeeded the Umayyid dynasty and reigned from ca. 749-932 C.E., retaining titular control during the Buyid and Seljuk dynasties until 1258 C.E.

adab. Manners, etiquette and respectful conduct, especially between Sufis.

adhan (azan). The Islamic call to prayer.

ahadith (sing. *hadith*). Sayings or oral traditions of the Prophet Muhammad recorded outside the Qur'an, and based on an *isnad* (chain of transmission from one witness to another).

'alam (pl. *'alamin*). World, Universe, or sphere of existence.

'alam-i arwah. The universe of souls, the timeless dimension where souls dwell before coming to earth—where each one pledged to uphold the Divine Truth on earth.

"*Alastu bi-Rabbikum?*" "Am I not your Lord?" The question asked by Allah to the souls when they were still "in the loins of Adam." (Qur'an 7:166)

'aleihi salaam. "Upon him be peace." A phrase customarily said

by Muslims after mentioning the name of a prophet.

alhamdulillah. "All praises are flowing to Allah." A common Arabic expression of thanks, employed frequently in Qur'an.

alif. The initial letter of the Arabic alphabet, equivalent to "A," a silent letter connoting spirit.

"*Ana'l-Haqq*". "I am the Divine Truth (or God)." A controversial ecstatic statement made famous by the tenth century martyr, Mansur al-Hallaj.

'arif. A wise person or learned Muslim scholar.

Ashk (*aşk*), *ashik*. Turkish word for passionate love, lover (*Ishq* in Arabic).

Ashki (*Aşki*). The Turkish Sufi name and poetical nom-de-plume of Muzaffer Efendi, meaning "the one who is always in love."

ayat (*ayah*) A sign or indication; may denote a verse from a *sura* (chapter) of the Qur'an.

B

Baba Turkish for father; used by Sufis to refer to a spiritual elder or sheikh.

baqa (*baka*) "Abiding in God;" a form of resurrection which the seeker experiences after having been lost in Allah (*fana-fi'llah*) In the first stage, *fana*, one "dies" to the limited self (during this lifetime). This is followed by the second stage, *baqa*, in which the Divine "comes alive" in one.

bala. Arabic for "yes."

baraka. The blessing or spiritual power of a holy person.

bayat (*bay'a*). Initiation; joining the right hand in allegiance with a Sufi sheikh to join a tarikat, after the ceremonial manner in which the Prophet received converts into Islam.

Bedevi (*Badawi*) *Topu*. A section of the standing dhikr in which the dervishes crowd in around the sheikh, while chanting powerfully; given as a gift to the Jerrahis from the practices of the Badawi tarikat.

Bismillah (*ir-Rahman, ir-Rahim*). "In the Name of God, (the Compassionate, the Merciful); an opening invocation found at the beginning of most suras of the Qur'an.

C

Caliph (*khalif*) "Successor; viceroy." A *khalif* or *Khalifa* (pl. *Khulafa*) is an initiating leader in a Sufi order, a deputy to the head sheikh. *Caliph* refers to the political and spiritual head of Islam who is a direct successor of the Prophet Muhammad, a position not overtly claimed after the fall of the Ottoman Empire in the 1920's.

Chelebi. An Turkish honorific title; may also refer to the head of the Mevlevi Order.

D

dergah. (Turkish)"The Sultan's court;" can refer to a main Sufi Lodge.

dhikr (*zikr*), *dhikrullah*. "Remembrance (of Allah);" can refer to the chanting of the names of God (especially *La ilaha illallah*); often repeated by Sufi groups in a circle or in lines.

dhikr al-mawt. The remembrance of death (the awareness of one's own mortality as a spiritual perspective).

dua. A prayer; a personal, often extemporaneous, divine supplication, frequently uttered with palms raised in prayer.

E

Efendi. (Greek) A Turkish honorific title similar to "sir;" may also indicate a grand-sheikh.

esma. Arabic for "name;" may refer to one of the 99 Divine Names from the Qur'an.

Estaghfirullah "I seek forgiveness from Allah;" a common Islamic phrase.

Eyvallah. Common Turkish phrase meaning, "All right," or "I accept (everything, as being from Allah)."

F

fana. "Annihilation," in *tassawuf* (Sufism), it refers to being lost or effaced in the sheikh, in the Prophet, or in God, a positive spiritual state of ego transcendence which may be followed by the station of *baqa* (being found or "subsisting" in God).

fana-fi'llah. "Lost or effaced in God." (See *fana* above)

Fatih. ("Conqueror"); an area of Istanbul, named after Mehmet II the Conqueror.

Fatiha. The seven line opening sura of the Qur'an; to recite the first sura, whose utterance—especially among Islamic mystics—is considered to contain great power of spiritual blessing.

Four worlds. The Sufis delineate four levels of reality: Shariat refers to the physical level, the realm of action, the exoteric religious law, the literal meaning of scripture. Tarikat refers to the level of heart, of feeling, the esoteric, oral tradition, the inner, allegorical meaning. Hakikat refers to the highest truth, beyond words, boundaries or creeds, the level of *being*, of oneness, transcending all duality. Marifat refers to the level of knowledge, of mystic realization, of integration with the Divine Will, the metaphorical meaning. Kabbalistic as well as Yogic tradition also delineates these four worlds.

G

Gabriel (*Jibra'il*) The angelic Divine Messenger who delivered the Qur'anic revelations from Allah Most High to the Prophet Muhammad.

H

hadith (pl. *ahadith*) An oral tradition or non-Qur'anic saying of the Prophet Muhammad.

hadith qudsi. A sacred hadith in which Allah speaks directly in the first person through the Prophet Muhammad.

hafiz. One who has memorized the entire Qur'an and can chant it by heart.

hajj. "Pilgrimage"; visiting Mecca during the Islamic month of Dhul-Hajj, with its rites, including circling the Ka'ba, visiting Mina, Arafat (and Medina); one of the five pillars of Islam.

Haji. One who has made the pilgrimage to Mecca and performed the rites of hajj is known as a *haji* (masculine) or *haja* (feminine).

hakikat (*haqiqa*) Ultimate Reality, the realm of highest truth, the One Source which transcends all duality or separation.

hal (pl. *Ahwal*), halat. A spiritual state or peak experience, especially an ecstatic one.

halal. That which is considered lawful or permissible in Islam (as opposed to haram, forbidden).

halvet (*khalwa*). A spiritual retreat; traditionally entailing forty days and nights of seclusion.

Halveti-Jerrahi (*Order*). A Turkish Sufi tarikat founded in Istanbul by Pir Nureddin al-Jerrahi ca.1704 C.E., a branch of the older Khalwati (Halveti) Order. The history of this order is chronicled in *The Garden of Mystic Love*, by the author.

Hanafi. One of the four Sunni schools of jurisprudence, or *madhahib*, founded by Imam Abu Hanifa (d.767 C.E.) of Kufa.

hanif. A believer in the One God (such as Abraham); the *hanifa* are mentioned in the Qur'an as pious monotheists in Arabia and elsewhere prior to historical Islam.

Haqq (*Hak*). "Truth" (Ultimate Truth or "God").

haram. That which is forbidden in Islam (can refer to certain acts or foods, such as pork).

haydariyya. A sleeveless vest worn by dervishes after the manner of Hazrat 'Ali.

Hayy. "Life" (the Divine Life which never dies).

Hazrat, Hazrati. "Presence"; an honorific title placed before the name of a revered, holy person.

hizmet. "Service"(duty); to serve Allah by serving and helping others.

hoja. (Turkish) A Muslim teacher.

I

Iblis. "The adversary," the name by which the Qur'an refers to the *shaitan*, Satan, or devil. In the Qur'an, Iblis is depicted as a rebellious jinn, rather than a fallen angel.

Ibrahim. Arabic name for the prophet Abraham (upon him be peace).

ilahi (pl *ilahiler*) Divine hymn; mystic poems which are sung by dervishes.

imam. One who leads prayers, or heads a congregation; in Shi'ism, an intercessory title (such as Imam 'Ali).

iman. Faith.

insha'llah. "If God wills it." A common Arabic expression.
Insan-i kamil. The perfect human being.

Isa. The Arabic name for Jesus (upon him be peace).

ishq (*ashk* or *aşk*). Love or desire.

istikhara (*istihare*). "Asking for the best choice;" a special two-rakat prayer before sleep (based on *sunna*), asking for divine guidance or dream resolution on some matter.

J

jalal. The powerful qualities (including wrath and splendor).

jamal. The gentle, beautiful qualities.

jami (*cami*), *Jami*. Turkish word for a "mosque"; a divine name meaning "the Collector;" also the name of a famous mystic poet.

jihad. To struggle (in the path of righteousness). The lesser jihad is outward, defensive warfare against an enemy or oppressor; the greater jihad is the inner struggle against the negative manifestations of the nafs or ego.

jinn. An unseen being of the subtle world (related to "genie" and "genius"), distinct from angelic beings.

Jum'a. Friday, The day of congregational prayer and worship in Islam.

K

Ka'ba. The central black, cubical shrine of Islamic pilgrimage, located in Mecca. It is considered to have been built by Abraham as the first temple to the One God.

Kabbala. The primarily oral Jewish mystical tradition; the *Zohar* and *Sefer Yetzirah* are part of its written corpus.

Karagümrük. The section of Istanbul where the main Halveti-Jerrahi dergah is located, now known as: "The Society for the Preservation of Turkish Cultural Music." ("Turk Tasavvuf Musikisi ve Folklorunu Arastirma ve Yasatma Vakfi").

Karbala. The place in Iraq where Husayn, the grandson of the Prophet, was martyred.

kaside. A mystic ode (often sung over the chanting of the divine names during dhikr).

khannas. The "whispering" inner urge to do evil, mentioned in Qur'an (Sura 114).

khutba. Sermon.

kitab. Book.

Kufr, *kafir*. One who rejects the faith.

L

La ilaha illallah. *Tawhid*; the quintessential Islamic declaration of unity: "Nothing exists except the One (*Al-Lah*); there is nothing worthy of worship but God, the Only Reality."

M

madrasa. An Islamic school or university of higher study.

madzub (*majdhub*). One who is appears "crazy" with divine love and attraction.

makam (*maqam*; pl. *makamat*). one's spiritual station or place (such as "the fourth level" of the seven levels; a musical mode (such as *hijaz* or *rast*), especially in Turkish and Arabic music.

malamat, malami (*melami*), *Malamatiyya, Malamiyya* The spiritual way of blame; a sect (also a makam on the Sufi path) in which the Malami purposely eschews outward displays of piety and religious convention so that the false ego will receive public contempt instead of praise. This cultivates humility and checks any "holier-than-thou" tendencies.

marifat (*ma'rifa*). "Knowledge"; one of the four levels in Sufism, associated with higher understanding and the living embodiment of Truth (*hakikat*).

masjid. A mosque, an Islamic place of worship.

medet. Help or aid; the Sufis often call out for spiritual assistance to Allah, a saint or a pir (ex. "Medet ya Hazrat Pir," meaning "Help us, O venerable Pir").

meshk (*meşk*). (Turkish) Musical practice; dervishes who gather for meshk usually sit, singing ilahis and chanting divine esmas, often with instrumental accompaniment.

mevlud. A poem by Süleyman Chelebi depicting the nativity of the Prophet Muhammad, which is sung by special singers on the Prophet's birthday or during a religious service to commemorate a departed soul.

meydan. An open space or circle; often associated with the area in a tekke where dervishes gather to make the ceremony of dhikr.

Mount Hira. The mountain near Mecca where the Prophet Muhammad meditated in a cave and received the first revelation of the Qur'an (also call *Jabal an-Nur*).

muezzin (*mu'azzin*) One who makes the call to prayer in a mosque or from a minaret.

muhabbet (*mahabba*). Spiritual love (*agape*); friendship.

muhib. One who loves; a sympathizer or friend of a dervish order.

murshid, *murshida*. "A guide" (from *rashid*), especially a Sufi spiritual teacher (male or female) or *sheikh*(*a*)

muslim. One who is submitted to the divine will (in peace).

N

nafs. The soul, inner self, ego, life-force; associated with the breath.

nafs al-ammara. The animal soul, one's carnal nature, the "lower," less civilized, or self-centered impulses, the commanding self; the lowest of seven levels of the soul or *nafs*.

Nasruddin Hoja (*or Mulla Nasruddin*) An often humorous fictional character in many Sufi teaching stories.

ney. A flute of reed, often utilized to accompany the Mevlevi turning ceremony (*sama*).

Nur (*i*) *Muhammad* (*i*) The Muhammedin Light, the first light of eternity through which creation was brought into existence, a concept first elucidated by the theologian, Tabari.

O

Ottoman. The Turkish empire, founded in the thirteenth century by Osman, which ruled most of the Islamic world until its final demise at the end of World War I.

P

PBUH - abbreviation for "Peace and blessings be upon him;" see also *salallahu 'aleihi wa salaam*, which is the same phrase in Arabic.

Q

Qahhar (*al-Qahr*) Esma (divine name) signifying Divine Sovereignty and Victory; the Overwhelming, Overarching aspect of the Divine.

qalbi. The Heart, the innermost part.

Qayyum. Divine esma signifying the Self-Subsisting and Everlasting.

Qur'an. The scripture of Islam, revealed by Allah, through the angel Gabriel, to the Prophet Muhammad over a course of 23 years.

Qur'an al-Karim. The Holy Qur'an.

qutb (*qutub*; pl. *aqtab* or *aktab*) The spiritual pole or axis, a saintly person, who may be known or hidden; one who has been divinely appointed as a leader of spiritual affairs in the world during their lifetime. Such a person often spiritually intercedes to help stop wars, mitigate disasters or bring succor to other souls.

R

R.A. - Radiallahu anhu; "May Allah's blessings be upon him."

Rabbi'l alamin. The Lord of the Worlds, the Lord of Countless Universes.

rak'a (pl. *rak'at*) A cycle of Islamic prayer; for instance, the morning *salat* consists of two *rak'at* (in each *rak'a*, one recites *tekbir* and Qur'an while standing, bows (*ruku*), performs two full prostrations (*sajda*), and after the second time, sits in the kneeling position).

rasul, Rasulullah. A prophet or divine messenger; "*Rasulullah*" (*Rasul Allah*) is a commonly used Islamic title referring to the Messenger of Allah, the Prophet Muhammad.

ruh. Spirit (or soul); Jesus (*Isa*) is known in Islam as *Ruh Allah* (the Spirit of God).

S

sadaqa. Alms or charity to the poor.

sajda (*sejda*). (Ritual) prostration, kneeling with forehead and palms to the ground (a part of Islamic prayers, and also found in other spiritual paths).

sakalayn (*sakaleyn*). One who has spiritual sight to see both worlds, as did the Prophet Muhammad (according to Qur'an)—refers to the two races of beings inhabiting the earth: humans (who are visible) and *jinn* (who are unseen).

"*(as-)salaam(u) 'aleikum.*" "(May) Peace be with you;" a common Islamic greeting, to which the response is: "*w'aleikum salaam*" ("And with you be peace.").

"*salallahu 'aleihi wa salaam.*" (abbreviated as s.a.w.s. or p.b.u.h.) "Peace and blessings be upon him;" a blessing of respect traditionally uttered by pious Muslims after mentioning the Prophet Muhammad; "*'aleihi salaam*" is said after mentioning any other prophet, and *radiallahu anhu* is said after the name of a man of great sanctity (*radiallahu anha* is said after the name of a saintly woman).

salat (*salah*). Prayer (*namaz* in Persian).

salawat. A blessing on the Prophet Muhammad, one of the most common being: "*Allahuma sali 'ala Sayyiddina Muhammad*" ("May Allah bless our master Muhammad").

sama (*sema*). "Listening"; a sacred ceremony involving uplifting spiritual music and dance (specifically among the Mevlevis, "the turn" or ceremony of the whirling dervishes).

Sayyid. Master or Lord; a title for a descendent of the Prophet Muhammad.

Sayyidina. "Our Master."

Shafi'i, Shafi'iyyah. A school of Islamic jurisprudence named after Muhammad ibn Idris al-Shafi'i (767-819 C.E.); it emphasized the legal authority of Qur'an and Sunna over *ijma* (community consensus) and *ijtihad* (individual judgment).

shahada. Bearing witness to the Divine unity and the authenticity of the prophetic message brought by Muhammad, the prerequisite declaration by which a person becomes a Muslim: "*Ashadu an La ilaha illallah wa ashadu anna Muhammadan rasulullah.*"

shaitani. Having a profane, decadent or lewd character (as in *shaitani* music).

shariat (*shari'a*) The sacred law; the basic religious observance and duties of Islam as revealed in Qur'an; the first of the four worlds or levels, shariat being the foundation of the other three (*tarikat*, *hakikat*, and *marifat*).

sheikh (pronounced *shaykh*). An elder or "old man" and leader of a community or village (*sheikha* is the female equivalent); a *murshid*, spiritual guide, or leader of a Sufi Community.

Shi'ia, Shi'ite (*Shi'i*). The smaller branch of Islam (prevalent today in Iran and Iraq) which separated from the main (Sunni) body of Muslims, in order to follow the spiritual leadership of Imam 'Ali ibn Abi Talib and his descendants, who include the twelve imams.

Sifaat Allah. The divine qualities or attributes of Allah.

sikke. A dervish headdress; a tall, conical tombstone-like hat worn by Mevlevis.

sohbet. (Turkish) Conversation, spiritual discourse by a teacher.

Sufi, *Sufism*. The mystical path of Islam, the religion of the heart; also referenced as *tasawwuf* and *tarikat* Possible related root words: "saf(a)" (Persian/Arabic for "pure" or "row"), "suf" (Arabic for "wool"), or "Sophia" (Greek for "wisdom").

sultan. Sovereign ruler or Lord (in an Islamic country).

sunna (*sunnat*). The customs, words and actions of the Prophet Muhammad, which serve as a model and precedent for good Muslim behavior, in addition to the Qur'an.

sura. A chapter of the Qur'an (which contains 114 suras).

T

takke. A white dervish cap.

tarikat, *tariqa* (pl. *turuq*). "The (mystic) path" of the heart; a Sufi order; one of the four worlds or levels in Islamic Sufism.

tasawwuf. Sufism, esotericism, the science of the soul (see "*Four Worlds*").

tawba. Repentance.

tawhid. To unify, to acknowledge the Divine unity (from the verbal noun, *wahhada*). The Arabic phrase of unity, "*La ilaha illallah*," is known as *tawhid* (*tevhid* in Turkish).

tayy-i mekan. To travel through time and space, so that one appears in a distant place.

tejelli (*tecelli*). A manifestation or unveiling of the Divine, for instance, in the human form; transfiguration.

tekke. A dervish lodge.

tesbih (*tasbih*). Dervish prayer beads; doing tesbih is repeating one's practice of dhikr or divine esmas; also the words "Subhan Allah" ("Glory to God") are called *tesbih.*

türbe, türbedar. (Turkish) Tomb, tomb-keeper.

turuq (sing. *Tarikat*). Sufi orders.

U

ujub. Spiritual pride or inflation.

Üsküdar. A section of Istanbul on the Asian side of the Bosphorus.

usul. A rhythmic pattern; among Sufis, may refers to the formal group recitation of their special liturgy (*wird*) and divine names (*esmas*) during meetings at their lodge.

V

vezir (*wazir* or *vizier*) Prime minister to the ruling sultan.

W

Wahid. The attribute of Divine Oneness.

wejd (*wajd*). Ecstasy; a state of spiritual upliftment.

waliyullah (pl. *awliya*). Friend of God; a spiritual master (saint).

Y

Ya Rabb. "O Lord."

Yathrib. The Arabian city to which Muhammad fled from Mecca; after the *hijra* it was renamed Medina.

Yusuf. Joseph in Arabic; in the Qur'an, the name refers to the Hebrew Prophet Joseph.

Z

Zulfikar. The famous sword of Hazrat 'Ali.

Zuleika. The wife of the Egyptian governor who loved the Prophet Joseph (*Yusuf*).

INDEX

U

W

Y

Z